Creation & Completion

Creation & Completion

Essential Points of Tantric Meditation

Jamgön Kongtrul Lodrö Thaye

Introduced, translated, and annotated by

Sarah Harding

Commentary by

Khenchen Thrangu Rinpoche

Wisdom Publications • Boston

Wisdom Publications
199 Elm Street
Somerville MA 02144 USA
www.wisdompubs.org

Library of Congress Cataloging-in-Publication Data
Koṅ-sprul Blo-gros-mtha'-yas, 1813–1899.
[Lam źugs kyi gaṅ zag las daṅ po pa la phan pa'i bskyed rdzogs kyi gnad bsdus. English]
Creation & completion : essential points of tantric meditation / Jamgön Kongtrul Lodrö Thaye ; introduced, translated, and annotated by Sarah Harding ; Commentary by Khenchen Thrangu Rinpoche.
p. cm.
Cover title: Creation and completion.
ISBN 0-86171-312-5 (alk. paper)
1. Meditation—Rñiṅ-ma-pa (Sect). 2. Meditation—Tantric Buddhism. 3. Rñiṅ-ma-pa (Sect)—Rituals. I. Title: Creation and completion. II. Harding, Sarah, 1951– III. Title.
BQ7662.6.K669612 2002
294.3'4435—dc21 2002003925

ISBN 0-86171-312-5

06 05 04 03 02
5 4 3 2 1

Cover design by Graciela Galup
Interior set in Garamond 10.8/14

Cover art: Detail of Vajradhara tangka from the Robert Hatfield Ellsworth collection.
Photo © John Bigelow Taylor, NYC.

Wisdom Publications' books are printed on acid-free paper and meet the guidelines for permanence and durability of the Committee on Production Guidelines for Book Longevity of the Council on Library Resources.

Printed in Canada.

Contents

Publisher's Acknowledgment

The Publisher gratefully acknowledges the Hershey Family Foundation for kindly sponsoring the publication of this book.

MARPA INSTITUTE

For Translators

Under the Spiritual Authority of
Khenpo Tsultrim Gyamtso Rinpoche

The end of this twentieth century is a time when people are extremely busy, whether engaged in their work, family, or assimilating a constant stream of new information. Finding a place for the practice of Dharma within such a complex and demanding world is not always easy, and so there is a need for clear, succinct presentations of meditation theory and practice.

This distillation of essence requires the most accomplished master, one who not only knows deeply a vast range of texts, but who has also realized the meaning of which they speak. Jamgön Kongtrul Lodrö Thaye was such a master. One of Tibet's greatest scholars, he was also a realized siddha, who through his compassionate desire to benefit sentient beings, composed this text on the central forms of practice within the Vajrayana, the creation and completion stages of meditation. There is an almost uncountable number of texts dealing with these topics, too many for any one person to study or practice, and so this text summarizing the key points is extremely useful. For new students, who do not know where to turn, it leads the way along a direct and clear path; and for old students, it gathers into one place and codifies the main points of myriad explanations.

Several years ago I suggested to Sarah Harding that she translate this composition, and I am very glad to see her work brought to completion. May it be the cause of immense benefit for sentient beings limitless in number.

Khenpo Tsultrim Gyamtso Rinpoche

Post Box 4017, Kathmandu.Nepal.

Preface

While in retreat from 1976 to 1980, I started reading Tibetan texts on the subject of visualization in an attempt to understand what it was that I was supposed to be doing, and why. There is a wealth of information in Tibetan, and my research proved to be rewarding and reassuring. Since the retreat, I've met many Western students of Tibetan Buddhism doing visualization practice but without the benefit of explanation. Although there is surprisingly little inquisitiveness—a sign, no doubt, of great faith—I felt a desire to help fill this gap in the transmission of the Dharma. In 1987, I translated a short text *(bskyed rdzogs nyams len mdor bsdus kyi gtam)* of uncertain origin on this subject to use as a teaching text. During this work, I asked Khenpo Tsultrim Gyamtso Rinpoche and his assistant Tenpa Gyaltsen for clarification on certain points. At that time, Khenpo Tsultrim introduced me to this text by Jamgön Kongtrul *(bskyed rdzogs gnad bsdus; Creation and Completion)* and suggested that I translate it. I found it listed in two separate tables of contents of Kongtrul's collected works as being located in volume *cha* of the Treasury of Vast Precepts *(rgya chen bka' mdzod)*. However, the diligent efforts of Susan Meinheit at the Library of Congress, and my own search through the library of the late Chögyam Trungpa Rinpoche, failed to turn up the actual pages. Later, information from Khenchen Thrangu Rinpoche revealed that this text had been missing ("borrowed" was the word) from the original volumes when the more recent woodblocks were being produced. So all that came into my hands was the mysterious photocopy from Khenpo Tsultrim.

It sat on my desk for years. In 1990, during a time of intense personal crisis, I turned for some reason to this text for refuge, translating furiously for several weeks. At the time I thought that if I could have only one book on a desert island, it would be this one. I reworked it over several years, asking questions of whatever generous and learned lama passed my way. In this regard, I would like especially to mention Bokar Rinpoche, successor to Kalu Rinpoche and holder of the Shangpa lineage, Khenpo Dönyö Rinpoche, Khenchen Thrangu Rinpoche, Khenpo Palden Sherab Rinpoche, and Khenpo Tsultrim Gyamtso Rinpoche. In checking the translation with the original, Tulku Thondup Rinpoche and Lobsang Lhalungpa were extremely generous. And in reading the English translation and the introduction, Dr. Reginald Ray, Joey Townsend, and Fletcher Chamberlain offered useful suggestions and encouragement. There were many others who contributed one way or another. I thank them all. Finally, with the support of Constance Miller and Emily Bower at Wisdom, it has at last reached some form of completion. In the translation of such a profound teaching, the work of improvement could have continued on for much longer, perhaps forever. But it seems time to share it with others, according to the original intention, and accept responsibility for any errors or mediocrity, praying that the original power comes through despite such failings. The effort is dedicated to the continuing beneficial influence of the activities of the great Kyabje Kalu Rinpoche.

Sarah Harding
Boulder, Colorado, 1996

Acknowledgments to the Revised Edition

The publisher wishes to thank Khenchen Thrangu Rinpoche for kindly allowing the inclusion of his commentary in this new edition of *Creation and Completion.* The commentary is based on an oral translation by Lama Yeshe Gyamtso that was transcribed by Jan Puckett and the staff of the Rigpe Dorje Center in San Antonio, Texas, where the teachings were given. Pema Tsewang Shastri input the Tibetan text in this new edition, and Lyn Miller and E. Gene Smith provided invaluable editorial assistance.

Technical Note

The problem of presenting Tibetan works to the English-speaking public is complicated, but I will attempt to clarify my logic here. The academic world uses a system of transliterating Tibetan into roman letters developed by Turrell Wylie at the University of Washington. This I have used in the notations for the benefit of those involved in Tibetan studies. But since the Wylie system is illegible to the uninitiated, I have also used my own phonetic system with Tibetan names and commonly known terms in the introduction and translation. There is no single system of English phonetics for Tibetan, due in part to the variety of Tibetan dialects, but mostly due to the fact that the English sounds just do not correspond exactly to the Tibetan. Therefore, my system is to write down as closely as possible what it sounds like to me when spoken by, say, a civilized Khampa, while still keeping it very simple. The only exceptions are words whose spellings have become commonly accepted, such as Rinpoche, rather than Rimpochay (and certainly not Rinbochay).

Sanskrit equivalents are given in the footnotes following the Tibetan, using the accepted diacritic notation. Diacritics have been dropped in the main text as unnecessary and not aesthetic. When no Sanskrit equivalent appears in the footnotes, it is because I was unable to find one. Occasionally, common Sanskrit words are used if they are more recognizable than their Tibetan or English equivalents, such as "buddha" or "karma." Only the first occurrence of a Sanskrit or Tibetan word is italicized. My purpose throughout is to try to present the impact and beauty of the original meaning without encumbering the reader with unnecessary impediments. English is an extremely rich, subtle, and flexible language, unjustly accused of being inadequate to convey spiritual truths. While we wait for some standard in the field of Buddhist studies, it seems best to employ that wealth for the sake of communication, rather than depend too much on the safety of foreign terms.

Introduction

The Tibetan text translated here is a concise yet thorough exposition of the essentials of Tibetan Buddhist meditation practice by one of the most brilliant minds of that tradition, Jamgön Kongtrul Lodrö Thaye (1813–99). The Tibetan title of the text is *lam zhugs kyi gang zag las dang po pa la phan pa'i bskyed rdzogs kyi gnad bsdus*, "The Essential Points of Creation and Completion That Will Benefit the Beginner Who Has Entered the Path." It is known to Tibetans simply as Kye Dzog Ne Dü *(bskyed rdzogs gnad bsdus)*, or "Essential Points of Creation and Completion." Creation (or development) and completion (or perfection)[1] refer to the two stages of meditation involving deity visualization practice, a meditation technique for which Tibetan Buddhism is widely known. The text is not a specific meditation in itself, but rather describes the meaning and effect of such practice, and in doing so the essential Buddhist outlook on the nature of mind and reality. It describes with masterful clarity the profound view and vast method within which meditation practice must occur.

Jamgön Kongtrul designed this text as a guide to meditation practice. It is written entirely in verse, in the style of the songs of realization and other inspirational spiritual literature of Tibet, following a very similar tradition in ancient India. It is not an in-depth analysis or scholarly treatise. Jamgön Kongtrul, a masterful scholar, was above all interested in the actual application of the teachings in meditation. His intention in this text was to convey just what was necessary for effective practice. The intention in translating and publishing it is the same: simply to make it available for people interested in Buddhist practice. Although each verse warrants a volume of commentary, this might just result in obscuring the essential points. So what is offered here is a minimum of commentary, just enough to provide some context.

Buddhism

The Buddhist teachings originated in India in the sixth century B.C.E. with Gautama, or Shakyamuni Buddha,[2] the prince who renounced his kingdom in search of wisdom. After an inner journey of many years, he experienced a total awakening, or enlightenment,[3] and went on to teach about this experience for forty-five years.

India at that time already had a strong tradition of contemplative practice, but these new teachings were unusual not only in their content but in that they reached across social and religious boundaries in their appeal. They offered to everyone equally the possibility of achieving liberation through personal effort. During the forty-five years that Buddha Shakyamuni traveled around India imparting his profound knowledge, many different aspects of it were presented in many different ways to a great variety of people. This special talent to present the truth *(Dharma)* in the way that is most practical and appropriate to a particular audience is called skillful means.[4] It is symbolically represented in the account of one of the Buddha's special qualities of speech: that he could deliver a discourse to a group of people all speaking different languages, and they would each hear it in their own language.

Three Turnings of the Wheel of Dharma

The First Turning

The great variety of Buddhist teachings that arose in India over the next millennium are classified into the three "turnings of the wheel of Dharma."[5] They are all said to originate with the Buddha Shakyamuni during different phases of his teachings, at different places, speaking to different audiences, sometimes simultaneously to different audiences. In the first phase, the four noble truths[6] were emphasized: the truth of suffering, its cause, its cessation, and the path to its cessation. Since the first pair describe the reality of our experience of life—cyclic existence *(samsara)*—and the second pair encompass all the modes of transcendence of it *(nirvana)*, there is nothing not included in this simple classification.

Among the important concepts revealed during this phase was the explanation of the totally dependent and interrelated nature of all phenomenal reality.[7] This is said to be the overarching vision that the Buddha experienced during the night of his awakening. If one can understand the intricate relationship of all phenomena, and particularly of one's own emotional and conceptual patterns, then the cycle of suffering can be broken. An in-depth analysis of the process of suffering also reveals that the notion of an intrinsically, independently existing "self" is at the bottom of it. This is considered to be a false notion, since upon direct examination through meditation and analysis, such a self cannot be found. Ignorance is the belief in this myth of the self and the dualistic thinking that it spawns. In protecting the self and distinguishing what is *other* than it, the emotional reactions of attachment and aversion along with many other "afflictive emotions"[8] occur. These in turn give rise to actions and their consequences *(karma).* These are the sources of suffering. So the idea of nonself[9] is another crucial idea presented in the first turning teachings. These concepts form the basis for all further developments in Buddhist thought.

The people who received, practiced, and accomplished the teachings of this early phase of Buddhism were called *arhats.*[10] This group includes most of the earliest disciples. The lifestyle that was stressed was one of renunciation and moral discipline, and the goal was to attain one's own liberation from the cycle of existence. These teachings developed over time into at least eighteen separate schools. Today they are represented by the School of the Elders *(Theravada),* prevalent in Sri Lanka, Burma, Thailand, and Cambodia. This path was later called the "Lesser Vehicle" *(Hinayana)* by other traditions.

The Second Turning

The second phase of teachings coincided with the wisdom literature,[11] a new phase of literature that began to spread between 100 B.C.E. and 100 C.E. and continued to develop for centuries. The two great ideas emphasized in this phase were emptiness and compassion.[12] Emptiness is a further development of nonself and of the interdependent nature of phenomena. Not only was the self discovered to be empty of any independent existence, but so too was all phenomena. The lack of independent existence of phenomena is emptiness, and this truth is called the absolute truth.[13] On an ordinary level, the interrelated existence of phenomena and the functioning of cause and effect (karma) are considered the relative truth.[14] To comprehend these two truths simultaneously is to maintain a "middle path" without falling into extreme notions of either existence or non-existence. With no ground to stand on and no concepts to cling to, the causes of suffering are no longer operating. This is wisdom, the opposite of ignorance, which must be perceived experientially through meditative practice, not only by philosophical contemplation.

Compassion is the recognition that other beings are embroiled in lives of suffering exactly because they lack this understanding of emptiness. Their suffering is not inevitable, but it is self-perpetuating unless insight into the cyclic pattern arises. The person who begins to comprehend the true nature of emptiness naturally feels less self-cherishing and develops concern for others who exist interdependently. Compassion in turn promotes the experience of selflessness. Thus compassion and emptiness, or wisdom, are seen as the two necessary qualities to cultivate together on the Buddhist path, like the two wings of a bird.

The people who received, practiced, and accomplished these teachings were called *bodhisattvas.*[15] The lifestyle emphasized was one of great compassion and good deeds for the sake of others, as well as meditative discipline. For this, a monastic life was not necessarily relevant, so laypeople could be equally involved. The goal was the full enlightenment of all sentient beings, and thus it came to be called the "Great Vehicle," or *Mahayana.*

The Third Turning

The third phase was again based on these same concepts, but with a further development, that of *buddha nature,*[16] the inherent potential for enlightenment. This seemed to spring out of the meditative experience of a radiant awareness, or knowing capacity, inherent in the mind that could not exactly be just empty. Speculation on emptiness can lead to the question of whether the essential nature of everything is empty of a concrete self and other dualistic notions, or whether everything is truly empty in and of itself. The direct experience of intrinsic awareness would tend to indicate the former, and this essence that could be experienced came to be called buddha nature. This nature is an integral part of every single sentient being and endows that being with the opportunity to become enlightened. Enlightenment then comes to mean the recognition and full realization of this true nature of the buddha that one already is.

The goal is still the liberation of all sentient beings, and so the teachings of this turning belong to the Mahayana, and the practitioners are bodhisattvas. The literature connected with this phase as well as with the first two turnings are called *sutras,*[17] the discourses attributed to Buddha Shakyamuni. The idea of buddha nature that developed in this last phase is crucial for an understanding of another kind of literature that existed in Buddhist India, that of the tantras.

Tantra

Tantra[18] refers to a special kind of literature of esoteric teachings and also to those teachings themselves and their practice. The path of tantra is also called *Vajrayana,*[19] the "Indestructible Vehicle." Thus it is often classified as a third vehicle, although it is actually part of the Mahayana since the intention is the liberation of all beings. Another name for it is the "secret mantra,"[20] reflecting the widespread use of special sounds and syllables called *mantras.* There were both Hindu and Buddhist tantras in ancient India, and it is unclear how much one influenced the other. The Buddhist tantras are said to have been taught by the Buddha Shakyamuni manifesting in various forms on specific occasions to special groups of adepts. The main emphasis in Buddhist tantras is the natural purity or intrinsic perfection of all being. The method for realizing this is to cultivate pure vision,[21] or sacred outlook, at all times. The lifestyle tends to emphasize the unconventional in order to break through ordinary barriers and personal inhibitions to a nonconceptual understanding of true nature. The techniques that are taught in the tantras are visualization of enlightened forms (deities and mandalas[22]) and cultivation of the subtle energies of the psychophysical body, along with recognition of the ultimate inherent nature. These two are the stages of creation and completion that are the subject of the text translated here.

Buddhism in Tibet

Buddhism in Tibet and the other Himalayan regions not only preserved all of these strands of Buddhist thought without denigration or contradiction, but it also maintained a tradition of actual practice incorporating all the vehicles in an effective way. In addition, it encompassed the practices of the native Bön religion already present in Tibet when it first spread there, thus becoming the rich treasure of spiritual wisdom that we still benefit from today.

Buddhism may have entered Tibet as early as the fifth century C.E., but it was during the reign of several religious kings from the seventh to ninth centuries that it became the established religion. King Trisong Detsen[23] invited the great scholar-monk Shantarakshita,[24] who founded the monastic lineage, and the tantric master Guru Padmasambhava,[25] who brought the esoteric teachings of Buddhism and subdued opposition from local forces. This first spreading of the Dharma in Tibet established the Nyingma, or Ancient, School,[26] which continues today. After a dark period, when the anti-Buddhist king Langdarma[27] suppressed the religion, the later spreading[28] took place in the eleventh century, with a new influx of great teachers from India and new translations of sacred texts. Eight main practice lineages[29] flourished, as well as many smaller ones. From those, the four main schools, which are well known today, were established: the Nyingma, Kagyu, Sakya, and Gelug.

Many great saints and scholars from these traditions have appeared continuously in the Himalayan regions and have contributed richly to the great treasury of Buddhist literature that had been brought from India and translated into Tibetan.

In terms of practical application, scholars such as Jamgön Kongtrul have simply classified all those teachings and practices into the two approaches of sutra and mantra,[30] representing, roughly, exoteric and esoteric. The sutra approach encompasses the general methods and ideas expressed in the three turnings of the wheel of Dharma. In our text, Kongtrul summarizes that approach with the famous verse:

> Doing no unvirtuous deed whatsoever,
> engaging in prolific virtuous activity,

> completely controlling one's own mind,
> this is the teaching of the Buddha.[31]

The approach of mantra (Secret Mantra Vehicle) or tantric Buddhism is basically the two stages of creation and completion. But to try to practice them without the ethical foundation and mental control gained through the sutra approach is considered useless, at best. Kongtrul thus advises us in this small meditation guide on ways to practice all of the characteristic methods of both approaches. He summarizes them into three techniques for dealing with the afflictive emotions: rejection, transformation, and recognition *(spang bsgyur shes gsum)*. These three techniques for dealing with emotions that would interfere with the meditation process clearly correspond to the three phases of teachings described above as the three turnings. Rejection of afflictive emotion reinforces the attitude of renunciation so important in the First Turning teachings. The second turning teachings are applied in transforming so-called negative states into conducive conditions on the spiritual path through meditations based on compassion and the realization of emptiness. Finally, recognition of one's own true nature, which is intrinsically pure and pervasive even within one's affects, represents the ideas of buddha nature expressed in the third turning *as they are applied* in the practices of secret mantra. In Tibetan Buddhism this involves primarily meditation using visualized forms representing the awakened mind: the deities and mandalas.

Deity Practice

Tibetan Buddhist spiritual practice centers around the deities in its devotional rituals and meditation techniques. It may be disconcerting for those who have heard that Buddhism is a "nontheistic" religion to discover an elaborate system of worship with a pantheon of goddesses and gods. It is for this reason that some other Buddhist schools have considered the Buddhism in Tibet to be corrupt or untrue to its original form. However, these deity practices are deeply rooted in the very foundations of Buddhist thought and represent an exceptionally skillful use of technique to evoke realization of those ideas on the deepest levels.

One can impute emptiness logically when an independent reality of the self or of other phenomena is sought and not found. One also experiences it directly through meditation when the mind abides without ideas of existence or non-existence or both or neither. Meditators experience emptiness as a kind of fullness. Emptiness allows for the unimpeded radiance of intrinsic awareness. In the experiential sense, then, it is not only a lack of something, but also a quality of knowing, or pristine cognition, a luminous quality that is the actual nature of the mind that can be experienced once the veils of concepts and emotions have been cleared away. This experience is often referred to as *clear light* or *radiance ('od gsal)* and also as "compassion." It is not something other than emptiness, for without emptiness it could not occur. It is the radiance-awareness that is the primordially pure basis of all manifestation and perception, the buddha nature.

This very nature of mind was always already there and is never corrupted or damaged, but only covered up by confusion. As such, it is the basis of spiritual practice, and also the goal or result. For this reason, tantra is called the resultant vehicle,[32] because the approach is to rediscover the result already within. Buddha is not found anywhere outside of the intrinsic state of one's own mind. In the traditional breakdown, then, of ground, path, and fruition, the ground is one's own true nature, the fruition is the discovery of that, and the path is whatever it takes to make the discovery. Kongtrul describes the identity of ground (basis) and fruition when he says:

> The basis of purification is the eternal, noncomposite realm of reality that fully permeates all beings as the buddha nature.[33]

Since every aspect of ourselves is intrinsically pure, the path can employ any method to bring us back to our own nature. The deities used in tantric practice are a manifestation of this pure nature. In one sense, they exist as a method to undermine our pathetic projection of ourselves and our universe as flawed, a way of connecting with our true human/buddha nature. At the same time, they *are* that nature.

Due to the complex process involved in engendering and maintaining a sense of a substantial self and of the world around us, we have lost touch with our basic nature. It is often explained that the actual emptiness nature of mind is misconstrued as a self, while the clear or radiant aspect is projected outward as the separate, external world of others.[34] As the confusion proliferates, the concepts of duality, feelings of attachment and aversion, and consequent karmic actions and imprints become self-perpetuating. Thus it is called cyclic existence and is "characterized by the experience of suffering."[35] But the essential nature of emptiness and clarity has never for a moment been absent.

In contemplative practice we can watch this process in our minds moment by moment and recognize how we create our world. Then there is the possibility of creating it consciously. Now, because of the complications of our confusion, we visualize the world and ourselves as a mixture of bad and good, creating a constant tension of dissatisfaction. But we could *choose* to regard it as continuously manifesting the basic purity of emptiness/awareness. The deities represent an alternate reality that more precisely reflects the innate purity of our minds. In any case we visualize and create a world with its beings. The tantric approach is to use whatever we have, whatever we do already, as the method. So we use this capacity of projection and creation, which is really the unimpeded radiance of mind, as the path of meditation, but with a radical shift. Instead of imperfect women and men, we have goddesses and gods embodying the buddha qualities. Rather than run-down houses, there are brilliant palaces in divine configurations. The whole sorry world, in fact, is the buddha realm of magnificent glory manifesting as the mandala pattern of enlightened mind.

Emptiness and pure awareness allow us to do this. Deity visualization may seem contrived, and it is acknowledged as such, but if the fact that we create our own version of reality is deeply understood, it is very reasonable. We perceive water as something to drink, a fish perceives it as something to live in. We perceive the world now as impure, but we might as well see it as pure, which is closer to the truth if one considers its essential nature. The deities are forms that display the immanence of buddha nature in everything. All the different ways of relating with deities are ways we already have of relating to our experience. In this sense, the practice of deity meditation is a skillful way of undermining our ordinary mistaken sense of solid reality and moving closer to a true mode of perception.

The natural array of perceptions and feelings that arises can be regarded differently through deity practice. For instance, in Jamgön Kongtrul's last example of transformation, when desire arises, it arises *as* the deity, and we relate to it, or to ourselves, in that form. The deity shares some familiar characteristics with desire, has the same energy, but is by nature a pure manifestation, untainted by ego's complications. The deity in this meditation might be an embodiment of pure (com)passion, such as Chakrasamvara,[36] and thus represent an aspect of enlightenment. But the process itself also recaptures and demonstrates that the essential nature of neurotic thought is none other than buddha nature, whatever its shape. By creatively using forms that recall innate purity, the habitual mistake of relating to thoughts and emotions as other than pure is reversed.

This does not mean that tantric deities are merely an abstract, symbolic form representing something other than themselves. This again would be a dualistic concept. They *are* enlightened form, and they are intrinsic as part of buddha nature. Even the specific forms are understood as an integral part of awareness. This is a difficult point to comprehend. Jamgön Kongtrul refers to this truth when he says:

> The basis of purification, which is this very buddha nature,
> abides as the body with its clear and complete vajra signs and marks.
> A similar form is used as the path and leads to
> the fruition of purification: that very divine form that existed as
> the basis.[37]

"A similar form...used as the path" is the deity visualized in creation-stage meditation. Such practice leads to the realization of that divine form as it already exists within the true nature of mind. The idea of the intrinsic qualities of enlightenment, including actual physical attributes, can be found in such early texts as the *Uttaratantra*[38] and other sutras and commentaries associated with the teachings ascribed to the third turning. Qualities and activity manifest from the fundamental enlightened nature in response to the needs of sentient beings, and yet are inseparable from that very nature, not something added on to it. In the *Uttaratantra*, thirty-two specific attributes of the form manifestation are listed, concluding with the reminder that they are intrinsic and inseparable:

> Those qualities of thirty and two
> are distinguished through the dharmakaya;

> yet they are inseparable like a gem's
> radiant color and its shape.[39]

Different dimensions or manifestations of the enlightened principle, buddha, are traditionally called *bodies (kaya).* The most common division is into three bodies.[40] The *body of reality (dharmakaya)* is the ultimate true nature, beyond concept. Buddha nature refers to the same thing when it is obscured by the incidental veils in sentient beings. Although itself without form, this body of reality manifests spontaneously in ways to benefit beings, just as our intrinsic awareness radiates naturally from emptiness. The enlightened manifestations are called the *form bodies (rupakaya).* They are the *body of perfect rapture (sambhogakaya),* only visible to those of high realization; and the *emanation body (nirmanakaya),* the actual manifestations of the Buddha to our normal perceptions. The Buddha Shakyamuni is said to be such an emanation body. The deities visualized in Tibetan meditation practice for the most part represent the body of perfect rapture. When visualized for purposes of meditation or ceremony, the deity is called *yidam,* that which binds the mind.

It is taught that the practice of visualizing deities plants the seed for our later manifestation of form bodies for the benefit of beings at the time of enlightenment. This is why the seemingly simple approach of directly apprehending the empty, radiant nature of mind is not enough. The body of reality alone would be the result of that apprehension. But that would be, in a sense, emptiness without form, and would accomplish only one's own purpose. The body of reality must be accessible somehow to sentient beings in whom it is still hidden. That is the natural function of the form manifestations. It is still necessary to work with the whole phenomenal world, form and emptiness inseparable.

The Guru

The single most important factor in effective tantric practice of any kind is the relationship between the practitioner and the spiritual master. Although a teacher is also stressed in the other approaches, it is only in the Mantrayana approach that this relationship *itself* forms the basis of a spiritual evolution. Thus the covenant *(dam tshig,* Skt. *samaya)* between master and disciple must be carefully guarded and honored at all times *from both sides* or the process won't work. Given the difficulties of relationships in general, and the delicacy and profundity of this tantric relationship in particular, it is not surprising that many misunderstandings and abuses have occurred, particularly in the West, where a committed, devotional relationship to another human being is quite alien and often confused with a personality cult. Although these problems require extensive consideration, here we are discussing the ideal.

The relationship with the guru informs both creation-stage and completion-stage practice. In the creation stage, it constitutes the connecting factor between one's own buddha nature and the visualized deity, which is always conceived of as essentially the guru. The guru becomes the external, identifiable form of the ultimate buddha. All buddha qualities are projected and identified with the guru. Longing and devotion directed toward the guru are so intensified that one is moved to the very core of one's being; one's heart is fully opened, providing the space for connection, that is, blessing, to occur. In the development of this relationship, there is more and more capacity for intimacy until finally full union takes place: the guru's mind and the disciple's mind are recognized as identical *(thugs yid dbyer med),* and all the enlightened attributes of the guru are reclaimed as one's own. This is the fruition of deity practice and specifically the recognition attained in the completion stage. As the hallmark of tantric practice, guru devotion employs as its means perhaps the most powerful factor of human existence—relationship—both to others and to "other" in an abstract sense. Working with the general projection of self and other, and even more, with all the feelings and affections one develops in relationships, deity practice skillfully uses these affects themselves in devotional practice in order to transcend them.

Ultimate completion stage is direct recognition of our fundamental nature, but it is impossible to approach with the conceptual mind. How can we even begin to recognize nonconceptual pure nature? It is like the eye trying to see the eye. The mystery of tantra is that the only *thing to do* is to pray to the guru for realization to dawn, because there is no other *thing to do.* A pithy text on great seal *(mahamudra),* a practice for realization of the ultimate nature, says:

Mahamudra has no cause;
faith and devotion are the cause of mahamudra.
Mahamudra has no condition;
the holy lama is the condition for mahamudra.[41]

In the usual sense of "cause," there is nothing that can cause mahamudra, the ultimate realization. The relationship of devotion is the only attitude that creates the condition for it to happen. This is why the guru plays such a crucial role in Vajrayana. In *Creation and Completion* the pre-eminent role of the guru relationship is indicated in the first line of homage to Jamgön Kongtrul's primary guru. It is taken for granted as the foundation of the practices that are being described. The consummating event in that guru-disciple relationship, the initiation or empowerment,[42] is not mentioned, but assumed. Without empowerment from the guru, the practitioner will not reap the benefits of deity practice. It is customary for a student to request a ritual empowerment for each deity to be practiced in order to be fully empowered both in the sense of permission to do the practice and of establishing the relationship and receptivity needed for such practice.

Creation Stage

Visualization practice works with our relationship to the phenomenal world of appearance and seeks to undermine its solidity and shift it into an alternate, awakened perspective. The word often used for this process is *jong wa (sbyong ba)*, which has a wide range of meanings, including to purify, purge, train, exercise, study, accustom, and cultivate. In this translation, "purify" is used in the sense of a thorough workover and radical shift. Four aspects of purification are mentioned as a framework for understanding. The basis, or ground, of purification is buddha nature. That which needs purifying or removing are the conceptual and emotional obscurations to this nature, which are merely incidental and not intrinsic to it. That which does the purifying is deity practice. The fruition of purification is full recognition of the ground.

The discussion of the actual purification process can be very obscure, and this text really only gives us some clues, as do most Tibetan lamas.

Apparently this is all that is really necessary for it to "work." Deity practice takes place within the framework of a ritual, liturgical text called a "means of accomplishment" *(sgrub thabs,* Skt. *sadhana).* There is great variety in the sequence of practices within these texts, depending on which level of tantra and which tradition they belong to.[43] Different relationships with the deity are cultivated, such as that of lord, friend, and sibling, and then total identification through visualization of oneself as the deity.[44] But there are many common aspects as well. The general idea is that the process and sequence of visualizations correspond exactly to certain experiences of our life cycle, and that through "re-envisioning" them in this pure way, the process is basically recreated or purified, and can be recognized as the pure display of radiant mind.

Jamgön Kongtrul mentions four visualization sequences[45] as corresponding to the four possible kinds of birth: womb, egg, moisture-warmth, or miraculous. The first sequence of five stages[46] purifying womb birth is given as an example to convey this idea. Beginning with the three meditative absorptions *(ting nge 'dzin; samadhi),* the first, absorption of suchness *(de bzhin nyid),* corresponds to the experience of death in one's previous life. This absorption is basically the meditation on emptiness, the pure ground from which everything arises. Along with this, the *all-appearing* or *all-illuminating absorption (kun snang),* corresponds to and purifies the previous experience of the intermediate state *(bar do)* between death and rebirth. This is the meditation of the clarity or compassionate aspect, the natural radiance of emptiness, the energy of the natural mind. Then the *absorption of the cause,* or *seed (rgyu),* corresponds to the process of conception in rebirth, the sperm and ovum coming together as the physical basis of the future body. Here it is described as the visualization of the sun and moon and lotus seat, the first appearance of form in the visualization process.[47] In its pure, enlightened aspect, it is the inseparability of the previous two, emptiness and its radiance, compassion. Then there is the visualization of the deity's seed syllable upon the seat, corresponding to the consciousness of the individual entering the womb with the combination of sperm and ovum. Just as all life begins with a seed or quintessence of that form, deities also emanate from a quintessential syllable or vibration. Then the visualization of the special implement or insignia *(phyag mtshan),* such as a vajra or a sword, representing the particular deity, corresponds to fetal growth in the womb, when one's distinctive characteristics begin to develop. Finally, the visualization of the complete body of the deity corresponds to and purifies the actual birth from the womb and the development into an individual. These five stages may also be correlated with the five wisdoms, the pure aspect of the five afflictive emotions.[48]

In the more complex deity practices, the process continues through many stages, all the stages of our life. Finally there may be full-blown visualization of the entire mandala palace and surrounding environment, including many other deities as retinue in the mandala. This mandala corresponds to our complex life, with all of its relationships to beings, and to the environment surrounding our notion of ourself in concentric circles of importance all around. We have already created this mandala, but without awareness. Recreating the process in visualization, we see how we did it in the first place, and how, as the natural process of the creative energy of mind, it is essentially pure already.

Three Aspects of the Creation Stage

Traditionally there are three aspects, or techniques, to develop in visualization practice: clarity, recollecting purity, and pride. *Clarity of form (rnam par gsal ba)* is the art of visualizing with steady, vivid precision. The deity is held in the mind clearly, yet is always empty of solid reality, like a vivid rainbow. This is not only a focus for achieving one-pointed attention *(rtse gcig)* and stillness *(zhi gnas,* Skt. *shamata),* but also provides instant feedback on the state of one's mind. It is immediately apparent that a relaxed mind is a necessary condition for sustained visualization, as it is for any kind of exercise in memory. Advice on how to cultivate this clarity is given in the text.

Recollecting the purity means knowing and remembering the symbolic meaning of each of the aspects of the visualized deity. These meanings are usually found in the course of the practice liturgy to refresh the memory for practice. For instance, the deity's legs crossed in vajra posture indicates abiding in the inseparability of cyclic existence and transcendence; sitting on a lotus indicates utter purity of the form manifesting for beings, like a lotus growing in a swamp but untouched by its filth. None of these details are arbitrary, and as manifestations of the body of reality, they are naturally meaningful and potent. As such, one might wonder if they are equally effective whether or not they are consciously remembered. It is interesting that in this text Jamgön Kongtrul goes against mainstream teachings in suggesting that all this recollecting might just interfere with the real meditation process, particularly for the beginner. He suggests that rather than cluttering the mind with these details, it is more important to simply recall that the mind projecting the empty, radiant deity is fundamental emptiness radiating its intrinsic qualities in the arising of hands, faces, and so on.

The third aspect to cultivate is called *pride of the deity* or *divine pride (lha'i nga rgyal)*. Generally, this means maintaining the deep sense of actually being the deity, pure and perfect in every way. It is not the feeling of dressing up in a costume and mask, assuming another weird form, or superimposing an alien personality on top of the old one. A sense of confidence in being the actual deity counteracts one's sense of ordinariness and frees one from all the limitations usually imposed by our mundane sense of self. As the deity, boundless compassion and wisdom are only natural, whereas normally we feel burdened by our own inadequacy in such matters. Many teachings emphasize this as the main point of deity practice. Even if the visualization itself is unclear, just this sense of actually being the deity achieves the purpose of the practice. However, pride of the deity is in no way to be confused with its opposite: ordinary, ego-oriented pride. Apparently Jamgön Kongtrul felt that this was very important: the two lines on the subject concern the benefit of meditating without (ordinary) pride.

Kongtrul's discussion of creation-stage practice ends with a description of the signs of accomplishment, such as the deity arising effortlessly at all times and even being visible to others. But even if these experiences don't happen and the visualization remains obscured, that obscuration itself is not different from the true spacious nature of mind itself. It always comes back to that. So the real accomplishment of the creation stage is the natural state of the completion stage.

Completion Stage

The true nature of mind and all phenomena is "beyond intellect and inexpressible."[49] There is no intentional effort that causes its realization except that, as the text says, "the power of devotion causes it to arise from within."[50] This makes it difficult to write about, but a few points need to be mentioned.

The creation stage undermines attachment to the solid, impure phenomenal world, but can still leave us with the traces of attachment to this new manifestation that we have created or perceived. So in the completion stage, the whole new wonderful world dissolves back into basic ground, from which it never really departed. In the context of relationship with life cycles mentioned above, this stage corresponds to death. Recognizing that the visualization was created in the first place by mind, empty and radiant, and dissolves back into it, purifies or prepares us for the process of actual death, when this realization can result in full awakening.

Within the context of meditation, there is no longer a visualized form to work with, but there is still mind. So the discussion of the completion stage begins with a description of the mental process itself, so that the practitioner can be aware of exactly what is happening. The tradition of examining and analyzing the mental process has been a mainstay of Buddhist practice since its inception. It is sometimes referred to as Buddhist psychology. In this text the discussion centers on the eight aggregates of consciousness,[51] a model of the perceptive process that emerged during the development of the Mahayana. The purpose of the detailed analysis is for the meditator to be able to recognize and interfere in the process at just that precise point before mental events imprint on the foundation consciousness and become karmicly effective. The thought process is not expected to cease, as in any case it is the natural, pure radiance of emptiness. But the product of attachment—that is, karma—must be prevented to achieve freedom from the process. Working with the mind in this way, cutting through the very creation process of our self-imposed cyclic existence, is fundamentally the same as the practices of working with the afflictive emotions described earlier in the text.

Various experiences arise as this method becomes effective, but the meditator is warned not to fixate on them, for they too are unreal, passing away like everything else. The one single tool that is stressed continuously to get through all manner of mental events, obstacles, distractions, and even positive meditative experiences is called *mindfulness*,[52] the ability to focus and know what is happening. Various ways of applying this mindfulness to different situations form most of the last part of this text.

Mindfulness develops initially in the meditation of calm abiding, which is held as the preparatory foundation for many practices that aim at direct realization of the mind's nature, such as the mahamudra and completion-stage practice in its broadest sense. Only mindfulness sees one through the whole way and is the final technique. Then "ultimately, even mindfulness itself does not exist."[53]

The exceptional esoteric instructions of great perfection *(dzogchen)*[54] are mentioned as an approach of total noncontrivance, requiring only naked awareness itself. Even the foundation of calm abiding is unnecessary. Kongtrul mentions this exceptional approach several times, as it is subtly, but profoundly, different. However, each mention comes with a note of warning, not in the sense of any doubt as to the edifying nature of the instructions, but to caution against the grave possibility of misconstruing these very fine points. Kongtrul claims it would be "better to tread the gradual path."[55]

Completion-stage meditation, the simple state of resting in intrinsic awareness, is rife with pitfalls and challenges. Methods for identifying and processing all of the experiences that could arise in this stage constitute the bulk of the literature on the subject. Otherwise, there is nothing to say.

One last clarification about the term itself: completion stage actually has two applications, and this could cause some confusion. In the context of this present teaching, it is the second of the two stages of deity practice, and usually corresponds to the actual dissolution of the visualization, where mind rests without contrivance in its own nature. Since this is ideally the ultimate realization, the term may take on a very expansive meaning.

The other use of the term is in describing a different series of meditation practices, more commonly known as yogas *(rnal 'byor)*, that involve working with the channels, chakras, seminal drops, and vital winds[56] in the psychophysical body. This includes such well-known practices as mystic heat *(gtum mo)*, ejection of consciousness *('pho ba)*, and dream yoga *(rmi lam)*, as well as techniques practiced with a partner to develop and deploy sexual energy *(phyag rgya)*. These are all called completion-stage practices. Some of these practices are mentioned briefly toward the end of the text. Since they involve a considerable amount of technique, including extensive visualization, it is not immediately apparent where the connection is with the formless, uncontrived apprehension of the natural state that is also called the completion stage in deity practice. They are, however, related.

According to the teachings of Vajrayana, there is an intimate relationship between the mind and the movement of vital energy or "wind" in the body. It is said that the mind rides the wind, or that mind and wind are inseparable. This can be noticed when calm abiding is stabilized. When the ultimate realization of true nature takes place, what happens on the psychophysical level is that the wind enters the central channel *(dbu ma,* Skt. *avadhuti)*, the main artery of movement of energy in the body. On the other hand, a practitioner may choose to work at it from the other side, that is, to cultivate these energies intentionally and cause the wind to enter the central channel through various physical techniques, spontaneously bringing about realization.

The first approach is termed the *path of liberation ('grol lam)* and the second the *path of method (thabs lam).* The first is the direct approach of recognizing mind nature, already described in the previous discussion of completion stage. Although it may seem more direct and, to some people, more attractive, it is evasive and difficult. It is one of the skillful methods of tantra to work first with the physical energies of the body, for there the mind will follow. The well-known yogi Milarepa[57] was an example of a practitioner of this path. But generally one practices both, often in conjunction, and, since the goal is the same, they are mutually supportive. This is the relationship between the two uses of the term, and one need only be informed of which method, form or formless, is under discussion. The relationship between the terms is explained in the following quotation from Gyurme Tsewang Chogdrup:

> ...to meditate [visualize and perceive] all the appearances without differentiation as the Buddha-bodies of the deities, (in form or structure) similar to the phenomena of the three existents [worlds], combined with great compassion and contemplation of the bliss of melting, which causes the three Buddha-bodies to mature (within oneself) is the essence *(Ngo-bo)* of the development stage... To merge the energy/air, mind and thoughts *(rLung Sems Yid)* into the central channel and to actualize the blissful and empty primordial wisdom directly is the essence of the completion stage... The stage of the training [yoga] on channels, energies, and subtle essence and the stage of (training in

> using) consorts (S. mudra) which cause the energies to enter, be maintained and dissolve into the central channel is not the actual completion stage, but since it causes one to achieve it, it is [also] called the completion stage.[58]

In addition to some of the completion-stage yogas, the text concludes with advice on other daily practices and techniques that enhance realization in spiritual life. Tantric practice is not an isolated technique used only for achieving altered states. These practices form a part of an entire lifestyle with a fully intact ethical basis that is assimilated into every aspect of daily living. This is the case with all Buddhist practice, and all the more so in Vajrayana, which seeks to radically alter our mode of perception to rediscover ourselves. Every moment must be steeped in awareness, and any method that enhances that must be employed. One must never lose sight of remembering impermanence, cultivating love and compassion and devotion, and acting with integrity and an awareness of karmic cause and effect. Creation-stage and completion-stage practices are set within this context of a wholly spiritual and awakened life. So it is said:

> Therefore the view is higher than the sky;
> karmic cause and effect is finer than flour.[59]

Jamgön Kongtrul[60]

Jamgön Yönten Gyamtso Lodrö Thaye[61] was one of the spiritual and literary giants of nineteenth-century Tibet. The scope of his accomplishment is enormous, and his tremendous influence in the religious development of the Himalayan region cannot be underestimated. He is renowned for his crucial role in the nonsectarian *(ris med)* movement of Eastern Tibet (Kham) that was revitalizing the religious life of the time. This cultural renaissance was an exciting period of spiritual and intellectual evolution that gave rise to a great many exceptional religious figures: Jamyang Khyentse Wangpo (1820–92), Mipam Gyamtso (1846–1912), and Chokgyur Dechen Lingpa ("Chokling" 1829–70), to name a few. Even among these great masters, Kongtrul's name looms large.

Kongtrul was largely successful in his lifetime in accomplishing the three main goals that characterized this eclectic nonsectarian movement: to preserve the various practice lineages that were verging on extinction, to discourage the narrow-minded sectarian bigotry that had plagued Tibet for centuries, and to re-integrate religious study and practice in a meaningful way in the lives of its practitioners. The acute necessity for these changes came as the result of the long history in Tibet of power politics invading the realm of religion and the resulting degeneration in authentic spiritual practice. Fortunately, the pure lineage of practice was never lost entirely, and throughout the history of the region there have continued to be great masters who have risen above sectarianism through the power of the true teachings. Jamgön Kongtrul is certainly such a one, and perhaps his own personal experiences with the unsavory side of religious politics and pettiness contributed to his greatness.

Kongtrul was born in December of 1813 in Rongyab in Kham, Eastern Tibet. He was raised by his mother, Tashi Tso, and her husband Sönam Pel, who was a village lama of the pre-Buddhist Bön religion. Kongtrul was thoroughly trained by Sönam Pel as a Bön priest, and quickly mastered that tradition. He described himself later as gentle and shy, but with an early spiritual propensity.[62]

Around the age of fourteen, his life and training were abruptly interrupted. Due to a local feud, authorities from Derge, the capital of the area, captured Sönam Pel and took him off to prison, where Kongtrul followed in order to help sustain him. There he made connections with some teachers of the Nyingma school, who were greatly impressed with his knowledge of Bön. This led to his acceptance into the Nyingma monastery of Shechen, which he entered in 1829 and received full monastic vows in 1832. The monastic institutions of Tibet were bastions of power and intrigue, and an established monastery with good connections could wield a great deal of power. Though Kongtrul was apparently quite happy with his studies at the Nyingma monastery, his exceptional talents caused him to be requisitioned as a secretary for a high lama of Palpung, a powerful Kagyu monastery. He moved there in 1833 and was advised to retake his monastic ordination under the principal head of that monastery, Situ Pema Nyinche.[63] Presumably the ordination he had received just one year earlier didn't "count" because it was from a different order.[64] His objections were overruled and the vows retaken. This occasion may have marked Kongtrul's first disillusionment with the petty sectarianism of the monastic world, but a further political maneuver was to follow. The Palpung lamas were concerned lest his outstanding qualities attract the attention of the Derge government, which could requisition him for its own purposes. So they devised a plan to install him as an incarnation[65] of a previous Palpung personage, which would assure his permanent position there. They chose the late servant of the previous Situ incarnation, a position not too high but still an incarnate lama, which would serve their purpose adequately. He was "recognized" as such and received the name "Kongtrul."[66]

Despite this background of political intrigue, Kongtrul sincerely regarded Situ Pema Nyinche as his primary guru[67] and Palpung Monastery as his seat. He continued his studies under this great lama, and came to consider himself as a holder of the Kagyu lineage. His primary interest had always been in actual meditation practice, so in 1842 he left the main monastery to take up residence in an old, abandoned retreat center nearby, which turned out to be near a sacred power site, known as Tsandra Rinchen Trak. This he eventually (1860) transformed into a three-year retreat center and designed a curriculum that is still the model for similar retreats today.

Before this, however, he had come to feel regret with what he considered a lapse in his connection with the Nyingma lineage, and he attributed this as the cause for later ill health and various mental and karmic obstacles. Gradually he worked through these problems, largely with the help of the great Jamyang Khyentse Wangpo and Chokling Rinpoche. The two of them recognized him as a revealer of hidden treasures *(terton)*,[68] and bestowed on him the name Tennyi Yungdrung Lingpa. During the latter part of his life, he fulfilled this role, bringing forth many new hidden treasures, often in conjunction with Khyentse. The relationship between Kongtrul and Khyentse, the two "Jamgön Lamas," was very profound and mutually inspiring, and it is often difficult to tell who was the guru and who the disciple. They became powerful forces in the entire region, and were able to pacify some of the conflicts that arose due to sectarian competition.

Kongtrul developed a profound faith in all aspects and lineages of the Buddha's teaching. All manifestations of the Dharma are for the benefit of beings, and rejecting any aspect of them basically amounts to rejecting the

Buddha's doctrine. The symptoms of the inner conflict caused by the sectarian and political problems seem to have been resolved by the time Kongtrul was forty years old, when he went on to establish the retreat center and continue his prolific writings. The program of the retreat included meditations from all of the practice lineages, some of which were disappearing within the overbearing monastic institutions of the four main schools. Thus through his teaching and writing, he preserved the rich variety of precious instructions of all lineages and fostered a sense of appreciation and mutual respect. The nonsectarian movement flourished in large part due to his contributions. It is still a powerful influence that all of the great lamas since Kongtrul have supported. The power of Kongtrul's influence will hopefully prevail in the West, where hints of ignorant sectarianism sometimes creep in.

Kongtrul continued his activities until the time of his death in 1899 at the age of eighty-seven. The enormity of Kongtrul's contribution was expressed by the late Dudjom Rinpoche as follows:

> So if we examine Jamgön Kongtrül's career, which produced over ninety volumes of wonderful scripture, it is as if he spent his whole life as an author.
>
> None the less, if one thinks of his teaching and propagation of the empowerments, guidance, esoteric instructions, recitational transmissions, and so forth, of the ancient and new sūtras and tantras, and transmitted precepts and treasures, without bias, it is as if he spent his whole life teaching and propagating. And, if one investigates how, beginning with the preliminary yogas of accumulation and purification, he experientially cultivated the stages of creation and perfection associated with inconceivable myriads of maṇḍalas, it seems as if he passed the length of his life in a retreat house sealed up with mud.
>
> Likewise, if one considers how Jamgön Kongtrül expanded the new monastic communities at the places of attainment in Tsandra Rincen Trak and Dzongshö Deshek Düpa, and how he renovated many old establishments, commissioned inconceivable numbers of new representations of the buddha-body, speech, and mind, performed more than one hundred and fifty rites of great

attainment involving maṇḍala clusters, offered worship to the Three Precious Jewels, and venerated the monastic community—in short, his legacy in connection with the ten modes of doctrinal conduct—it is as if he passed his whole life diligently engaged in the sphere of work and activity. In these ways [his career] was inconceivable, within only the reach of those who are truly sublime.[69]

Literary Works

The collected literary works *(gsung 'bum)* of Jamgön Kongtrul Lodrö Thaye take up ninety volumes in the complete Palpung edition. Traditionally they are divided into five collections, called the Five Great Treasuries *(mdzod chen lnga)* listed below, and they fulfill the early prediction of Jamyang Khyentse Wangpo that Kongtrul would produce five such treasures. Most of them were collected during the time of Kongtrul's administration of the retreat center near Palpung, and many works were composed for the specific study program there. Together the Five Great Treasuries represent the entire range of Buddhist philosophy and practice of all the sects. Their very composition and arrangement is a testimony to Kongtrul's nonsectarian approach. His intention in bringing together this vast collection was to reveal the essential similarities of the various approaches as well as to preserve them.

1. *The Encompassment of All Knowledge (shes bya kun khyab)* or *Treasury of Knowledge (shes bya mdzod)*[70] in three volumes covers the full range of Indo-Tibetan knowledge, from the formation of the universe up to the history of Buddhist lineages and practices in Tibet. It includes the common sciences and all the philosophical viewpoints as well as religious history. This masterpiece in itself would have been a stupendous accomplishment for one person's life.
2. *The Treasury of Kagyu Mantra (bka' brgyud sngags mdzod)* in four or six volumes is a collection of esoteric teachings and practices from two transmissions of the Kagyu—Marpa and Ngog—as well as some from the Nyingma.

3. *The Treasury of Precious Treasure (rin chen gter mdzod)* in sixty or sixty-three volumes is not just a reproduction of the older cycles of treasure texts that are still extant, as is sometimes thought, but contains smaller basic texts, supplementary works, new liturgical texts, and introductory instructions for other treasures, all pertaining to the Nyingma.[71]
4. *The Treasury of Instructions (gdams ngag mdzod)* in ten volumes is a systematic presentation of the most important instructions of all the different lineages, especially of the Eight Great Chariots of Practice.
5. *The Extraordinary Treasury (thun mong ma yin pa'i mdzod)* and its auxiliary *The Treasury of Vast Precepts (rgya chen bka' mdzod)*, comprising ten volumes, contains Kongtrul's own revealed treasures as well as many other writings that don't belong in any of the other Treasuries.

The text translated here is a tiny drop in this vast, deep ocean.

Creation & Completion: The Root Text

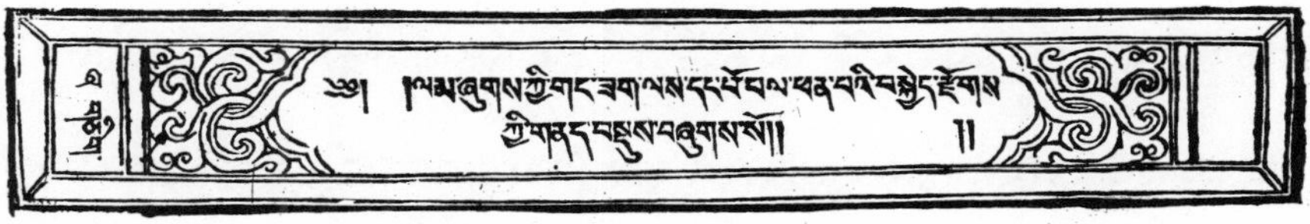

NOTE ON TEXT

In preparing this volume of the Tibetan text, the publisher has checked it against the *Tsibri Parma* edition, published by Ladakh Tripon Trulshik Pema Chogyal (1876–1958). Obvious misprints have been corrected, and variant readings from the *Tsibri* print have been added in small gray script. In most cases the readings from Khenpo Tsultrim Gyamtso's manuscript are preferable.

༄༅། །ལམ་ཞུགས་ཀྱི་གང་ཟག་ལས་དང་པོ་པ་ལ་ཕན་པའི་བསྐྱེད་རྫོགས་ཀྱི་གནད་བསྡུས་བཞུགས་སོ།། །།

༄༅། །རྟག་བརྟན་ཡོངས་སུ་གྲུབ་པ་ཟག་མེད་ཀྱི། །བདེ་སྟོང་ཏིང་འཛིན་སྒོ་བརྒྱ་སྤྲོ་བསྡུ་ལ། །རྣམ་པར་རོལ་པ་མཚོ་སྐྱེས་རྡོ་རྗེ་དང་། །དབྱེར་མེད་པདྨ་ཉིན་བྱེད་དབང་པོར་འདུད། །སྙིགས་མའི་རང་མདངས་མངོན་པར་ཤར་བའི་སྐབས། །ཐ་མལ་རྨོངས་པ་བདག་འདྲས་ཟབ་རྒྱས་དོན། །ཁྱད་པས་ཅི་བྱ་རང་ཉིད་ངལ་བའི་རྒྱུ། །འོན་ཀྱང་རྡོ་རྗེ་མཆེད་པོས་བཀའ་གནང་དང་། །རང་འདྲའི་རྨོངས་པ་འགའ་ལའང་ཕན་པའི་གཏམ། །དཔལ་ལྡན་བླ་མའི་བྱིན་རླབས་ཁོ་ན་ལ། །བརྟེན་ནས་གང་ཤར་བཀག་མེད་ལྷུག་པར་སྨྲ། ༈ །རྙེད་དཀའི་དལ་འབྱོར་རིན་ཆེན་ད་རེས་ཐོབ། །ཐ་མལ་སྐྱེ་བོ་མ་ལུས་ཆོས་དང་མཇལ། །སངས་རྒྱས་དངོས་སྣང་བླ་མས་རྗེས་སུ་བཟུངས། །ཆོས་ཀྱི་ཡང་སྙིང་གང་ཟབ་བལྟ་བ་དང་། །བླ་མའི་ཁྲིད་ནས་སུ་བཟང་འདོམ་འདེམ་པས་ཆོག །རང་དབང་ཡོད་དུས་ཆོས་མཐུན་རྐྱེན་མ་ལུས། །འཇོམས་པའི་དུས་འདིར་གཞན་དོན་མ་འགྲུབ་ཀྱང་། །རང་མགོ་ཐོན་ཙམ་ཉམས་ལེན་མ་བྱས་ན། །ནམ་འཆི་ཆ་མེད་འཆི་ཚེ་ཆོས་མ་གཏོགས། །ཅིས་ཀྱང་མི་ཕན་འཁོར་ལོས་སྒྱུར་རྒྱལ་གྱི། །དཔལ་འབྱོར་ཡོད་ཀྱང་མལ་གྱི་ཤུལ་དུ་ལུས། །

The Essential Points of Creation and Completion That Will Benefit the Beginner Who Has Entered the Path

I bow to Pema Nyinje Wangpo[72]
inseparable from the Lake-born Vajra,[73] who manifests
the infallible absorption of bliss-emptiness, steady and everlasting,
emanating and resolving in a hundred ways.

In the face of these disturbing times,
an ordinary stupid person like myself becomes exhausted
trying to explain the deep and vast meaning!
Nevertheless, my vajra friend[74] has implored me,
and maybe it would help a few fools like me.
So I rely only on the blessings of the glorious guru
and speak freely without reservation.

You now have the precious opportunity of human life, so difficult to find;
not just as an ordinary person, but one who has encountered the Dharma
and been accepted by a teacher, the personal appearance of the Buddha,[75]
you can seek the most profound quintessence of Dharma
and choose the finest from among the gurus.
While you have this chance, and all conditions conducive to Dharma
have accrued, even if you do not achieve others' welfare,
at least practice for your own sake.
Otherwise, at the time of death, and that time is uncertain,
there is nothing whatsoever that can help other than Dharma.
Even the wealth of a universal monarch[76] just gets left behind on the death bed.
Positive and negative actions adhere to the consciousness,
and not knowing what to do, even regret won't help.

རྣམ་ཤེས་དཀར་ནག་ལས་ཀྱི་རྗེས་སུ་འབྲང་། །ཅི་བྱས་གཏོལ་མེད་འགྱོད་ཀྱང་མི་
ཕན་པས། །ད་ལྟ་ཉིད་ནས་ཕྱི་གཡོལ་མེད་པ་རུ། །སྒོ་གསུམ་དགེ་བའི་ལས་ལ་
འབད་པར་འཚལ། །ཉམས་ལེན་རྨང་རྡོ་ངེས་འབྱུང་ཁོ་ན་ཡིན། །ཉམས་ལེན་
འཇུག་སྒོ་དད་པ་ཁོ་ན་ཡིན། །ཉམས་ལེན་གཞུང་ལམ་སྙིང་རྗེ་ཁོ་ན་ཡིན། །ཉམས་
ལེན་སྲོག་ཤིང་རྩེ་གཅིག་སྒྲུབ་རྒྱུགས་ཡིན། །ཉམས་ལེན་འབྲལ་མེད་བག་ཡོད་དྲན་
ཤེས་ཡིན། །ཉམས་ལེན་གེགས་སེལ་དཀོན་མཆོག་བློ་གཏད་ཡིན། །ཉམས་ལེན་
ཐོགས་འདོན་བླ་མར་མོས་གུས་ཡིན། །ཉམས་ལེན་འཁྲུལ་མེད་བླ་མའི་གདམས་
ངག་ཡིན། །ཉམས་ལེན་གནད་འདུས་རྩ་གསུམ་གཅིག་དྲིལ་བ། །ཞི་དང་ཁྲོ་བོའི་
དཀྱིལ་འཁོར་མ་ལུས་པར། །བླ་མའི་རོལ་པར་ཤར་ན་གཅིག་ཆོག་ཡིན། །དབང་
པོ་ཡང་རབ་སྦྱངས་པ་སྔོན་སོང་དང་། །མོས་གུས་ཚད་དུ་ཕྱིན་དང་སྐྱེས་ཆེན་
མཆོག །དེ་དག་རྣམས་ནི་རིམ་རྩོལ་མ་བྱས་ཀྱང་། །ཆོས་ཉིད་བདེན་པ་གཟིགས་
པ་འཐད་རུང་བྱུང་ཡིན། །དེ་ལས་གཞན་ཀུན་འཕགས་པ་ཀླུ་སྒྲུབ་ཀྱིས། །ཇི་སྐད་སྟེང
གསུངས་བཞིན་ཐོས་པས་བསམ་བྱུང་བསྐྱེད། །བསམ་པས་སྒོམ་ཉམས་བསྐྱེད་དེ་
གོ་རིམ་བཞིན། །རྣམ་གཡེང་སྤངས་ཏེ་རྟག་ཏུ་བརྩོན་བྱས་ན། །དང་པོ་ཐོས་པ་ལས་
བྱུང་ཤེས་རབ་ཀྱིས། །འཁོར་འདས་ཆོས་ཀྱི་མཚན་ཉིད་སྤྱི་ཙམ་རྟོགས། །བསམ་
པས་འཁྲུལ་སྣང་བདེན་འཛིན་རགས་པ་ཞི། །སྒོམ་པས་སེམས་ཐོག་ཁོ་ཐག་ཆོད་པ་
སོགས། །སྔ་མ་སྔ་མས་རྒྱུ་བྱས་ཕྱི་མ་བསྐྱེད། །དེ་དག་མི་ལྡན་རྒྱུ་མེད་འབྲས་

From this very moment on, without delay,
you must strive to practice virtue with body, speech, and mind.

The only foundation stone of practice is renunciation.
The only gateway of practice is faith.
The only approach to practice is compassion.
The life-tree of practice is single-minded application.
Constant practice is conscientious mindfulness.
The removal of obstacles to practice is to rely on the Three Jewels.[77]
The enhancement of practice is devotion to the guru.
Unmistakable practice is the guru's instruction.
The one essential point of practice is that the Three Roots[78] combined
and all of the peaceful and wrathful mandalas[79]
arise as the guru's display—this one thing is sufficient.

The most gifted individuals are those who have developed in previous lives,
have already reached the full capacity of devotion, and are born as great, superior beings.
For them, even without following the stages of practice,
it is still possible to perceive the truth of reality.[80]
For all others, it is as the noble Nagarjuna[81] said:
Listening to Dharma engenders contemplation,
and contemplation gives rise to the meditation experience—this is the sequence.
So if you abandon distraction and continuously apply effort,
first the intelligence[82] that comes from listening
will result in comprehension of the general characteristics of the phenomena of cyclic existence and its transcendence.[83]
Then, contemplation will pacify blatant grasping to the reality of illusory appearances,
meditation develops the definitive direct experience of mind, and so on.
Thus the previous stages act as causes for the arising of the latter.
When this is not the case, it is like desiring results without any cause.
You may claim that your accumulation, purification, and practice are most excellent,
bemoaning the hardships of a practice that is merely conjectural.

འདོད་ལྟར། །བསགས་སྦྱངས་སྒྲུབ་ཚུགས་ཤིན་ཏུ་བཟང་ངོ་ལོ། །ངེས་ཤེས་མེད་པའི་ཉམས་ལེན་སྡུག་ཡུས་ཆེ། །དེ་འདྲས་ཉམས་མྱོང་བློ་ཐག་ཆོད་མི་འགྱུར། ། ཐག་མ་ཆོད་པས་ཐེ་ཚོམ་དང་དུ་ལུས། །ཐེ་ཚོམ་ཁོ་ན་མཆོག་གི་བར་ཆད་ཡིན། ། ཐོས་བསམ་སྒོམ་པས་བློ་ཐག་ཆོད་པའི་ཚེ། །ཁྲིད་ཀྱི་བསྒོམ་འདེས་དམྱལ་བར་འགྲོ་ཟེར་ཡང་། །ཡ་ང་ཁ་འཕྲིག་འཁྲིག་མི་སྐྱེ་ཐག་ཆོད་ལགས། །རྒྱལ་བས་གསུངས་པའི་ཆོས་ཚུལ་མཐའ་དག་གི །གནད་དོན་བསྡུ་ན་རང་སེམས་འདུལ་ཐབས་ལགས། །སེམས་ཀྱི་ཉམས་ལེན་དང་པོའི་འཇུག་སྒོ་ནི། །ངེས་འབྱུང་ཁོ་ན་མེད་ཐབས་མེད་པ་ལགས། །ངེས་འབྱུང་གཤའ་མ་སྐྱེས་ན་བྱ་བྱེད་ཉུང་། །བྱ་བྱེད་ཉུང་ན་བྱར་མེད་དོན་དང་ཉེ། །བྱར་མེད་མངོན་དུ་གྱུར་ཚེ་གནས་ལུགས་ཡིན། །དེ་ལས་གཞན་དུ་སངས་རྒྱས་ཡོད་མི་སྲིད། །ལྷ་སྒོམ་སྒྲུབ་པའི་དབྱེ་བ་གྲངས་མང་ཡང་། །རང་གི་སེམས་ཀྱི་སྟེང་དུ་ཚུར་བསྡུ་ན། །གནས་ལུགས་གཞི་རྩ་ཆོད་པ་ལྟ་བ་ཡིན། །དེ་དོན་རྒྱུད་ལ་སྦྱོར་བ་སྒོམ་པ་ཡིན། །གང་ཤར་ལྟ་སྒོམ་རྩིས་ཟིན་སྤྱོད་པ་ཡིན། །ཡིན་ལུགས་མངོན་དུ་གྱུར་པ་འབྲས་བུར་འདོད། །འཁྲུལ་པའི་རྩ་བ་ཕྱི་རོལ་སྣང་བ་ལ། །རང་གི་སེམས་ཀྱིས་བདེན་པར་འཛིན་པ་ཡིན། །བསྐྱེད་རིམ་རྫོགས་རིམ་ཅི་དང་ཅིར་བསྒོམ་ཡང་། །འཁྲུལ་སྣང་བདེན་ཞེན་བཟློག་ཐབས་ཁོ་ན་སྟེ། །ཆགས་སྡང་ཨ་འཐས་བག་ཆགས་མ་ཟློག་ན། །བསྒོམ་པ་དོན་མེད་ཕྱི་བ་ཁང་ཉལ་འདྲ། །བཅོས་མ་ཀུན་བརྟགས་རྒྱ་ཆེ་བསྐྱེད་པའི་རིམ། །རྣལ་མ་ཡོངས་

This kind of experience will not lead to conviction.
Without conviction, you are stranded in doubt,
and doubt is the only supreme obstacle.
When conviction arises through listening, contemplating, and meditating,
even if someone says "this meditation will send you to hell,"
rather than being frightened, you will be supremely confident.

The essential point of all the modes of Dharma taught by the Buddha
can be epitomized as a method to subdue one's mind.
The entryway into the initial mind practice
is surely renunciation, without which there is no way.
If authentic renunciation arises, compulsive activities will be few;
if activities are few, the significance of non-action will be near.
When non-action is realized, it is the true nature.[84]
There is no other buddha outside of that.

There are many categories of view, meditation, and action,
but when applied to one's own mind,
the view is absolute conviction in the true nature;
meditation is assimilating that meaning in one's being;
and action is recognizing anything that happens as that view and meditation.
It follows that the fruition will be the actualization of things as they are.

The root of delusion is one's own mind grasping
external appearances as being truly existent.
Whatever creation or completion stage meditations are employed,
all are intended as methods to reverse this attachment to the reality of deluded appearance.
If stubborn habits of attachment and aversion are not reversed,
then meditation is as meaningless as a gopher hibernating in a hole.
Creation stage is the vast imaginary nature of contrivance
and completion stage is the profound perfectly existent nature of genuine condition.[85]
These are the names and definitions that have been taught.
They are also described as with and without elaboration, respectively.

གྲུབ་ཟབ་པ་རྫོགས་རིམ་གྱི། །མིང་གི་རྣམ་གྲངས་སོ་སོའི་ངེས་ཚིག་སྟོན། །སྤྲོས་
བཅས་སྤྲོས་མེད་ཉིད་ཀྱང་དེ་བཞིན་ནོ། །གང་ཟག་བློ་རིམ་མཆོག་དམན་ལ་
དགོངས་ནས། །བསླུ་མེད་རྒྱལ་བའི་དགོངས་པ་ཕོ་ནའི་ཕྱིར། །བཟང་ངན་དབྱེ་རྒྱུ་
མེད་ཀྱང་རང་རང་གི །བློ་དང་བསྟུན་ནས་ཉམས་སུ་ལེན་པ་གནད། །ཐབས་མང་
དཀའ་བ་མེད་པ་སྔགས་ལམ་ནས། །དབང་རྣོན་ཤེས་རབ་ཆེ་བའི་གང་ཟག་གིས། །
བྱེད་སྤྱོད་ཐམས་ཅད་ཚོགས་གཉིས་ཕོ་ན་ལས། །དོན་མེད་འགྱུར་བ་སྤུ་ཙམ་མེད་ན་
ཡང་། །རྨོངས་པ་ལོག་ལྟ་ཅན་གྱི་སྤྱོད་ཡུལ་མིན། །ཅིར་ཡང་སྣང་བདེན་ཞེན་ཆུང་
ཞིང་ཐབས་ལམ་ལ། དད་པ་མོས་གུས་ཡིད་ཆེས་གཏིང་ཚུགས་སྐྱེ། །འདུན་པ་
བསྒྱུར་བའི་གནད་ཀྱིས་འཛིན་མཁས་ན། མཆོག་ཐུན་དངོས་གྲུབ་ཐོས་པའི་མགྲོན་
ལས་མྱུར། ༄ །ཆོས་རྣམས་ཐམས་ཅད་བདེན་པ་གཉིས་ཀྱིས་བསྡུས། །དེ་ཡང་
ཀུན་རྫོབ་བདེན་པ་འཁྲུལ་ངོར་བདེན། །དོན་དམ་བདེན་པ་གཤིས་ངོར་བདེན་པ་
ཡིན། བདེན་པའི་གཏན་ཚིགས་བསླུ་བ་མེད་ལ་བརྗོད། །བདེན་གཉིས་དབྱེར་མེད་
ཆུ་ཟླ་ལྟར་ཤེས་ན། །དེ་ལ་འཁྲུལ་པའི་སྣང་བ་ཟད་ལ་ཉེ། ༄ །དྲང་ངེས་ལམ་
གྱིས་སངས་རྒྱས་བསྒྲུབ་པ་ལ། །བསླུ་བ་མེད་ཀྱང་ལམ་ཐག་ཉེ་རིང་ཡོད། །དཔེར་
ན་བགྲོད་བྱ་ལྷ་སའི་གནས་གཅིག་ལ། །རྐང་པས་ཕྱིན་དང་མཁའ་ལ་འཕུར་བ་
འདྲ། །ཉེ་ལམ་ཡིན་ཀྱང་གང་ཟག་བློ་ཞེན་ན། །ཟབ་ཁྱད་རྒྱུས་མི་ཐོན་ཐ་མལ་དང་དུ་
ལུས། །འོག་མ་ཁྱད་བསད་གོང་མ་མི་ཐེན་པར། །སྟོང་སྐད་འདོན་ནས་རྒྱུ་འབྲས་

Since they are both exclusively the infallible intention of the victorious ones
who recognize the different capacities of individuals,
there is no question of division into good and bad.
The point is to do practice appropriate to one's own intellect.

In the mantra approach,[86] with its many methods and few austerities,
a person of sharp faculties and high intelligence
may gather the two accumulations during all activities
and never do even a trace of anything meaningless.
This is not, however, the sphere of activity for a fool with mistaken views.
With little attachment to the reality of whatever arises,
deeply rooted devotion and belief in the path of methods,
and tenacity in pursuing the significance of the goal,
ordinary and supreme mastery will come quicker than a summoned guest!

All phenomena are subsumed under the two truths:
the relative truth is true with respect to delusion,
and the absolute truth is true with respect to true nature.
The definition of "truth" is that it is without deception.
If you know that the two truths are inseparable, like the moon in water,
then the extinction of deluded appearance is close at hand.

There is no doubt that both the provisional and definitive paths[87] lead to buddhahood,
but there are shorter and longer paths.
For instance, the destination may be a single place, such as Lhasa,
but you could either go on foot or by flying through the air.
Even on the short path, a person with meager intelligence
will not discover the distinctive wisdom, but will be left among the ordinary.
Disdaining the lower and unable to grasp the higher,
talking of emptiness, such a person will neglect cause and effect,
mouthing on about the view while in a state of self-deception.
It would be better to concentrate on the gradual path.

ཁྲིད་བསད་དེ། །ལྟ་བ་ཁ་ཁྱེར་ཕྱིར་རང་གིས་རང་ཉིད་བསླུ། །དེ་འདྲས་རིམ་བགྲོད་ལམ་ལ་འབད་ན་ལེགས། ༈ །འཇུག་པའི་ལམ་ཡང་མདོ་ལམ་དང་སྔགས་ལམ་གཉིས། །ཞུགས་པའི་ཐབས་ལ་རྒྱ་ཆེ་གྲངས་མང་ཡང་། །སྡིག་པ་ཅི་ཡང་མི་བྱ་དགེ་བ་སྤྱོད། །རང་སེམས་འདུལ་ལ་མདོ་ཡི་ཉམས་ལེན་འདུས། །བསྐྱེད་རྫོགས་རིམ་གཉིས་བསྒོམ་པ་སྔགས་ལུགས་ཀྱི། །ཉམས་ལེན་འདུས་ཞེས་ཐམས་ཅད་མཁྱེན་པས་གསུངས། །དེ་ཡང་ཆོས་ཀུན་རྩ་བ་སེམས་ཡིན་པས། །ཐོག་མ་ཉིད་དུ་རང་སེམས་འདུལ་བ་གནད། །སེམས་མ་ཐུལ་བའི་བསྙེན་སྒྲུབ་རྟེན་བཞེངས་སོགས། །ཚེ་རབས་བསགས་ཀྱང་བྱང་ཆུབ་ཐོབ་མི་འགྱུར། །སེམས་དུལ་ཞེས་པ་ཉོན་མོངས་འདུལ་བ་ཡིན། །ཉོན་མོངས་འདུལ་ཐབས་སྤང་བསྒྱུར་ཤེས་གསུམ་འདུས། །ཉོན་མོངས་སྤོང་བ་ཐུན་མོང་མདོ་ཡི་ལམ། །འདོད་ཆགས་མི་སྡུག་ཞེ་སྡང་བྱམས་པ་དང་། །གཏི་མུག་གཉེན་པོར་རྟེན་འབྲེལ་བསྒོམས་པས་སྤངས། ། ཉོན་མོངས་བསྒྱུར་བ་ཐུན་མིན་གསང་སྔགས་ལམ། །འདོད་ཆགས་སྐྱེས་ཚེ་འོད་དཔག་མེད་པའམ། །ཞལ་སྦྱོར་ཧེ་རུ་ཀ་ཡི་ལྷ་ཞིག་བསྒོམ། །འདོད་ཆགས་རྟོག་པ་ཡི་དམ་ལྷ་རུ་བསྒྱུར། །ཉོན་མོངས་གཞན་ལའང་དེ་ཡིས་འགྲེ་བར་བྱ། ༈ །ཉོན་མོངས་རང་བཞིན་ཤེས་པ་ཁྱད་པར་ལམ། །འདོད་ཆགས་རྟོག་པ་ལམ་ལམ་ཤར་བའི་ཚེ། །ངོ་བོ་གཅེར་གྱིས་བལྟས་པས་རང་སར་ཡལ། །བདེ་སྟོང་དབྱེར་མེད་ཕྱག་རྒྱ་ཆེན་པོ་འཆར། །སོ་སོར་རྟོག་པའི་ཡེ་ཤེས་ཞེས་ཀྱང་བྱ། །གདོད་ནས་སྤང་

In entering the path, there is both the sutra approach and the mantra approach,
and there are a vast number of methods for following them.
The omniscient one taught that to do no unvirtuous deeds whatsoever,
to practice virtue, and to control[88] one's own mind summarizes sutra practice,
and meditation on the two stages of creation and completion
summarizes mantra practice.
Since the mind is the root of all phenomena,
it is crucial to control it right from the start.
Doing recitation and visualization practices without mental control
could go on for lifetimes without resulting in enlightenment.
What is called "mental control" means controlling afflictive emotions.[89]
Methods of controlling afflictive emotions can be subsumed into three: rejection, transformation, and recognition.
Rejecting these emotions is the ordinary approach of the sutras.
Desire is renounced through contemplation on repulsiveness, hatred through contemplation on love,
and stupidity through meditation on interdependent relationship.[90]

The uncommon approach of mantra is to transform afflictive emotions.
When desire arises, you meditate on Amitabha[91]
or a deity such as Heruka[92] in union.
The desirous thought is transformed into the deity.
The other deluded emotions are treated in the same way.

The exceptional approach is to recognize the true nature of afflictive emotions.
When desirous thoughts arise vividly,
looking directly at their essence, they subside in themselves.
This is the dawning of mahamudra,[93] bliss and emptiness inseparable.
It is also called the pristine wisdom of discernment.[94]
There has never been anything to reject, nor to accept,
nor to transform; everything is contained within mind.
Know that there is no other intention of a buddha
than simply the uncontrived mind itself.

དུ་མེད་ཅིང་སྣང་དུ་མེད། །བསྒྱུར་དུ་མེད་ཅིང་ཐམས་ཅད་སེམས་སུ་འདུས། །
སེམས་ཉིད་མ་བཅོས་བཞག་ན་སངས་རྒྱས་ཀྱི། །དགོངས་པ་དེ་ལས་གཞན་མེད་
ཞེས་པའོ། ༈ །དེ་གསུམ་སྟན་ཐོག་གཅིག་ཏུ་ཉམས་བླངས་ཐབས། །རྒྱལ་བ་
ཡང་དགོན་པ་ཡི་བཞེད་པ་ནི། །དཔེར་ན་འདོད་ཆགས་རྟོག་པ་སྐྱེས་པའི་ཚེ། །
སྐྱེས་མ་ཐག་ཏུ་དེང་ནས་བྱུང་ཚུབ་བར། །བདག་གིས་གི་འདོད་ཆགས་རྟོག་པ་རང་
རྒྱུད་པ། ཐེད་རེ་སྐམ་དུ་སྤུང་སེམས་བརྟན་བསྟེན་པར་བྱ། །དེ་ནས་ནམ་མཁའ་ཁྱབ་
པའི་སེམས་ཅན་རྣམས། །འདོད་ཆགས་རྟོགས་པ་རང་རྒྱུད་པར་སར་གཡེང་བས། །
སྡུག་བསྔལ་མི་བཟད་སྤྱོད་བ་གང་ཡིན་དང་། །ཆོས་མཛད་བཤེས་གཉེན་རྣམས་ཀྱི་
ཐུགས་རྒྱུད་ལ། །འདོད་ཆགས་རྟོག་པས་བར་ཆད་ལ་སོགས་པ། །ཐམས་ཅད་
རང་གི་དེ་ལ་ཁྱབ་ཀྱིས་བསྡུས། །འགྲོ་རྣམས་ཐམས་ཅད་འདོད་ཆགས་སེམས་
བྲལ་བསྒོམ། །བདག་གི་འདོད་ཆགས་རྟོག་པ་འདིར་བརྟེན་ནས། །འགྲོ་རྣམས་རྡོ་
རྗེ་འཆང་གི་གོ་འཕང་ལ། །འགོད་ཕྱིར་རིམ་གཉིས་སྒོམ་པར་བྱ་སྙམ་དུ། །སྐད་
ཅིག་བདེ་མཆོག་ལྷ་བུའི་ཧེ་རུ་ཀ །ཡབ་ཡུམ་ཞལ་སྦྱོར་རྒྱན་རྫོགས་གསལ་བར་
བསྒོམ། །དེ་ཡང་ཡབ་ལ་རིག་པ་རྩིལ་གྱིས་གཏད། །ཧ་ཅང་ཡུམ་གྱི་རྣམ་པ་
གསལ་དྲག་ན། །ད་དུང་འདོད་ཆགས་དུག་རོ་ལྷང་ཉེན་ཡོད། །དེས་ན་གནས་
སྐབས་ཐིག་ལེ་འཚོར་བ་དང་། །མཐར་ཐུག་རང་སེམས་འདོད་ཆགས་དབང་དུ་
ཤོར། །ཕྱིར་ཡང་ལྷ་སྐུ་བསྒོམས་བསྒོམ་ནས་ཉོན་མོངས་སོགས། །འཇིག་རྟེན་རྣམ་

There is a method for practicing all three of these approaches in one sitting,
according to Gyalwa Yangön.[95]
With thoughts of desire, for example,
as soon as they arise think: "From now on until enlightenment
I will do away with these ordinary thoughts of desire."
In this way establish an attitude of rejection.
Then imagine that whatever ordinary disturbing thoughts of desire
in the minds of all beings throughout space,
causing unbearable experiences of suffering,
as well as the thoughts of desire causing obstacles to
the minds of spiritual guides who are practicing Dharma,
are all gathered into your own desire,
and the minds of all beings become free of desire.
Then, thinking that by using these very thoughts of desire,
you will practice the two stages
in order to place all beings in the state of Vajradhara,[96]
meditate that you instantly become a heruka such as Chakrasamvara,[97]
masculine and feminine in union, with all the adornments.
When you identify your awareness with the masculine
and visualize the form of the feminine too intimately,
there is still the danger that the toxic effect of desire will resurface,
resulting initially in loss of vital energy[98] and
ultimately in coming under the power of desire.
In general, it is inappropriate to pursue mundane thoughts
and afflictive emotions while meditating on a deity.
Imagine that your root guru, magnificent and powerful,
is in your heart on a lotus and moon seat.
Pray sincerely again and again for the blessing that
the thoughts of desire that occur in your mind
arise as the pristine wisdom of discernment.
Then look directly at your own mind
as the inseparability of the deity, the guru, and the emotion.
The meditation should be maintained from the time
the emotion arises just until it is resolved.
Afterward, do a prayer to perfectly dedicate the merit, such as

རྟོག་རྗེས་སུ་འབྲང་མི་རུང་། དེ་ཡི་ཐུགས་ཀར་པད་ཟླའི་གདན་སྟེང་དུ། །རྩ་བའི་
བླ་མ་མཛེས་བརྗིད་ལྡན་པར་བསྒོམ། །བདག་རྒྱུད་ལ་སྐྱེས་འདོད་ཆགས་རྟོག་པ་
འདི། །སོར་རྟོག་ཡེ་ཤེས་འཆར་བར་བྱིན་གྱིས་རློབས། །ཁ་ཞེ་མེད་པར་ཡང་ཡང་
གསོལ་བ་གདབ། །དེ་ནས་ལྷ་དང་བླ་མ་ཉོན་མོངས་གསུམ། །དབྱེར་མེད་རང་
སེམས་ཉིད་ལ་ཐིག་གེར་བལྟ། །བསྒོམ་ཡུན་རིང་ཐུང་ཉོན་མོངས་སྐྱེས་ནས་
བཟུང་། །ལམ་དུ་མ་སོང་ཚོད་ཙམ་སྐྱོང་ནས་མཐར། །དགེ་འདིས་འབྲེལ་བའི་
སེམས་ཅན་མ་ལུས་དང་། །ཆོས་མཛད་རྣམས་ཀྱིས་ལམ་བར་ཆད་སོགས། །ཉོན་
མོངས་འདོད་ཆགས་རྟོག་པ་ཀུན་ཞི་ནས། །བདེ་སྟོང་ཕྱག་རྒྱ་ཆེན་པོ་མངོན་གྱུར་
ཤོག། །ཅེས་པའི་བསྔོ་སྨོན་རྣམ་པར་དག་པ་བྱ། །ཞེ་སྡང་གཏི་མུག་ལ་ཡང་དེས་
དེའི་འགྲེ་ཞིང་། །ཞེ་སྡང་ཞི་བའི་ལྷ་བསྒོམ་ཁྱད་པར་གནད། ༔ །ཐ་མལ་འཁྲུལ་
སྣང་བཟློག་ལ་བསྐྱེད་རིམ་སྟེ། །དེ་ཉིད་བདེན་ཞེན་བཟློག་ལྡོག་ལ་རྫོགས་རིམ་
གཙོ། །ཚེ་གཅིག་རྡོ་རྗེ་འཆང་དངོས་སྒྲུབ་པ་ལ། །བསྐྱེད་རྫོགས་ཡ་བྲལ་སོང་བས་
དོན་མི་འགྲུབ། །བསྐྱེད་རྫོགས་ཟུང་འཇུག་ཟབ་མོའི་ལམ་ཡིན་ཀྱང་། །རྣམ་རྟོག་
འགྱུ་བ་སྒོམ་དུ་མ་ཤར་བར། །ཟུང་འཇུག་དངོས་གཞི་མི་འོང་རེས་འཛོག་བྱ། །
བཙོས་པའི་ཟུང་འཇུག་བློས་བྱས་ཡིན་པས་སྤྱངས། ༔ །དེ་ཡང་བསྐྱེད་རིམ་སྒོམ་
བསྒོམ་པར་བྱེད་པ་ལ། །སྦྱང་གཞི་སྦྱང་བྱ་སྦྱོང་བྱེད་སྦྱངས་འབྲས་ཀྱི། །གོ་དོན་
ཕྱོགས་མགོ་ཙམ་ཞིག་ཆགས་པར་དགོས། །སྦྱང་གཞི་ཆོས་དབྱིངས་རྟག་བརྟན་

"By this virtue may the thoughts of desire of
all deluded sentient beings
and obstacles to the stages and paths of Dharma practitioners be eliminated,
and the bliss-emptiness of mahamudra be actualized."
Apply this kind of meditation to hatred and stupidity as well.
For pacifying hatred, it is especially effective to meditate on a deity.

Creation stage is mainly for undermining the deluded appearance of ordinary reality,
and completion stage for undermining attachment to the reality of that creation stage itself.
The actualization of Vajradhara in a single lifetime
will not be achieved if creation and completion are separated.
Even though the unity[99] of creation and completion is the profound approach,
until the movement of thoughts arises *as* meditation,
it is not the real practice of unity, so you should alternate their practice.
Contrived unity is a mental fabrication and should be abandoned.

In the meditation of creation stage, there are four aspects
of which you should gain at least some understanding:
the basis of purification, that which is to be purified, that which purifies, and the result of purification.
The basis of purification is the eternal, noncomposite realm of reality[100]
that fully permeates all beings as the buddha nature.[101]
Sentient beings thus also possess the qualities of the body of reality,[102] such as the marks and signs,
that exist as an integral aspect of awareness: this is the basis for purification.
That which is to be purified is the incidental blemish of delusion
arising from ignorance without beginning, which obscures this buddha nature.
An example would be the sun obscured by clouds.
The sunshine is the capacity to manifest inherent qualities.
The clouds are incidental blemishes that could clear away.
Emotional and cognitive obscurations and those of meditative absorption are what is to be purified.

འདུས་མ་བྱས། །བདེ་གཤེགས་སྙིང་པོས་འགྲོ་ཀུན་ཡོངས་ལ་ཁྱབ། །ཆོས་སྐུའི་ཡོན་ཏན་མཚན་དཔེ་སོགས་ཀྱང་ལྡན། །ཡེ་ཤེས་རང་ཆས་བཞུགས་པ་སྦྱང་གཞི་ཡིན། །སྦྱང་བྱ་ཐོག་མེད་དུས་ནས་མ་རིག་པས། །གློ་བུར་འཁྲུལ་པའི་དྲི་མས་གཤེགས་སྙིང་བསྒྲིབས། །དཔེར་ན་ཉི་མ་སྤྲིན་གྱིས་བསྒྲིབས་པ་བཞིན། །ཡོན་ཏན་རང་ཆས་མངོན་རུང་ཉེ་ཟེར་འདྲ། །དྲི་མ་གློ་བུར་བསལ་རུང་སྤྲིན་དང་འདྲ། །སྙོམས་འཇུག་ཉོན་སྒྲིབ་ཤེས་སྒྲིབ་སྦྱང་བྱ་ཡིན། །སྦྱོང་བྱེད་དབྱིབས་ཀྱི་རྣལ་འབྱོར་གྲངས་མང་ཡང་། །མངལ་སྐྱེས་སྒོང་སྐྱེས་དྲོད་གཤེར་སྐྱེས་པ་གསུམ། །མངོན་བྱང་ལྔ་བསྐྱེད་རྡོ་རྗེ་བཞི་བསྐྱེད་དང་། ཚིག་གསུམ་གྱིས་བསྐྱེད་པ་སོགས་ཀྱིས་སྦྱངས། །བརྫུས་སྐྱེས་སྐད་ཅིག་དྲན་རྫོགས་བསྐྱེད་པས་སྦྱངས། །མཁས་པས་སྦྱར་ཤད་མི་མཐུན་གྲངས་མང་ཡང་། །མདོར་བསྡུས་གང་ཡང་འགལ་མེད་ཤེས་པས་འཐུས། །དང་པོར་མངོན་རྟོགས་བསྒོམ་ནས་བསྡུ་རིམ་ཡན། །ཚོ་གའི་རིམ་པ་སོ་སོར་ཡོད་པ་ཡང་། །སྦྱང་གཞི་བདེ་གཤེགས་སྙིང་པོ་དེ་ཉིད་ལ། །སྦྱང་བྱ་བྱིས་པའི་རྣམ་ཤེས་ཞུགས་ནས་བཟུང་། །བཙས་ནས་འཆི་བའི་བར་གྱི་འཁྲུལ་པ་སྟེ། །གསར་རྙིང་ཚོ་གའི་རིམ་པ་མི་འདྲ་ཡང་། །ཉོན་མོངས་འཁྲུལ་པའི་དྲི་མ་སྦྱངས་ལ་གཅིག །དཔེར་ན་མིག་ནད་བཅག་བུ་ཐུར་མས་བཅོས། །ཁ་ནང་མཁུར་བ་ཀང་ཚ་ཀྱང་བསིལ་དྲོད་སོགས། །ནད་ལ་གཉེན་པོ་སོ་སོར་དགོས་པ་བཞིན། །སྦྱང་བྱའི་གྲངས་ལྟར་སྦྱོང་བྱེད་དེ་མཚུངས་སྟེ། །མིག་ལ་ཐུར་མས་བཅོས་སམ་སྨན་གྱིས་

That which purifies are the many different form yogas,[103]
such as the creation of the five actual enlightening factors, the four vajras, and the three rituals,[104] which purify, respectively,
womb birth, egg birth, and moisture-warmth birth.
Miraculous birth is purified by the instantaneously complete creation.
Although scholars have applied many conflicting explanations,
we could summarize in the knowledge that there is nothing really contradictory.
From the initial meditation on the deity visualization[105] up to the dissolution,
each ritual has its own sequence, but to generalize:
the basis on which purification takes place is the buddha nature itself;
that which is purified is the delusion of the infant consciousness from the time it enters and is born
through the time of the intermediate state of death.[106]
There are different ritual sequences in the old and new traditions,[107]
but with respect to purifying the blemishes of deluded emotion they are the same.
For instance, for disease of the eyes one primarily uses a scalpel,
or orally administers cooling or warming substances for imbalances in heat or cold,
the particular remedy depending on the kind of disease.
There are as many methods of purification as there are problems to be purified.
For the eyes, whether they are restored with instruments or healed with medicine,
for relieving the pain and suffering, it is the same.
Similarly, there are various ritual sequences in the new and old traditions,
but insofar as they all purify the thoughts of afflictive emotions, there is no difference.
Briefly, the way in which the rituals purify is as follows:
Meditation on the absorption of suchness purifies the previous death experience.
All-arising absorption purifies the mental body of the intermediate existence.
Absorption of the cause, meditation on the lotus, sun and moon seat,

གསོལ། །མིག་གི་ཟླུག་རྡུ་སེལ་ལ་གཅིག་པ་བཞིན། །གསར་རྙིང་ཆོ་གའི་རིམ་པ་ཐ་དད་ཀྱང་། །ཉོན་མོངས་རྟོག་ཚོགས་སྦྱངས་ལ་ཁྱད་པར་མེད། །དེ་ལ་ཆོགས་སྦྱང་ཚུལ་མདོར་བསྡུས་ན། །དེ་ཉིད་བསྒོམས་པས་སྤྱར་གྱི་འཆི་སྲིད་སྦྱོང་། །ཀུན་ཉིད་བསྒོམས་པས་བར་སྲིད་ཡིད་ལུས་སྦྱོང་། །རྒྱུ་ཉིད་པད་ཉི་ཟླ་བའི་གདན་བསྒོམས་པས། །ལུས་རྟེན་ཕ་མའི་ཁུ་ཁྲག་དཀར་དམར་སྦྱོང་། །ས་བོན་བསྒོམས་པས་རྣམ་ཤེས་ཞུགས་པ་སྦྱོང་། །ཕྱག་མཚན་བསྒྱུར་དང་སླར་ཡང་ས་བོན་བསྒོམ། །མེར་མེ་ལྷར་ལྷར་གོར་གོར་ལ་སོགས་སྦྱོང་། །སྐུ་ཡོངས་རྫོགས་པས་ལུས་གྲུབ་བཙས་པ་སྦྱོང་། །གནས་གསུམ་བྱིན་རླབས་སྒྲོ་གསུམ་བག་ཆགས་སྦྱོང་། །མངོན་བྱང་ལྷ་ཡིས་མངལ་སྐྱེས་སྦྱོང་ཚུལ་སྟེ། །གཞན་དག་ལ་ཡང་དེ་ཡིས་རིགས་འགྲེ་བྱ། །གསང་སྔགས་བླ་མེད་རྒྱུད་སྡེ་འགའ་ཞིག་ནས། །རྒྱུ་ཡི་རྡོར་འཛིན་འཆི་སྲིད་འོད་གསལ་དང་། །འབྲས་བུའི་རྡོར་འཛིན་བར་སྲིད་གྲུབ་པ་དང་། །མཁའ་གསང་ནས་སྦྲོས་སྦྲོད་ཁུ་རྡུལ་རླུང་གསུམ་པོ། །འདྲེས་པའི་བག་ཆགས་ལུས་རྟེན་སྦྱོང་བ་དང་། །འབྲུ་གསུམ་རིམ་ཡལ་སྣང་མཆེད་ཐོབ་གསུམ་སྦྱང་། །ཐིག་ལེས་སྣང་བ་དཀར་དམར་སྦྱོང་བ་སོགས། །མང་ཡང་འདི་ཙམ་ཤེས་པས་དེ་དག་ཁྲོལ། །ཡེ་ཤེས་བཅུག་པ་འཕྲུལ་སྤྱོད་བསླབ་པ་སྦྱོང་། །དབང་བསྐུར་རྒྱས་གདབ་ཕ་སྐལ་ཐོག་པ་སྦྱོང་། །ཕྱག་བཤགས་མཆོད་བསྟོད་ཡུལ་ལ་ལོངས་སྤྱོད་སྦྱོང་། །འཛབ་བསྙེན་བཟླས་པས་ངག་གི་ལོང་གཏམ་སྦྱོང་། བསྡུ་རིམ་སྐྱེ་བ་དེ་ཡི་འཆི་སྲིད་དང་། །ལྷ་

purifies the physical base, the parents' sperm and ovum, white and red.
Meditation on the seed syllable purifies the entering consciousness.
The transformation into implements and again the meditation on the seed syllables
purifies the fetal stages of round, oval, oblong, and so on.
The fully complete form purifies the birth of the developed body.
The blessing of the three places purifies the habitual patterns of the body, speech, and mind.
This manner of the five enlightening factors purifying womb birth[108]
can be applied in a similar way to the others.
In some of the highest yogatantras[109] of secret mantra,
the "cause vajra holder" corresponds to the clear light[110] of the death experience,
the "result vajra holder"[111] to achieving the intermediate existence,
and the emanation from the organs in union corresponds to the habitual pattern of sperm, ovum, and vital wind[112] combining, and purifies the physical basis of existence.
The sequential absorption of the three letters purifies the three stages of experience: appearance, increase, and attainment;[113]
and the vital drops purify the white and red appearances,[114] and so on—
there is much more, but just knowing this much illuminates the rest.
The entrance of the wisdom beings[115] purifies skilled activities and trainings.[116]
Sealing with the empowerments[117] purifies the inheritance of one's birthright.
Homage, confession, offerings, and praise purify the enjoyment of sense objects.
Recitation of the mantra purifies irrelevant speech.
The dissolution phase purifies the death experience of that life,
and the reappearance in the deity's form purifies the intermediate existence.
Without going further, this summarizes it.
The initial going for refuge and generation of the intention of enlightenment,[118] and the concluding dedication and aspiration
are indispensable in the Great Vehicle[119] approach.
Consecration of offerings, feast gatherings, and so on
are additional ways through which you can effortlessly complete the two accumulations.[120]

སྐུར་ལྡང་པས་བར་སྲིད་སྦྱོང་བ་སོགས། །རྒྱུས་སྦྱོར་མི་བྱ་འདི་རུ་མདོ་ཙམ་མོ། །
སྔོན་དུ་སྐྱབས་སེམས་རྗེས་སུ་བསྔོ་སྨོན་ནི། །ཐེག་ཆེན་ལམ་ལ་མེད་ཐབས་མེད་པ་
སྟེ། །མཆོད་པ་བྱིན་རླབས་ཚོགས་ཀྱི་འཁོར་ལོ་སོགས། །འབད་མེད་ཚོགས་
གཉིས་རྫོགས་པའི་ཡན་ལག་གོ །དེ་ཡང་སྦྱང་གཞི་བདེ་གཤེགས་སྙིང་པོ་ཉིད། །
རྡོ་རྗེ་མཚན་དཔེ་གསལ་རྫོགས་སྐུར་བཞུགས་པས། །དེ་དང་འདྲ་བའི་རྣམ་པ་ལམ་
བྱེད་ཀྱིས། །སྦྱངས་འབྲས་གཞི་ལ་ཡོད་པའི་ལྷ་སྐུ་ཉིད། །མངོན་གྱུར་བྲལ་བའི་
འབྲས་བུ་མཐར་ཐུག་ཆོ། །རྡོ་རྗེ་འཆང་གི་གོ་འཕང་ཐོབ་ཅེས་ཟེར། ༔ །བསྐྱེད་
རིམ་རྒྱས་བསྡུས་ཇི་ལྟར་བསྒོམ་ཡང་རུང་། །རྣམ་པ་གསལ་བས་སྣང་ཡུལ་ཞེན་པ་
སྦྱོང་། །རྣམ་དག་དྲན་པས་གདོས་བཅས་མཚན་འཛིན་བྲལ། །ང་རྒྱལ་བརྟན་པས་
ཐ་མལ་ངར་འཛིན་གཞོམ། །དེ་ཕྱིར་དང་པོར་དབུ་དང་ཕྱག་ཞབས་སོགས། །རེ་རེ་
བཞིན་དུ་གསལ་འདེབས་ཅུང་གོམས་ནས། །སྐུ་གཟུགས་ཡོངས་རྫོགས་ལམ་
གྱིས་གསལ་བར་བསྒོམ། །བསྒོམས་ཀྱང་མི་གནས་རྣམ་རྟོག་འཕྲོ་འདུག་ན། །
ཕྱག་ན་རྡོ་རྗེ་ལྟ་བུར་རིག་པ་གཏད། །རྒོད་ན་སྐྱིལ་ཀྱང་བྱིང་ན་གཙུག་ཏོར་གྱི། །ནོར་
བུ་ལྟ་བུར་རིག་པ་གཏད་ནས་བསྒོམ། །དེ་ནས་ཧ་ཅང་རྣམ་རྟོག་མི་འཕྲོ་ཡང་། །
རྣམ་པ་མི་གསལ་ལྟོག་པ་འདྲ་འདུག་ན། །མིག་སྟུར་ཐང་ཀའམ་ནི་སྟེར་སོའི་སྐུ། །
བཟོ་བྱེད་ལེགས་ལ་ཚོན་བཀྲག་ལྡན་པར་ཞགམ། །རྣམ་རྟོག་མི་འཕྲོ་དེ་ལ་ཡུན་རིང་
བལྟ། །དེ་མ་ཐག་ཏུ་རང་ལུས་དེ་འདྲར་བསྐྱེད། །དེ་ནི་སྟུར་གྱི་སྒོམ་དེ་བོགས་ཐོན་

The basis of purification, which is this very buddha nature,
abides as the body, with its clear and complete vajra signs and marks.
A similar form is used as the path and leads to
the fruition of purification: that very divine form that existed as the basis.
At the time of ultimate fruition of actual freedom,
this is called "obtaining the state of Vajradhara."

Whether one meditates on an elaborate or concise version of creation stage,
there are three main points:
Clarity of form purifies attachment to the appearing object,
recollecting the purity[121] frees one from clinging to corporeality,
and maintaining pride vanquishes clinging to ordinary self.
As to the first, initially visualize each individual part, such as the head,
hands, feet, and so on,
and when somewhat used to that, meditate clearly on the entire form.
When meditation is not stable, and thoughts come and go,
focus your awareness on an implement, such as the vajra in the hand.
If you are languishing, focus on the crossed legs, and if sinking,
focus on something like a jewel in the deity's crown.
Then if there aren't so many active thoughts, but
the form is unclear and murky,
set before you a picture or statue
that is well made and appropriately painted,
and, without thinking, look at it for a long time.
Then immediately generate your own body in that image.
This will enhance the former meditation.

You may recollect the appropriate purities,
but this mental exercise might just add to discursive thoughts.
For the beginner it will become the cause of unclear, scattered meditation.
It is better to meditate on the deity's form as empty and light, like a rainbow,
and to know that the one who is doing that is one's own mind.
Mind itself, intrinsically free of a basis, is emptiness,
and the demonstration of its special qualities
is the arising of forms of faces, hands, and ornaments.

འགྱུར། ༔ །རྣམ་དག་སོ་སོ་ཉིད་ནས་དྲན་བྱས་ཀྱང་། །བློ་ཡི་བཅོ་བསླང་བགྲང་རྣམ་
རྟོག་སྟོན་རྫོལ་མ་ཡིན། །ལས་དང་པོ་ལ་མི་གསལ་འཕྲོ་རྐྱེན་བྱེད། །དེ་བས་ལྷ་སྐུ་
སྣང་གསལ་འཇའ་ཚོན་ལྟར། །དེ་ཉིད་བྱེད་མཁན་རང་གི་སེམས་ཡིན་ཏེ། །སེམས་
ཉིད་གདོད་ནས་རྩ་བྲལ་སྟོང་པ་ཉིད། །དེ་ཡི་ཡོན་ཏན་ཁྱད་པར་སྟོན་བསྟན་པ་ལ། །
ཞལ་ཕྱག་རྒྱན་གྱི་རྣམ་པ་ཤར་ཞེས་བསྒོམ། ༔ །ང་རྒྱལ་མ་བསྒོམ་བདག་འཛིན་རྩ་
བ་ཆོད། །བདག་འཛིན་ཞིག་ཆེ་རང་སེམས་གར་གཏད་ཀྱང་། །དེ་ཡི་ངོ་བོར་ཁྲིག་
གེར་ཤར་བ་ཡིན། །དེ་ལྟར་བསྐྱེད་རིམ་རྩོལ་བས་བསྒོམ་པ་ཡིས། །བསྒོམ་པའི་ཚེ་
ན་དངོས་སྣང་ནུས་པ་བསྒྲིབ། །མ་བསྒོམ་ལྟར་འཆར་གསལ་སྣང་ཆུང་དུ་ཡིན།
བསྒོམ་དང་མ་བསྒོམ་བསྒོམས་མེད་པར་འཁྲུལ་སྣང་ཀུན། །ལྷ་དང་གཞལ་ཡས་
འཆར་བ་གསལ་སྣང་འབྱིང་། །རང་གིས་ལྷ་བསྒོམ་བསྒོམས་གཟུགས་ཅན་གཟུགས་
མེད་ཀྱིས། །རང་ཉིད་ལྟར་མཐོང་གསལ་སྣང་ཆེན་པོ་སྟེ། །ཚིང་ལུགས་རྣམ་པར་
སྨིན་པའི་རིག་འཛིན་ཐེར། ༔ །ལྷ་སྐུ་གསལ་ཡང་རང་སེམས་གསལ་སྣང་ཡིན། །
མི་གསལ་བློ་ཡི་རྩོམ་པའང་རང་སེམས་ཡིན། གསལ་འདོད་ཡང་སྒོམ་བསྒོམ་བྱེད་
པའི་མཁན་པོའང་སེམས། རང་སེམས་ཡེ་ཤེས་བླ་མ་ལྷ་ཡང་ཡིན། །ཐམས་ཅད་
སེམས་སྣང་སེམས་ཉིད་མ་བཅོས་པ། །རིམ་གཉིས་ལམ་གྱི་གཅེས་གནད་མཐར་
ཐུག་སྟེ། །བསྐྱེད་པའི་རིམ་པ་མང་པོ་ཅི་བསྒོམ་ཡང་། །མ་ཡེངས་ཙམ་གྱི་དྲན་
རིག་གསལ་ཐེབ་ན། །གསལ་ན་གསལ་སྟོང་རྟོགས་ན་རྟོགས་སྟོང་འཆར།

Do not meditate on pride; cut through the root of ego-clinging.
When ego-clinging is destroyed, wherever one's mind focuses,
its essence arises vividly.
In this way, by meditation on the creation stage with effort,
while actually meditating, the impact of "real" appearances will be diminished,
and without meditating, the deity arises.
This is the lesser experience of luminous appearance.[122]
When all deluded appearances, regardless of meditating or not,
arise as the deity and divine palace, it is intermediate luminous appearance.
When you meditate on the deity and form and formless beings see you as that deity,
it is the great luminous appearance, called a maturation knowledge-holder[123] in the Ancient tradition.

The clear form of the deity is the luminous appearance of your own mind,
and the unclear, dissatisfying experience is also your mind!
So also, mind is the one who desires clarity and tries again,
and mind is the wisdom deity and guru.
Everything is mind's appearance, and yet mind itself is uncontrived.
The beauty of this ultimate essential point of the approach of the two stages
is that no matter which of the many creation stages you do,
if you apply clear awareness and mindfulness that is merely undistracted,
when the meditation is clear, it arises as clarity-emptiness and when obscure, as obscurity-emptiness!

In general, creation stage is a contrivance,
but the path of contrivance leads to the authentic natural state.
With the mental conviction of the lack of reality in the root or ground
of deluded grasping to deluded appearance,
resting in a pristine state is completion stage itself, the actual natural state.
The first stage is the provisional meaning and the latter the definitive meaning.

It is said that if you understand mind, knowing this one thing illuminates everything,

༈ །སྤྱིར་ནི་བསྐྱེད་པའི་རིམ་པ་བཅོས་མ་ཡིན། །བཅོས་མའི་ལམ་གྱིས་རྣལ་མའི་དོན་ལ་ཁྲིད། །འཁྲུལ་སྣང་འཁྲུལ་འཛིན་གཞི་རྩ་མ་གྲུབ་པར། །བློ་ཐག་ཆོད་པས་མ་བཅོས་སོར་བཞག་ནི། །རྫོགས་རིམ་ཉིད་དེ་རྣལ་མ་དངོས་ཡིན་ནོ། །སྒྱུ་མ་དྲང་དོན་ཕྱི་མ་ངེས་དོན་ཡིན། །སེམས་དོན་ཤེས་ན་གཅིག་ཤེས་ཀུན་གྲོལ་ཏེ། །སེམས་དོན་མ་ཤེས་ཀུན་ཤེས་གཅིག་ཧྲུག་སྡུག་ཟེར། །སྟོང་ཉིད་རུང་ན་ཐམས་ཅད་ཀུན་རུང་ལ། །སྟོང་ཉིད་མི་རུང་ཐམས་ཅད་མི་རུང་ཞེས། །སློབ་དཔོན་ཆེན་པོ་འཕགས་པ་ཀླུ་ཡིས་གསུངས། །ཕྱག་རྫོགས་དབུ་མ་སྤྲོས་བྲལ་དོན་དམ་དང་། །རྒྱལ་བའི་དགོངས་པ་གདོད་མའི་གནས་ལུགས་དང་། །ཤེས་རབ་ཕར་ཕྱིན་ལྟ་སྒོམ་སྤྱོད་པ་སོགས། །ཐ་སྙད་མིང་གི་རྣམ་གྲངས་ཐམས་ཅད་ཀུན། །དོན་ལ་སེམས་ཉིད་དངོས་པོའི་གཤིས་ལུགས་ཉིད། །ཅིར་ཡང་མ་གྲུབ་བློ་འདས་བརྗོད་བྲལ་བ། །དེ་ཉིད་གཅིག་པུར་འདུ་ཚུལ་གསུངས་པ་ལགས། ༈ །དེ་ལྟར་སེམས་དོན་སྒོམ་པར་བྱེད་པ་ལའང་། །མོས་གུས་སྟོབས་ཀྱིས་ནང་ནས་ཤར་བ་ལ། །དགོས་པ་མིན་ཀྱང་གང་ཟག་ཕལ་རྣམས་ཀྱིས། །བསྒོམ་བྱ་སེམས་ཀྱི་གནས་ལུགས་ཙུང་ཟད་རེ། །མ་ཤེས་ལུང་མ་བསྟན་ལ་བསྒོམ་པར་སྲིད། ༈ །རྣམ་ཤེས་ཚོགས་བརྒྱད་མ་དག་འཁྲུལ་སེམས་ཡིན། །དེ་ཡི་ངོ་བོར་དག་པའི་ཀུན་གཞི་གནས། །དེ་ལ་ཉིད་སྒྲས་སྒྲས་བསྟན་ཕྱིར་སེམས་ཉིད་བྱ། །སྒོ་ལྔའི་རྣམ་པར་ཤེས་དང་དྲུག་པའི་ཡིད། །ཉོན་ཡིད་ཀུན་གཞིའི་རྣམ་ཤེས་བཅས་པ་ལ། །ཚོགས་བརྒྱད་ཞེས་སུ་རང་བྱུང་ཀུན

but if you don't understand mind, knowing everything obscures the one thing.
The great master Noble Nagarjuna said it this way:
"Where there is appropriate understanding of emptiness, all things are appropriate,
and if there is no appropriate understanding of emptiness, nothing is."
All of the various designations, such as
mahamudra, dzogchen,[124] middle path,[125] unembellished, ultimate,
enlightened intention of the victorious ones, intrinsic nature,
perfection of wisdom, view, meditation, and action, and so on,
indicate that mind itself and the true nature of objects
have no true reality whatsoever and are beyond intellect and inexpressible.
This one point could well be the synopsis of all teachings.

In bringing about meditation on the nature of mind in this way,
the power of devotion causes it to arise from within,
and more is really unnecessary. However, most ordinary people
know very little about the meditation subject—the nature of mind—
and their meditation could prove ineffectual.

Deluded mind consists of the eight impure groups of consciousness.[126]
The essence of that abides as the pure foundation.[127]
In order to indicate the suchness of *that*, the term "mind itself"[128] is used.
The All-knowing Rangjung[129] held that
the eight groups are the five sense consciousnesses, the mental consciousness,
afflictive mind, and the foundation consciousness.
Since the "instantaneous mind"[130] conditions all of those,
when counted together, there are also held to be nine groups.
The sutras mention many terms such as "appropriating consciousness,"
"deluded mind," "cognitive obscuration," and "foundation consciousness."
Since it is taught that the intrinsic nature of the foundation is virtue,
it is essentially self-liberated buddha nature.
It is not the foundation itself that is removed, but it abides as the foundation of what is removed.

མཁྱེན་བཞེད། །དེ་མ་ཐག་ཡིད་དེ་ཀུན་འདུ་བྱེད་ཕྱིར། །ཟུར་དུ་མི་འདྲེན་ཚོགས་དགུར་བཞེད་པའང་ཡོད། །མདོ་ལས་ལེན་པའི་རྣམ་ཤེས་གསུངས་པ་དང་། །འཁྲུལ་པའི་སེམས་དང་ཤེས་བྱའི་སྒྲིབ་པ་དང་། །ཀུན་གཞིའི་རྣམ་ཤེས་མིང་གི་རྣམ་གྲངས་ཡིན། །ཀུན་གཞི་ངང་ལུགས་དགེ་བ་ཞེས་གསུངས་ཕྱིར། །དེ་ཡི་ངོ་བོ་རང་གྲོལ་བདེ་གཤེགས་སྙིང་། །བྲལ་བྱའི་གཞི་མིན་བྲལ་བའི་གཞི་རུ་གནས། །དེ་ཡང་རྣམ་ཤེས་ཚོགས་བརྒྱད་ཐག་ཁྲ་ལ། །སྦྲུལ་དུ་འཛིན་ལྟར་གཤིས་ལ་མི་གནས་པས། །འཁྲུལ་དུས་ཉིད་ནས་རང་གི་ངོ་བོས་སྟོང་། །ནམ་ཅམ་འཁྲུལ་ན་ཐོག་མ་མེད་པ་ནས། །ལྷན་ཅིག་སྐྱེས་པའི་མ་རིག་པ་ཡིས་སྒྲིབ་བསྒྲིབ། །དེ་ཡང་དཔེར་ན་མེ་ལོང་གསལ་བ་ཡི། །དྭངས་པའི་ཆ་ནི་བདེ་གཤེགས་སྙིང་པོ་ཡིན། །གཡའ་ཁམས་ཡོད་པ་ཀུན་གཞིའི་རྣམ་ཤེས་སམ། །ཤེས་བྱའི་སྒྲིབ་པ་ལྷན་སྐྱེས་མ་རིག་ཟེར། །གཡའ་དྲིས་གོས་ལྟར་ཀུན་གཞིའི་རྣམ་ཤེས་སྟེང་། །བག་ཆགས་བསགས་པ་ཉོན་མོངས་སྒྲིབ་པ་ཡིན། །རྣམ་ཤེས་དེ་ཡི་ངོ་བོ་སྟོང་པ་ལ། །བདག་ཏུ་འཛིན་ཅིང་གསལ་ཆ་ཡུལ་དུ་བཟུང་། །དེ་མ་ཐག་པའི་ཡིད་ཀྱིས་ཚོགས་དྲུག་གཡོ། །ཡུལ་དང་དབང་པོ་གཉིས་ཀ་འཕྲད་རྐྱེན་བྱེད། །རང་ལ་གཞན་དུ་མེད་ཀྱང་གཉིས་སྣང་དབང་། །དཔེར་ན་མིག་གིས་གཟུགས་སུ་མཐོང་བ་དང་། །མིག་ཤེས་དེ་ལས་གཞན་པའི་གཟུགས་མེད་ཀྱང་། །གསལ་ཆ་གཟུགས་དང་སྟོང་ཆ་དབང་པོར་འཁྲུལ། །དེ་མ་ཐག་པའི་ཡིད་ཀྱིས་མཚམས་སྦྱར་བྱེད། །མིག་གི་ཤེས་པ་རྟོག་

So, for instance, the eight consciousness groups are like a variegated rope
that is perceived as a snake, though that is not its true character:
From the very first moment of this delusion, it was itself essentially empty.
It is from beginningless time
that co-emergent ignorance has obscured true nature.
For example, the clear and limpid aspect
of a mirror is the buddha nature,
and the tarnish on it is the foundation consciousness,
also called cognitive obscuration or co-emergent ignorance.
Like the coat of tarnish, the foundation consciousness wears
the collection of habitual patterns, the obscuration of afflictive emotions.
The essentially empty nature of consciousness
is identified as the self, and objective reality is projected onto its luminous aspect.
The instantaneous mind moves the six consciousness groups
and causes the meeting of object and organ.
Though nothing other than mind itself, the appearance of duality predominates.
For example, when the eye perceives a form,
although there is no form outside of the eye consciousness,
the luminous aspect is mistaken for form and the empty aspect for the organ.
The instantaneous mind function coalesces the process:
eye consciousness initially arises undeluded, free of concept,
but instantaneously it is suppressed and
the feeling of duality arises, and with it the mental sixth consciousness.
Experiencing happiness, suffering, or neutrality,
the discriminations of attachment, aversion, and ignorance arise, and this is the afflictive mind.
Then through rejection or acceptance, the foundation consciousness is imprinted
with the accumulation of karmic action, also called formation.[131]
When the sixth mind is counted together with the instantaneous mind,
perceiving externally with the five senses, it is the object;
when the afflictive mind functions with the instantaneous mind,
directed inward, it leaves habitual patterns in the foundation.

བྲལ་མ་འཁྲུལ་སྐྱེ། །དེ་མ་ཐག་པས་དེ་འགགས་གཟུང་འཛིན་གྱི། །ཚོར་བ་སྐྱེས་ཚེ་དུག་པའི་ཡིད་ཀྱང་ལངས། །བདེ་སྡུག་བཏང་སྙོམས་སྤྱོད་པས་ཆགས་སྡང་དང་། །རྨོངས་པའི་འདུ་ཤེས་སྐྱེ་བ་ཉོན་ཡིད་ཡིན། །སྤྱང་བླང་བྱས་ནས་ཀུན་གཞིའི་རྣམ་ཤེས་སྟེང་། །ལས་བསགས་པ་ལ་འདུ་བྱེད་ཤེས་ཞེས་ཀྱང་ཟེར། །དུག་ཡིད་དེ་མ་ཐག་ཡིད་ལ་བསྒོམས་བསྒོངས་ན། །སྒྲོ་ལྔ་ཁ་ཕྱིར་བལྟས་པས་ཡུལ་ཡིན་ལ། །ཉོན་ཡིད་དེ་མ་ཐག་ཡིད་ལ་བསྒོམས་བསྒོངས་ན། །ནང་དུ་ཁ་ཕྱོགས་ཀུན་གཞིར་གཞི་བག་ཆགས་འཇོག །དེར་འཇོག་ལས་ནི་ལུང་མ་བསྟན་པར་གནས། །རྣམ་པར་མ་སྨིན་བར་དུ་ཆུད་མི་ཟ། ༈ །རྣམ་དཀར་དགེ་བའི་ཕྱོགས་ཀྱི་བག་ཆགས་ནི། །ཀུན་གཞིའི་རྣམ་ཤེས་སྟེང་དུ་བསགས་མི་ནུས། །དེ་ཚེ་ཉོན་ཡིད་རྣམ་བྱང་ཤེས་ཡིད་སྒྱུར་སྒྱུར་དང་། །གཉེན་པོ་ཡིན་ཕྱིར་ཡེ་ཤེས་སྟེང་དུ་འཇོག །དགེ་བའི་སེམས་པ་ཀུན་གཞིའི་ཡེ་ཤེས་ཀྱི། །རང་མདངས་ལས་བྱུང་དགེ་རྩ་བསགས་པ་ཡང་། །བྲལ་བའི་རྐྱེན་དང་རྣམ་སྨིན་རྒྱུར་འགྱུར་ལས། །བར་མ་དོ་རུ་ཆུད་ཟོས་འགྲོ་མི་སྲིད། །ཀུན་གཞི་ཕྱི་ཡི་ཡུལ་དང་ནང་དབང་པོ། །བར་གྱི་ཤེས་པ་ཀུན་གྱི་རྒྱུ་རུ་བྱེད། །ཉོན་ཡིད་སྤྲིན་བཞིན་ཚོགས་དྲུག་ཆར་ལྟ་བུ། །ལས་བྱས་པ་རྣམས་ཆུ་བོ་བག་ཆགས་ཀྱི། །ཀུན་གཞི་རྒྱ་མཚོའི་དཔེ་ཡིན་དེ་ཀུན་རྒྱུན། །འབྲེལ་བར་བྱེད་པ་དེ་མ་ཐག་ཡིད་ཡིན། ༈ །ཉམས་ལེན་པ་རྣམས་ཀུན་གཞིའི་རྣམ་ཤེས་ལས། །དེ་མ་ཐག་ཡིད་ལངས་པ་ཙམ་ཉིད་ལས། །དེ་རྒྱུན་མི་མཐུད་དེ་ཡི་སྟེང་དུ་བཞག །དེ་ལ་སྐད་ཅིག་དང་པོར་

Left there, the karma abides without effect
as unavoidable potential until it ripens.

Habitual patterns of totally pure virtue
cannot be accumulated as imprints on the foundation consciousness.
In this case, the afflictive mind becomes the fully purified mind,
and since that is the remedy, virtue is imprinted on pristine wisdom.
Virtuous thoughts arise from the intrinsic radiance of foundation wisdom.
This accumulation of the roots of virtue
becomes the condition of freedom and cause of complete fruition[132]
and also cannot be interrupted or lost.
With the foundation functioning as the cause of the outer objects, inner sense faculties,
and all the consciousnesses in between,
the afflictive mind is like the clouds, the six groups like rain,
the karmic actions are the rivers, and
habitual patterns of the foundation are the ocean.
In this example, the agent that connects all of this in some kind of continuity is the instantaneous mind.

For the practitioner, this means that just as soon as the instantaneous mind barely arises from the foundation consciousness,
without any extension of duration, you should place the attention directly upon it.
This is called liberation in the first moment, or
vanquished at first sight,[133] in certain doctrinal terms.
When the sixth mind consciousness and afflictive mind have just arisen,
and are recognized through mindfulness and liberated in their own place,
it is called liberation in the second or third moment.

However, since that discursive thought is the dynamic energy of mind,
it is impossible for thoughts of attachment and aversion not to arise.
However, if you rely on mindful awareness, discursive thoughts cannot accumulate karma.
It is like pouring water into a vase with a hole in the bottom.

གྲོལ་ཞེས་དང་། །ཆོས་སྐད་འགའ་ལ་འབུར་འཛོམས་མགོ་ཐུག་ཟེར། །དྲུག་པའི་ཡིད་དང་ཉོན་ཡིད་ལངས་ཙམ་ནས། །དྲན་པས་ཟིན་ཚེ་རང་སར་གྲོལ་བ་ལ། །སྐད་ཅིག་གཉིས་པ་གསུམ་པར་གྲོལ་ཞེས་གསུངས། །འོན་ཀྱང་རྣམ་རྟོག་སེམས་ཀྱི་རྩལ་ཡིན་པས། །ཆགས་སྡང་རྟོག་པ་མི་ཤར་མི་སྲིད་ཀྱང་པས། །དྲན་ཤེས་བརྟན་ན་ལས་བསགས་མི་ནུས་ཏེ། །བུམ་པ་ཞབས་རྫོལ་ནང་དུ་ཆུ་ལྷུག་འདྲ། །འཁྲུལ་རྟོག་རིག་པ་ཕྱེད་ཆ་མཉམ་ཉམས་པ་ལ། །སོར་རྟོག་ཉིད་ཀྱིས་ཞེན་རྟོག་གཞིལ་ཞེས་གསུངས། །དཔེར་ན་རྩྭ་སྦུར་ཕྲ་མོ་མེས་ཟིན་འདྲ། །མེ་དང་རྩྭ་སྦུར་གཉིས་ཀར་སྡང་ན་ཡང་། །སྐད་ཅིག་ཉིད་ལ་མེ་རུ་འགྱུར་བའི་ཕྱིར། །མེ་ཡིན་བྱས་ཀྱང་ཆོག་པ་ཏེ་བཞིན་ནོ། ༄ །མདོར་ན་ད་ལྟ་ཅི་ཡང་མི་དྲན་པའི། །ནག་ཐོམ་ལུང་མ་བསྟན་ཏུ་གནས་པ་ནི། །ཀུན་གཞིའི་རྣམ་ཤེས་ཤེས་བྱའི་སྒྲིབ་པ་ཡིན། །ལྷན་སྐྱེས་མ་རིག་ཅེས་པའང་དེ་ལ་བྱ། །ཡུལ་དབང་གཉིས་འཕྲད་ལམ་གྱི་དུང་ལྟ་བུའི། །གཟུགས་མཐོང་སྐད་ཅིག་མིག་ཤེས་རྟོག་མེད་ཟེར། །དེ་ལ་རིག་པའི་རྐྱེན་གྱིས་ཚོར་བར་གསུངས་། །དུང་དཀར་ལེགས་ལ་ཡིད་སེམས་དགའ་བ་སོགས། །ཆགས་སྡང་སྐྱེ་དུས་ཉོན་ཡིད་སླེབས་པ་ཡིན། །འདུ་ཤེས་ཞེས་གསུངས་དེ་ལས་འདུ་བྱེད་སོགས། །རྟེན་འབྲེལ་བཅུ་གཉིས་སྲིད་པའི་འཁོར་ལོ་བསྐོར། །མིག་ཤེས་ཡིད་ཤེས་བཀག་ཀྱང་མ་ཁེག་ལ། །ལས་ཀྱི་བག་ཆགས་བསགས་པའི་ནུས་པ་མེད། །ཕྱི་མ་ཉོན་ཡིད་དབང་དུ་ཤོར་བ་ན། །ལྟ་སྒོམ་སྤྱོད་པའི་གནད་མེད་ཐ་མལ་པ། །

The deluded thought and the aspect of awareness that distinguishes it are equal,
for the discriminating thought itself measures the thought of attachment.
It is like fire alighting on fine grass husks:
although the fire and the husks appeared as two things,
they instantly become just fire.
So it could be called simply fire.

In short, our present state of neutrality,
the darkness of total lack of awareness,
is the cognitive obscuration of foundation consciousness.
It is also called co-emergent ignorance.
When an object and the sense organ meet, such as seeing a conch shell on the road,
in the first instant of seeing the form, the eye consciousness is said to be without concept.
But due to that contact, what is called "feeling" occurs,
and then, if it is a nice white conch, mental pleasure, and so on.
At this point, with the arising of attachment or aversion, afflictive mind has arrived.
From what is called "perception" comes "formation," and so on:
through the twelve interdependent links[134] the wheel of existence turns.
Even if you tried to block eye consciousness and mental consciousness, they wouldn't cease,
but they don't have the power to accumulate karmic habitual patterns.
But when finally afflictive mind has taken over,
for an ordinary person without recourse to view, meditation, and action,
habitual patterns imprinted on the foundation will accumulate.
For that reason you should try not to fall under its power.
The instantaneous mind is the one that connects this whole process, like the force of water.
If you understand the significance of the eight groups in this way,
and are skilled in applying it directly to practice,
you can cut through the dualistic relationship of the six groups and their objects,
and then the six sense objects will not have the power to disturb meditation.

ཡིན་ཕྱིར་ཀུན་གཞིའི་སྟེང་དུ་བག་ཆགས་གསོག །དེ་ཕྱིར་དེ་ཡི་དབང་དུ་མ་ཤོར་འཆོལ། །དེ་རྒྱུན་འབྲེལ་བྱེད་དེ་མ་ཐག་ཡིད་དེ། ཆུ་ཡི་ཤུགས་འདྲ་དེ་ལྟར་ཚོགས་བརྒྱད་ཀྱི། །གནད་ཤེས་ཉམས་ལེན་སྐྱོང་སྐྱོལ་དུ་འཛུད་མཛུད་མཁས་ན། །ཚོགས་དྲུག་ཡུལ་ལ་གཟུང་འཛིན་འབྲེལ་ཆད་པས། །ཡུལ་དྲུག་རྐྱེན་གྱིས་མཉམ་བཞག་གཡོ་མི་ནུས། །དབང་ཤེས་ནང་དུ་ལྡོག་པར་རྟོམ་རྟོན་པ་ཡིན། །དེ་ཚེ་རླུང་བཅུ་ལས་སུ་རུང་བའི་རྟགས། །དུ་བ་སྨིག་རྒྱུ་སྒྲ་གཅན་ལ་སོགས་འཆར། །དངོས་སྣང་ནུས་པ་ཉམས་པས་སྒྲིབ་མེད་དུ། །ལྷ་སྐུ་ཐིག་ལེ་ལ་སོགས་གྲངས་མེད་པར། །ཕྱི་ནང་རང་ལུས་རང་སེམས་གར་གཏད་དུ། །རེ་དོགས་བྱ་རྩོལ་མི་དགོས་ཤུགས་ཀྱིས་འཆར། །དྲོད་ཐོབ་རྟགས་སུ་རྣམ་གཡེང་ལོང་གཏམ་དང་། །བྱ་བྱེད་འབྲེལ་འདྲིས་འདྲེས་སྤྱོད་པར་འཇུག་མི་སྤྲོ། །རྣམ་གཡེང་མེད་པའི་དབེན་པ་ཁོ་ན་འདོད། །རྣམ་རྟོག་རྒྱུན་ཆད་ནམ་མཁའ་གཡའ་དག་འདྲ། །ལུས་ངག་ཡིད་ལ་བདེ་གསལ་མི་རྟོག་ཉམས། །དཔག་མེད་འཆར་ཡང་ངེས་ཤེས་ཕྱོགས་རེ་བས། །ལམ་རྟགས་ཙམ་ལས་ས་ཟིན་གང་ཡང་མེད། །ཡུལ་དུ་བྱས་ཚད་སྐྱེ་གནས་འཕོ་འགྱུར་ཅན། །བརྟག་མི་ཐུབ་པར་གྲུབ་བརྙེས་ཡོངས་ཀྱིས་བཞེད། །རང་བྱུང་ཡེ་ཤེས་ཡུལ་མེད་ཟང་ཟངས་ཐལ་དུ། །མངོན་གྱུར་ཉིད་ལ་རྟོགས་པའི་ཡེ་ཤེས་བཏགས་རྟགས། །དེ་ཚེ་ལྟ་སྒོམ་སྤྱོད་པའི་ཞེ་འདོད་ཟད། །ཐ་མལ་ཤེས་པ་དེ་ཀའི་ཐོག་ཏུ་བབ། །སྔར་ནས་ཡོད་པ་ད་རེས་ཐག་ཆོད་པས། །བྱ་བ་ཟིན་པའི་སྐྱེས་བུ་བློ་བདེ་ལྟར། །འབད་རྩོལ་

This is the beginning of turning the sense organs and their
consciousnesses inward.
At that time, the signs that the ten vital winds[135] have matured
are experiences of smoke, mirages, eclipses, and so on.
The power of "real" appearances is diminished; and without obscurity,
countless deities, spheres, and so on appear wherever you focus,
outwardly and inwardly, in your body and your mind,
automatically arising without effort, expectation, or anxiety.
As a sign of attaining warmth,[136] you are no longer interested in
useless communication and associations,
and you desire only to remain in solitude without distraction.
The flow of thoughts is cut off and, like the clear sky,
boundless experiences of bliss, clarity, and nonthought[137] arise in body,
speech, and mind.
However, these are only signs on the path, a few approximations of
confidence,
and have nothing whatsoever to do with attainment of higher stages.
When these experiences are objectified, they are subject to arising, ceasing,
and changing,
and cannot be permanent, according to all adepts.[138]
True actualization of the open spaciousness of inherent wisdom without
object
is termed "the pristine wisdom of realization."
At that time, the desires and aversions of view, meditation, and action are
exhausted,
and one simply falls directly upon ordinary mind.
With the absolute conviction of recognizing what has been there all along,
like a contented person who has finished all work,
all effort is dropped: it is the ultimate fruition.

Deceiving appearances appear in variety as non-appearance.
Though appearing to appear, being essentially without reality, they
are empty.
Of mind itself, luminous awareness without foundation, free of basis,
you cannot say anything in regard to existence or non-existence.
In the levels higher than mahayoga,[139] the sublime view is that total purity

ཞིག་པ་འབྲས་བུའི་མཐར་ཕྱུག་གོ། ༈ །སྣང་བ་རྫུན་སྣང་མེད་བཞིན་སྣ་ཚོགས་སྣང་། །སྣང་བཞིན་ངོ་བོ་མ་གྲུབ་སྟོང་པ་ཡིན། །སེམས་ཉིད་གསལ་རིག་གཞི་མེད་རྩ་བྲལ་ཏེ། །ཡོད་མེད་ལ་སོགས་གང་དུའང་བརྗོད་མི་ནུས། ༈ །མ་ཧཱ་ཡོ་ག་ཡན་ཆད་རྣམ་བྱང་དང་། །སྡུག་བསྔལ་བདེན་པ་དབྱེར་མེད་ལྷ་བས་འཕགས། །རིམ་གཉིས་བསྒོམས་པས་དོན་དམ་མངོན་གྱུར་ཚེ། །ཀུན་རྫོབ་གཞི་མེད་རྩ་བྲལ་རང་ཡལ་འདོད། །དེ་ཕྱིར་སྣང་སེམས་གཉིས་བསྲེས་འཁོར་འདས་ཆོས། །ཅིར་ཡང་མ་གྲུབ་ཅིར་ཡང་འཆར་ཞེས་ན། །ཐོས་བསམ་གནད་དུ་སོང་བའི་གདན་ཚིགས་ཡིན། ༈ །རྫུན་སྣང་དེ་དག་སྦྱང་བསྒྱུར་སོར་བཞག་སོགས། །བསྐྱེད་རྫོགས་དམིགས་བཅས་དམིགས་མེད་ཐབས་དུ་མས། །སྦྱོང་སྦྱོར་ཚུལ་ཉམས་ལེན་ཀུན་གྱི་གཅེས་གནད་ནི། །དུས་གསུམ་རྣམ་རྟོག་རྒྱུ་ཡི་གཉེར་མ་འདྲ། །ཟད་པ་མེད་པ་དེ་རྗེས་མི་འབྲང་བར། །གང་ལ་མཉམ་པར་བཞག་བྱ་དེ་ཉིད་ལ། །བཟོ་གནས་མཁན་པོས་སྐུད་པ་འཁེལ་བ་ལྟར། །སྒྲིམ་ལྷོད་བར་མ་ཁམས་དང་བསྟུན་མཁས་ཀྱིས། །དྲན་པའི་རྒྱང་སོ་ཡང་ནས་ཡང་དུ་འཛུག །ཐུང་ཟད་གོམས་པས་དྲན་གྲངས་ཇེ་མང་འགྲོ། །རྩེ་གཅིག་ལ་སོགས་ཉམས་རྣམས་རིམ་གྱིས་སྐྱེ། །སེམས་སམ་རིག་པའི་སྙིགས་མ་ཞེས་བྱ་བ། །ཐ་མལ་འོག་འགྱུར་མི་བཏང་གསལ་དངར་འདོན། །བྱིང་རྒོད་གཉིས་ལས་འོག་འགྱུ་གནོད་ཚབས་ཆེ། །སེམས་ཀྱི་རང་བཞིན་རྩད་བདར་ཆོད་པའི་ཚེ། །དུ་མར་སྣང་ཡང་གཅིག་ལས་མེད་པ་དང་། །གཅིག་པུ་དེ་

is inseparable from the truth of suffering.[140]
When the absolute is actualized through meditation on the two stages,
it follows that the relative, which is without foundation and basis, automatically disappears.
Therefore, all phenomena of cyclic existence or transcendence, included within both appearance and mind,
have no reality whatsoever but arise in any way whatsoever.
When this is realized, it is proof that listening and contemplating have hit the mark.

The many techniques of creation and completion, both with and without visualization,
such as rejecting or transforming or resting in deceiving appearances,
are purificatory methods, and that is where the value of all practice lies.
Thoughts of past, present, and future are like ripples on water, never ending.
Without pursuing them, whatever the subject of concentration is,
upon that itself, like a master craftsperson spinning yarn,
not too tight or too loose, but just right for the material,
the wise direct their watchguard of mindfulness again and again.
When somewhat used to that, mindfulness will grow stronger,
and the progressive experiences, such as one-pointedness,[141] will arise.
Don't fall into the so-called residue of mind or awareness,
the ordinary mental undercurrent, but rather intensify the clarity.
The undercurrent can be more harmful than both sinking and scattering.[142]

When you establish for certain the true nature of mind,
many things arise, yet they are not other than the one.
That one thing also cannot even be grasped by objective clinging.
Looking at it, it is not seen, being without color or shape.
This is a sign of its being without foundation, free of basis, and beyond intellect.
Its essence is empty, its nature clarity,
and its dynamic play of compassion arises without inhibition.
Indeed, it is the three bodies[143] that have been spontaneously present all along.

ཡང་བཟུང་བས་མི་ཟིན་ཞིང་། །བལྟས་པས་མི་མཐོང་ཁ་དོག་དབྱིབས་མེད་པ། །
གཞི་མེད་རྩ་བྲལ་བློ་འདས་ཡིན་པའི་རྟགས། །དེ་ཡི་ངོ་བོ་སྟོང་ལ་རང་བཞིན་
གསལ། །ཐུགས་རྗེའི་རོལ་རྩལ་འགག་པ་མེད་འཆར་བ། །སྐུ་གསུམ་ཉིད་དུ་ཡེ་
ནས་ལྷུན་གྲུབ་ལགས། ༈ །རྣམ་རྟོག་བཀག་ཀྱང་ཁེག་པ་མི་འོང་བས། །མ་
བཀག་གཅིག་ཤར་གཉིས་ཤར་ཤར་དུ་རྒྱུག །ཤར་ཚེ་གར་འགྲོར་བཏང་ནས་རྒྱང་
སོ་རྒྱུགས། །དེ་ཚེ་འགྲོས་མི་ཆེད་ཚུར་ལ་ལོག །དཔེར་ན་རྫིང་ལས་འཕུར་བའི་བྱ་
རོག་བཞིན། །མེ་རོ་ལྡོད་དེ་རྒྱ་མཚོ་བཞིན་དུ་གནས། ༈ །དྲན་པ་ཡེངས་མེད་
གནས་པ་འཁོར་ཡུག་རྣམས། །ཙུང་ཟད་འབྱུང་དཀའ་གོམ་སྒོམ་ཤུགས་ཆུང་བས་
ལེན། །འོན་ཀྱང་སྣ་སུན་མི་བྱེད་རྒྱུན་སྐྱོང་གནད། །གནས་པ་བརྟན་ཡང་ཀྱང་འཛིན་
ཞེན་ཞེས་མ་གྲོལ་ན། །ཁམས་གསུམ་ཉིད་ལས་འཕགས་པར་མི་ནུས་ཀྱང་། །རྟོག་
པའི་རང་ངོ་རྣམ་རྟོག་དོན་མ་རྟོགས་འགྱུ་ཚས་སྒྱུར། །ཆུ་སྟོང་གཡོ་བས་ཟླ་གཟུགས་མི་
མཐོང་འདྲ། །དེ་ཕྱིར་ཐོག་མར་ཞི་གནས་ཉམས་བསླབས་ནས། །རྗེས་ལ་ལྷག་
མཐོང་བསྒོམ་པ་ཐུན་མོང་ལམ། ༈ །སྤྱིར་ནི་ཕྱག་ཆེན་མན་ཆད་སེམས་ལམ་
བྱེད། །རྫོགས་ཆེན་ཐུན་མོང་པའང་དེ་ཕྱོགས་མཐུན། །ཐུན་མོང་མ་ཡིན་མན་ངག་
སྡེ་པ་ནི། །རིག་པ་ལམ་བྱེད་ཉིད་དུ་གསུངས་པའི་ཕྱིར། །ཞི་གནས་ལམ་ནས་
འཇུག་དགོས་ངེས་པ་མེད། །རིག་པ་རྗེན་པ་སྒྲོ་སྐུར་བྲལ་བ་ཉིད། །རང་ངོ་འཕྲོད་ན་
དེ་ལ་གོམས་པས་ཆོག །འོན་ཀྱང་རང་ངོ་འཆུག་མེད་མ་འཕྲོད་ན། །མན་ངག་ཟབ་

You try to block thoughts and yet they are not blocked—
first one unblocked thought arises, then a second—let them arise.
When they arise, send them wherever they go and stand guard.
Since there is no place for them to go, they have returned,
like a crow who has taken off from a ship.
Rest like the movement of swells at sea.

Undistracted mindfulness and continuous mental abiding
may be difficult, and you must proceed by small steps.
Nevertheless, it is crucial to maintain the effort without becoming discouraged.

If abiding is stabilized but attachment to it is not released,
you will not be able to surpass the three realms,[144]
and the facade of realization will be whisked away by the movement of thoughts.
One cannot see the moon's reflection in disturbed water.
Therefore, first develop the experiences of calm abiding,
and then meditate on superior insight;[145] this is the normal approach.

Generally, everything up to the mahamudra is termed "mind path."
Common dzogchen is also included in this.
The class of exceptional esoteric instructions[146]
is said to be the "awareness path,"[147] and as such,
it is not definite that one must begin with calm abiding.
When the nature of naked awareness itself, without exaggeration or denial,[148] is revealed,
it is sufficient just to become accustomed to that.
However, if the true nature is not unerringly revealed,
then even the profound esoteric instructions will be difficult to assimilate.
In that case, it is better to tread the gradual path.

"Nonmeditation," "nondistraction," "abandoning mental doings,"
"maintaining whatever arises," "ordinary mind,"
and "free of intellect" all mean uncontrived.

ཀྱང་རྒྱུད་ཐོག་ལོན་པར་དཀའ། །དེ་འདྲས་རིམ་བགྲོད་ལམ་ལ་འབད་ན་ལེགས། །
སྒོམ་མེད་ཡེངས་མེད་ཡིད་བྱེད་སྤངས་པ་དང་། །གང་ཤར་སྐྱོང་དང་ཐ་མལ་ཤེས་
པ་དང་། །བློ་བྲལ་རྣམས་ནི་མ་བཅོས་པ་ཡི་དོན། །གནས་འགྱུ་གང་ཡང་རིག་ན་
བཅོས་མི་དགོས། །ཡང་དྲན་བྲལ་ཡང་འཛོག་རྟོག་པ་ཉིད་འཁྲུལ་ལུགས། །རིག་
ཙམ་དེ་ཡི་སྟེང་དུ་འཛོག་པ་ལ། །གང་ཤར་སྐྱོང་ཞེས་གྲུབ་བརྙེས་ཡོངས་ཀྱི་ལམ། །
ཉམས་ལེན་རྒྱུད་ལ་སྦྱོར་ཚུལ་དབུ་མ་དང་། །ཞི་གཅོད་ཕྱག་ཆེན་རྫོགས་ཆེན་ཐུན་
མོང་གི། །རྣམ་རྟོག་གང་ཤར་དེ་ལ་བཟོ་མེད་དུ། །གཅེར་གྱིས་བལྟས་པས་གྲོལ་
བ་ལམ་དུ་བྱེད། །རྫོགས་ཆེན་མན་ངག་སྙིང་ཐིག་ལམ་ལས་ནི། །གང་ཤར་རྣམ་
རྟོག་རིག་མཁན་རང་ངོ་ལ། །མང་ནང་དུ་བལྟས་པས་ཆོས་ཉིད་ངོ་བོ་མཇལ། །
འཁྲུལ་སྣང་རྣམ་རྟོག་གཏད་མེད་རང་སར་ཡལ། །སྤྲོ་མ་ཁ་ཕྱིར་ལྟ་བལྟ་བས་གཉིས་
འཛིན་ཡོད། །ཕྱི་མ་ནང་བལྟས་གཉིས་མེད་ཉིད་ཡིན་ཅེས། །མཁས་གྲུབ་བླ་མ་
འགའ་ཡི་ཞལ་ལས་ཐོས། །དེ་ལྟ་ན་ཡང་རྣམ་རྟོག་གྲོལ་ཚུལ་གྱིས། །རིམ་པ་
གསུམ་ལ་ངེས་ཤེས་ཉམས་སྐྱོང་དགོས། ༈ །དེ་ཡང་བི་མ་ལ་ཡི་བཞེད་པ་ལྟར། །
རྣམ་རྟོག་སྔ་ཕྱི་མེད་པར་གྲོལ་བ་ནི། །བུ་ཆུང་དག་གིས་ལྷ་ཁང་མཐོང་བ་འདྲ། །
ན་མཐོང་ཙམ་ཉིད་ལས་བཟང་ངན་ཡིད་བྱེད་མེད། །རྣམ་རྟོག་གང་ཤར་རང་སར་
གྲོལ་བ་ནི། །སྦྲུལ་གྱི་མདུད་པ་ནམ་མཁར་ཞིག་པ་འདྲ། །ཤར་ཙམ་ཉིད་ནས་
གཉེན་སྙིང་པོ་མེད་པར་ཞིག། །རྣམ་རྟོག་ཕན་གནོད་མེད་པར་གྲོལ་བ་ནི། །ཁང་

Whatever abiding or moving is perceived, it is unnecessary to fabricate anything.
Again minding and again concentrating is certainly adding deluded thought onto itself.
Focusing directly upon bare awareness,
called "maintaining whatever arises," is the path of all the adepts.

In the ways of applying practice to one's being, such as the middle way,
pacification and severance,[149] mahamudra, and common dzogchen,
whatever thoughts arise, without making anything out of them,
you look nakedly right at them, and they become the path of liberation.
In the path of the heart-drop[150] esoteric instruction of dzogchen,
you look inwardly right at the one who perceives whatever thoughts arise,
and you encounter the essence of reality.
Deluded appearance and thoughts disappear in their own ground without your paying attention to them.
I have heard several learned and accomplished gurus say
that the former is focusing outward with dualistic clinging,
while the latter is focusing inward and is truly nondualism.
Even if that is so, the methods of liberating thoughts
must include definite experiences in the three stages.[151]
Thus, according to Vimalamitra,[152]
liberation without an initial and subsequent thought
is like a child looking around in wonderment in a temple:
there is no mental construct of good or bad made from the initial perception.
Liberation in its own ground of whatever thought arises
is like the snake's knot disappearing in space:
as soon as it appears, it disappears without need of a remedy.
Liberation in thoughts, being neither helpful nor harmful,
is like a burglar raiding an empty house:
whether it occurs or not, there is neither loss nor gain.

In short, the essential meaning is this: understand the essential points of meditation;
do not fall under the power of mediocrity in external manners;

སྟོང་ནང་དུ་རྐུན་མ་ཕྱིན་པ་འདྲ། །བྱུང་དང་མ་བྱུང་གཉིས་ཀ་ཐོབ་ཤོར་མེད།
༄ །གནད་དོན་བསྡུ་ན་ཉམས་ལེན་གནད་ཤེས་ནས། །ཕྱི་རྐྱོལ་ཐ་མལ་དབང་དུ་མི་
གཏོང་བཞིན། །ནང་གི་འབད་རྩོལ་ཟེ་ཙམ་གློད་ཚོག་པ། །བརྟན་པ་ཐོབ་པའི་རྟགས་
སུ་མཁྱེན་པར་མཛོད། །སྒོམ་མེད་ཟེར་བའང་འབད་རྩོལ་ཟད་པ་ཡིན། །གནས་
ལུགས་བསྒོམ་རྒྱུ་མེད་ཀྱང་གོམས་རྒྱུ་ཡོད། །གོམས་པའི་ཆེད་དུ་ཟ་ཉལ་འགྲོ་སྡོད་
སོགས། །སྤྱོད་ལམ་ཀུན་ལ་ཡེངས་དབང་མི་བཏང་གཅེས། ༄ །གཅིག་པུར་
གནས་ཚེ་ལྷོད་ཅིང་རང་དོ་སྐྱོང་། །མང་པོ་ཚོགས་ཚེ་དྲན་རིག་གསལ་དར་
འདོན། །དྲན་རིག་དོ་བོ་ཅི་ཡང་མ་གྲུབ་པས། །གཏད་སོ་མེད་ཀྱང་རང་རྒྱུགས་
འཛིན་རྒྱུ་ཡོད། །རིག་སྟོང་ཡིན་པས་ཚོད་ཚེ་འཛིན་ཙུང་ཟད་དཀའ། །དཀའ་ཡང་
གོམས་ན་དོ་ཤེས་འཕྲད་ལྷར་འོང་། །སྣང་གྲགས་རྟོག་གསུམ་སྣ་ཚོགས་ཅི་ཤར་
ཡང་། །ཀོ་ཡི་རྣམ་འགྱུར་ཉིད་ལས་རྩལ་ཙམ་མེད། ༄ །ཐུན་མིན་ཨ་ཏི་ཡོ་གའི་
མན་ངག་ལས། །སེམས་དང་རིག་པའི་ཤན་འབྱེད་ཅེས་གསུངས་པ། །དྲན་པས་
འོད་གསལ་རང་དོ་མི་ཟིན་པས། །རྟོགས་པའི་ཆ་ཡོད་འགྲུ་དྲན་ཚོད་དཀའ་
སེམས། །ཤེས་པའི་ཡུལ་ཚོས་མེད་འོད་གསལ་རང་དོ་མཐོང་། །དྭངས་ཆ་མར་མེ་
ལྷར་གནས་ཕྱི་མ་སྟེ། །སྟོངས་སྐྲག་ལྷ་བུས་ཡུལ་མེད་ལམ་ལམ་པ། །འཆར་ཚེ་དེ་
དོས་བཟུང་བས་ངེས་ཤེས་སྐྱེ། །རིག་པའི་འགྱུ་སྟོང་སྐྱེ་མེད་གྲོལ་ཅེས་གསུངས། །
དཔེ་མཐོང་སྟོང་སྐད་མ་ཡིན་བླ་མ་ཡི། །ཞལ་ནས་བརྒྱུད་པའི་གདམས་པ་སྙིང་

and inwardly, exert effort tempered just right.
These should be understood as the signs of obtaining stability.
Nonmeditation is the exhaustion of effort.
Although there is nothing to meditate on, there *is* something to get used to.[153]
For the sake of habituation, while eating, resting, going, or staying,
in all activities, it is crucial not to give in to distraction.

When alone, you can relax and maintain true nature.
When in a crowd, the powers of mindfulness, awareness, and clarity need to be carefully guarded.
Since mindful awareness in essence has no true existence,
there is nothing to attend to, but there is something to establish.
Since it is awareness-emptiness, it is somewhat difficult to establish,
but once you are used to it, it will be like meeting an old acquaintance.
Whatever appearances, sounds, or thoughts occur,
there is not one iota that is not an aspect of awareness itself.

The esoteric instructions of exceptional atiyoga[154] speak of
the distinction between mind and intrinsic awareness.
Mindfulness cannot grasp the nature of clear light—
this abstruse aspect, with movement and memory, that is difficult to cut through, is mind.
With no object of cognizance, the nature of clear light is seen—
this radiant aspect that abides like a candle is the latter.
It is like a sudden fright without a known object,
but when it is recognized, confidence is established.
It is said that awareness is empty of movement, unborn, and liberated.
These are not just the words of emptiness seen in books.
They are the direct oral precepts of the lineage gurus that are like the heart's blood.
They are not revealed to those of broken commitment, sophists, and so on—
the protectors[155] of mantra keep a sharp watch!

Uncontrived reality does not need to be sustained continuously:

ཁྲིག་འདྲ། །དམ་ཉམས་ཁ་ཁྲེར་ཕྲིར་སོགས་ལ་མི་སྨོན་པ། །སྤུགས་ཀྱི་སྤྱུང་མས་བྱེ་ར་ལྷུང་ལྷུང་ཡོད། །ཆོས་ཉིད་མ་བཅོས་པ་ལ་རྟག་ཏུ་ནི། །ཏུ་རེ་མི་དགོས་ཕོག་ཞོག་ཅིག་དྲན་པ་ཡིས། །ཆོག་ཅེས་བཀའ་བརྒྱུད་གོང་མའི་ཞལ་ནས་གསུངས། །

ངོ་བོ་བསྒོམ་པས་བསྐལ་མང་ལས་སྒྲིབ་རྣམས། །དག་ཅིང་ལྷུང་ཡང་དབུ་མར་རང་བཞིན་དུ། །ཚུད་པ་ལ་སོགས་ཕན་ཡོན་བརྗོད་ལས་འདས། །རང་ངོ་ཤེས་ན་གཅིག་ཤེས་ཀུན་གྲོལ་ཡིན། །གློ་སྟོབས་ཆུང་ཚེ་གཏན་གཏད་མེད་སྐྱོང་དཀའ་ན། །བསྐྱེད་རིམ་སོགས་ལ་དྲན་འཛིན་རང་ཁམས་བསྟུན། །གཏན་གཏད་མེད་སྐྱོང་ལ་དབྱིངས་རིག་བསྲེས་བསྲེ་བ་ཡི། །ཐོགས་འདོན་དོན་ནམ་མཁའི་དཀྱིལ་དང་རྒྱ་མཚོའི་གཉིང་། །རྩ་བ་བསྲེག་ལ་དྲན་པའི་གསལ་འདེབས་བྱ། །དེ་ཚེ་རིག་སྟོང་མཐའ་དབུས་མེད་པར་འཆར། ༔ །སྟོང་ཉིད་ཞི་གནས་ལུང་མ་བསྟན་གསུམ་པོར། །ནོར་དོགས་གསུངས་པས་དང་པོར་སྟོང་ཉིད་ནི། །ཡོད་མེད་སྐྱེ་འགག་རྟག་ཆད་མཐའ་བྲལ་དོན། །དམིགས་བསམ་བརྗོད་བྲལ་རིག་ཐོག་སྐྱོང་ལ་ཟེར། ༔ །ཞི་གནས་རྣམ་རྟོག་འཚུབ་མ་རབ་ཞི་ནས། །མཐའ་དབུས་མེད་པར་འབྱུང་ཤེས་པ་ཁད་ཆགས་པ། །རླབས་དང་བྲལ་བའི་རྒྱ་མཚོ་བཞིན་དུ་གནས། ༔ །ལུང་མ་བསྟན་ནི་དྲན་རིག་ཤེད་ཉམས་ནས། །འགྱུ་བ་ཕྲ་མོའི་རྗེས་སུ་འབྲང་ཤེས་བྱས་ཏེ། །དྲན་རིག་སླེབ་དུས་ཕྱི་བལྟས་བྱས་འདྲ་འོང་། །རྩྭ་ཕུབ་གསེབ་ཏུ་ཆུ་བླུག་མི་མངོན་པ། །རྩྭ་ཕུབ་མེད་པར་སླེབ་དུས་མཐོང་དང་འདྲ། ༔ །མཉམ་བཞག་གཞག་སྐབས་སུ་ལུང་

the initial incident recalled is sufficient.
It was taught by the previous Kagyu[156] masters
that by meditating on the essence, the karmic obscurations of many eons
are purified, and furthermore, the vital wind enters the central channel[157] automatically.
There are other benefits too great to speak of.
If you know your own nature, it is the knowledge of the one thing that liberates all.
When your mental powers are weak, and maintaining without focusing on something is difficult,
practice developing mindfulness in creation stage and other techniques that are in keeping with your condition.

In sustaining nonfocusing, the mixing of basic space and intrinsic awareness
is enhanced by mixing the source, mind, with the center of space
or the midst of the ocean to illuminate mindfulness.
At that time, awareness-emptiness without center or circumference arises.

Three things are said to pose the danger of misunderstanding:
emptiness, calm abiding, and neutrality.
Emptiness means freedom from the extremes of existence and nonexistence, birth and cessation, eternalism and nihilism.
It is called an experience in awareness, unimaginable, inconceivable, and ineffable.

Calm abiding is thoroughly pacifying the churning of thoughts
and resting the mind evenly, without center or circumference,
abiding like the ocean without waves.

Neutrality is when the power of mindful awareness weakens,
and you pursue the subtle mental movements.
When mindful awareness arrives, it is more like hindsight.
It is like water flowing through grass:
you see it only when it comes out the other side.

During meditation, if a state of neutrality occurs,

མ་བསྟུན་བྱུང་ན། །ཐེར་ལ་འདོན་ཞེས་དྲན་རིག་གྲིམ་ཆ་བསྐྱེད། །ནག་ཐོམ་བྱུང་ན་ལྷུང་རོ་བསལ་བ་དང་། །བཟླས་བརྗོད་སྐད་མཐོ་གཡོ་འགུལ་སོགས་ཀྱིས་སེལ། ༈ །ཞི་སྣང་རྟོག་པ་ལམ་ལམ་འཆར་བའི་ཚེ། །རྗེན་པར་བལྟ་ཞིང་བཟོ་མེད་བཞག་པ་ན། །ཕན་གནོད་མེད་པར་རང་ས་དེ་རུ་ཡལ། །དེ་ལས་གཞན་དུ་རང་བྱུང་ཡེ་ཤེས་མེད། །བཟོ་མེད་ངང་དུ་ལམ་ལམ་འཆར་བ་དེ། །རྣམ་པ་ཞི་སྣང་ངོ་བོ་ཡེ་ཤེས་ཡིན། །ཞི་སྣང་ཡལ་རྗེས་སྟོང་མདངས་ཚོལ་མི་དགོས། །སྟོང་ཞིང་དམིགས་མེད་དེ་ལ་ཟུང་འཇུག་ཟེར། །རྡོ་རྗེ་སེམས་དཔའ་སོགས་ཀྱང་དེ་བཞིན་ནོ། །ཉོན་མོངས་འདོད་ཆགས་སོགས་ལའང་རིགས་འགྲེ་འཚལ། ༈ །ཡང་དག་དོན་ལ་བསྒོམ་བྱ་སྒོམ་བྱེད་མེད། །དྲན་པ་གཅིག་པུས་ཆོག་ན་ཉམས་ལེན་སྟེ། །མཐར་ཐུག་དོན་ལ་དྲན་པ་ཉིད་ཀྱང་མེད། །དྲན་གཞི་དབྱིངས་སུ་དག་ཚེ་ཡེ་ཤེས་བརྗོད། །བུད་ཤིང་ཟད་ཚེ་མེ་ཡང་ཡལ་བ་བཞིན། །འཁྲུལ་པ་ཟད་ཚེ་གཉེན་པོ་ཉིད་ཀྱང་ཞི། །འདི་ནི་འཕགས་པ་རྣམས་ཀྱི་སྤྱོད་ཡུལ་ལགས། ༈ །བསྒོམ་པ་མ་ཡིན་མི་བསྒོམ་པ་ཡང་མིན། །བསྒོམ་པ་མིན་ཏེ་དམིགས་གཏད་གང་ཡང་མེད། །མི་བསྒོམ་མིན་ཏེ་ཡོངས་སུ་བཏང་བ་མེད། །ཆོས་ཉིད་རང་ངོ་ཤེས་ཙམ་དེ་ཐོག་འཇོག །དེ་ལ་བློ་ཡི་བསམ་བྱ་ཡོད་མིན་ཏེ། །དོན་དམ་བློ་འདས་དམིགས་མེད་ཡིན་པས་སོ། །རྣམ་རྟོག་ཡུལ་དང་འབྲེལ་འདྲིས་མ་ཆད་ན། །མ་བཅོས་ཟེར་ཡང་འཁྲུལ་པ་བཟློག་མི་ཐུབ། །ལྟ་མཁན་ནང་དང་བལྟ་ཡུལ་ཕྱིར་ཆད་པ། །རང་ཤར་རང་གྲོལ་ཟེར་ཡང་

single it out, that is, tighten up the mindful awareness.
When dark torpor sets in, clear out the stale breath[158]
and wake up by chanting, shouting, swaying, and so on.

When angry thoughts arise vividly,
if you look at them nakedly and rest without fabrication,
they will vanish in their own ground without harm or benefit.
Self-arising wisdom is none other than that.
That vivid arising within a state of nonfabrication
takes the form of anger but is essentially pristine wisdom.
In the wake of the vanishing anger, the radiance of emptiness need not be pursued.
That emptiness without frame of reference *is* what's called "unity,"
as are Vajrasattva[159] and the others.
Apply this also to the afflictive emotions, such as desire and so on.

In the completely perfect sense, there is no meditation and nothing to meditate on.
When mindfulness alone is enough, it is the peak of practice.
In the ultimate sense, even mindfulness itself does not exist.
When the basis of mindfulness is absolved in basic space, we speak of wisdom.
As when fuel is used up the fire is also extinguished,
when delusion is used up the remedy itself is eliminated.
This is the sphere of activity of all noble ones.

It is not meditation, nor is it nonmeditation.
Not being meditation, there is nothing at all to focus on,
and not being nonmeditation, there can be no distraction.
Simply place the mind on the bare apprehension of the nature of reality.
This is not a thought-object of the rational mind,
because the absolute is beyond intellect and without reference point.
If the intimate connection between thought and object is not severed,
although you call it "uncontrived," it cannot reverse delusion.
Severing the inner perceiver and the external object
may be called self-arising self-liberating, but it is still duality.
When there is no antidote, it is self-arising self-liberating.

གཉིས་འཛིན་ཉིད། །གཉེན་པོ་མེད་ན་རང་ཤར་རང་གྲོལ་ཡིན། ༈ །རང་གི་སེམས་ཉིད་མ་ལ་སྣང་བ་བུ། །ཆུ་ལས་ལ་ཆུ་བུར་བརྡོལ་བཞིན་ཞེན་པ་ལས། །སྣང་བ་ཤར་ཡང་གཉིས་མེད་རོལ་ཤེས་ན། །སྣང་སེམས་མ་བུ་འཕྲད་ཅེས་དེ་ལ་བྱ། །འཁོར་འདས་བཟང་ངན་རྟོགས་དང་མ་རྟོགས་ཀུན། །སྲིད་སྣང་མི་རྟེད་ཡེ་སྟོང་ཡེ་རྫོགས་འགྱུར། །ལྷ་སྒོམ་སྒྲུབ་པ་ཐམས་ཅད་དེ་ལ་འདུས། །བསྲུང་བྱའི་དམ་ཚིག་རྣམས་ཀྱང་དེར་འདུས་པས། །དེ་ཕྱིར་རྫོགས་ཆེན་ཨ་ཏི་ཡོ་ག་ལས། །མི་བསྲུང་བསྲུང་བའི་དམ་ཚིག་བཞིར་གསུངས་པ། །བསྲུང་མཚམས་མེད་པས་མེད་པའི་དམ་ཚིག་ལ། །གཟུང་དང་འཛིན་པ་བྲལ་བས་ཕྱལ་པ་ཡིན། །ཐམས་ཅད་སེམས་སུ་རྫོགས་པས་གཅིག་པུ་སྟེ། །ལྷག་མེད་དེ་ལ་རྫོགས་པས་པ་ལྷུན་གྱིས་རྫོགས། །དུས་གསུམ་རྒྱལ་བའི་དགོངས་པའི་མཐར་ཐུག་གོ ༈ །ཐོ་རེངས་གཉིད་སད་དུས་ཀྱང་རྨི་ལམ་ལ། །རྟོག་དཔྱོད་ལ་སོགས་རྣམ་རྟོག་བསྡུ་སྒྲིལ་ཀུན། །མི་བྱེད་ཉམས་ལེན་གསལ་འདེབས་དྲན་པའི་ངང་། །བཞག་ཚེ་དེ་ཉིད་རིག་པའི་དྭངས་སྙིགས་ཕྱེད། ༈ །སྲིད་སྣང་མི་ཤེས་ཆོས་ལ་མི་གུས་དང་། །བག་མེད་པ་དང་ཉོན་མོངས་མང་བ་བཞི། །འདི་བཞི་འཛོམ་ན་ཉེས་ཉེ་ལྟུང་ཆར་བཞིན་འབེབས། །ལྟུང་བ་འབྱུང་བའི་སྒོ་བཞི་ཕྱེས་པ་འདྲ། །དྲན་ཤེས་བག་ཡོད་ཉིད་དང་མ་བྲལ་ན། །ཉོན་མོངས་རྣམས་ཀྱང་ཡེ་ཤེས་ཆེན་པོར་འགྱུར། །གཞན་ཀུན་དགེ་བར་འགྱུར་པ་སྨོས་ཅི་དགོས། །ལམ་ཁྱེར་གནད་ཀུན་དྲན་པའི་ལག་ཏུ་ཡོད། །དྲན་པ་མེད་ན་ལམ་ཁྱེར་

One's very own mind is the child appearing to the mother.
Like bubbles rising out of water, appearances arise out of attachment,
and yet if you know that it is the play of nonduality,
then this is what is meant by appearance and mind being the meeting of mother and child.
You won't find acceptance or rejection of cyclic existence and transcendence, good and bad, realized and unrealized—
emptiness and completion were always present.
All view, meditation, and action is included in that,
and since all the commitments to preserve are also included in that,
the dzogchen atiyoga teaches
four commitments[160] to preserve that are kept by not preserving.
Being without interruption in preservation is the commitment of "nonexistence,"
being free of duality is "evenness,"
everything being perfect in mind is "singularity,"
and this completion in itself without anything else is "spontaneously perfect."
This is the ultimate intention of the victorious ones of the three times.

Don't bother with examination of dreams when awakening at dawn
and all the other methods of welcoming discursive thinking.
Resting within mindfulness during illuminated practice,
the brilliance and murkiness of today's awareness will separate out.

Not understanding rejection and acceptance; lack of devotion in Dharma,
careless, compulsive behavior, and excessive afflictive emotion—
if these four are present, faults and downfalls will fall like rain.
It is as if the four trapdoors to downfalls are wide open.
But if you maintain cautious mindful awareness,
even the afflictive emotions will turn into great wisdom;
what need to mention that all else becomes virtue?
All the essential points of daily-life applications[161] are held by mindfulness.
Without mindfulness, you won't even remember these applications,
and their mere existence is of no benefit whatsoever.
You must proceed directly with a direct attitude.

མི་དྲན་པས། །ཡིན་པ་ཙམ་གྲིས་ཕན་ཐོགས་ཅི་ཡང་མེད། །ཐད་ཀ་ཐད་ཀའི་འདུ་
ཤེས་རྗེས་ཟིན་དགོས། །སྤྱོད་ལམ་ཀུན་ལ་བག་ཡོད་བསྟེན་པ་ནི། །ཐུབ་དབང་ཉིད་
དང་འབྲལ་མེད་འགྲོགས་པ་འདྲ། །བཟའ་བཏུང་ཨོཾ་ཨཱཿཧཱུྃ་གིས་བདུད་རྩིར་
སྦྱངས། །དྲོ་ཡི་གོང་དུ་དཀོན་མཆོག་རྗེས་དྲན་པའི། །མདོ་ཡི་ཚིག་གི་ཉི་རྒྱུས་
བསྡུས་གང་རུང་བཏོན། །རང་ལུས་ལྷར་གསལ་སྤྱི་མགྲིན་སྙིང་ག་རུ། །ཁྲོ་བོ་རིག་
འཛིན་ཞི་བ་རིགས་བརྒྱའི་ལྷ། །གཙོ་བོ་རྩ་བའི་བླ་མ་དབྱེར་མེད་བསྒོམ། །པ་སྤྱིའི་
བུ་གང་རིག་འཛིན་མཁའ་འགྲོ་སོགས། །ཉིལ་གོང་ཁ་ཕྱེས་བཞིན་དུ་བཞུགས་མོས་
ལ། །དྲན་དང་ཤེས་བཞིན་ཆགས་སེམས་ཞེན་མེད་པར་སྤྱད། །བཟའ་བཏུང་ཐ་
མལ་མཐོང་ཡང་སྐྱོན་མེད་དེ། །ཅི་ཟོས་ཚོགས་ཀྱི་འཁོར་ལོར་འགྱུར་པ་ཡིན། །
ལམ་ཁྱེར་གཞན་ལ་བླ་མའི་རྣལ་འབྱོར་དང་། །བྱང་ཆུབ་སེམས་སྤྱོད་སྦྱོངས་བསྐྱེད་
རིམ་རྫོགས་རིམ་སོགས། །གང་འདོད་བསྒོམ་པ་བླ་མའི་ཞལ་ལས་ལོངས།

༄༅ །འདུས་བྱས་མི་རྟག་ཟག་བཅས་སྡུག་བསྔལ་བ། །སྣང་འདས་ཆོས་རྣམས་ཞི་
བ་སྟོང་པ་ཉིད། །འདི་བཞི་ལྟ་བ་བཀའ་རྟགས་ཕྱག་རྒྱ་ལགས། །ཛམ་ལྷར་གཏོར་
མ་འཕྲོག་མར་ཆད་བུ་དང་། །འཇུར་གེགས་ཁ་འབར་མ་ལ་ཆུ་སྦྱིན་ཏེ། །བཞི་འདི་
སྤྱོད་པ་བཀའ་རྟགས་ཕྱག་རྒྱ་ལགས། །ལྟ་སྤྱོད་ཕྱག་རྒྱ་བརྒྱད་པོ་འདི་འཛིན་ན། །
རྒྱལ་བའི་རྗེས་འཇུག་ཡིན་ལ་མི་འཛིན་དེ། །གོང་གི་སློབ་མ་མིན་ཞེས་ཐུབ་པས་
གསུངས། །བོད་ཁམས་སྐྱབས་པའི་མགོན་པོ་ཨོ་རྒྱན་ཡིན། །རྣམ་ཐར་བཀའ་དྲིན་

Relying on cautious attention in all activities
is like having Shakyamuni himself as your constant companion.

Consecrate food and drink as nectar with OM AH HUNG,[162]
and before lunch recite the brief or extensive verses of
The Sutra of Recalling the Jewels.[163]
Imagine your own body as a deity, and in the crown, throat, and heart centers,
the hundred wrathful deities, knowledge-holders, and peaceful deities,[164]
and meditate mainly on inseparability with your source guru.
Imagining your pores filled with knowledge-holders, dakinis,[165] and so on,
like a bursting bag of sesame seeds;
in a state of deliberate mindfulness, partake without attachment.
It doesn't matter if you see it as ordinary food and drink;
whatever you eat will become a sacred feast.[166]

Other applications for daily living are guru yoga,[167]
bodhisattva activities,[168] creation and completion stage practices, and so on.
You can receive whatever meditation you desire from your guru.

All that is composite is impermanent, all that is corrupt is suffering,
transcending misery, all phenomena are peace and emptiness—
these are the four seals that distinguish the genuine Buddhist view.[169]
Offering food cakes[170] to Jambhala,[171] a pinch of food to the Plunderer,[172]
and water to the Constricted Throat and Blazing Mouth spirits[173]—
these are the four seals that distinguish genuine Buddhist activity.
If you uphold these eight seals of view and action,
you are a follower of the victorious ones, but if not,
you are not a disciple—this was taught by Shakyamuni.

The lord of refuge in Tibet and Kham[174] is Orgyen.[175]
Remembering his kindness and life example, supplicate him.
Tibet's deity of good fortune is the Great Compassionate One.[176]
Diligently recite the six-syllable mantra.[177]

The profound essential points for wisdom to arise naturally are these:

དྲན་པས་གསོལ་འདེབས་འཚོལ། །བོད་ཀྱི་ལྷ་སྐལ་ཐུགས་རྗེ་ཆེན་པོ་ཡིན། །
བཟླས་པ་ཡིག་དྲུག་ཉིད་གཉིས་ལ་འབད་པར་འཚོལ། ༔ །ཡེ་ཤེས་རང་ཤར་འགྲོ་
བའི་གནད་ཟབ་ནི། །གཟུང་འཛིན་རླུང་རྣམས་རང་བཞིན་དག་པའི་ཕྱིར། །འབད་
རྩོལ་མེད་པར་བར་གྱི་རླུང་སྦྱོར་དགང་། །ཅིར་སྣང་ཡེ་ཤེས་འཆར་བའི་སྒོ་ཡིན་
ཕྱིར། །ཀ་དྷི་ཤེལ་གྱི་རྩ་ཆེན་ནམ་མཁར་ཕྱེ། །གང་ཤར་གཏད་མེད་ངང་དུ་གྲོལ་
བའི་ཕྱིར། །རང་སེམས་སྙིང་པོ་ཡི་གེ་ཧཱུྃ་ལ་གཏད། །གནད་ཀྱི་ཁྱད་པར་དེ་གསུམ་
དང་ལྡན་ན། །དཀའ་བ་མེད་པར་གདོད་མའི་རྒྱལ་སར་གཤེགས། ༔ །གཞན་
ཡང་ནངས་སྔ་ལངས་མ་ཐག་པའི་ཚེ། །རླུང་རོ་གསལ་ནས་འབྱུང་གནས་འཇུག་པ་
གསུམ། །ཧཱུྃ་ཨཱཿཨོཾ་སྦྱར་ཉེར་གཅིག་བརྒྱ་སོགས་བསྲུང་། །ཉིན་པར་རླུང་རྣམས་
དེ་བཞིན་ཡིན་པར་མོས། །ཉལ་ཁར་འབྱུང་འཇུག་གནས་གསུམ་འདྲ་གསུམ་
སྦྱར། །མཚན་གྱིས་ཀྱི་དབུགས་རྣམས་དེ་བཞིན་ཡིན་པར་མོས། །དེས་ནི་ཉི་ཁྲི་ཆིག་
སྟོང་དྲུག་བརྒྱའི་རླུང་། །སྔགས་འགྱུར་དཀའ་བ་མེད་པར་ལྷ་བསྙེན་ཐེམ།
༔ །ཆོས་ཀྱི་རྒྱལ་པོ་མཉམ་མེད་དྭགས་པོ་ཡིས། །ང་བོ་མཐོང་ནས་འཇམ་རླུང་
ཙུང་ཟད་རེ། །བཟུང་ཞིང་ཡིད་བཟླས་ཟབ་མོར་མི་ཆེ་དྲིལ། །སྐབས་སུ་བླ་མར་
གསོལ་གདབ་ཐུགས་ཡིད་བསྲེ། །དེ་ལས་གཞན་པའི་ཟབ་ལམ་མེད་པར་
གསུངས། ༔ །ཉལ་དུས་སྤྱི་བོའི་བླ་མ་སྙིང་དབུས་དྲངས། །དྲན་རྟོག་འཕྲོ་འདུ་
བསམ་བློ་ཀུན་སྤངས་ཏེ། །མོས་གུས་གསོལ་བཏབ་ཡེངས་མེད་ངང་དུ་སྐྱོད། །

Since the vital winds of duality are naturally pure,
effortlessly hold the intermediate wind.[178]
Since whatever appears is the door to the arising of wisdom,
open the great crystal *kati* channel[179] to the sky.
Since whatever arises is liberated without focusing on it,
focus on the letter HUNG as the essence of one's mind.
If you possess these three special essential points,
you will easily arrive at the primordial place of the victorious ones.

Additionally, in the morning as soon as you rise,
having cleared away the stale breath, apply HUNG AH OM
to the exhaling, pausing, and inhaling, counting twenty-one or a hundred times.
Imagine that all your breathing during the day is like that.
When going to sleep, apply the three letters to exhaling, inhaling, and pausing,
and imagine that all your breathing during the night is like that.
By doing this, your daily 21,600 breaths become mantra
and the deity's recitation requirement is fulfilled without hardship.[180]

The king of Dharma, the unsurpassable Dagpo,[181]
said that there is no more profound approach than
looking at the essence and holding a few "gentle" breaths
while doing profound mental recitation, thus incorporating it with human life,
and occasionally praying to the guru and blending your minds.

When retiring to sleep, draw the guru from above your head into the center of your heart,
abandon the coming and going of thoughts, memories, and all mental activity,
and relax into a state of undistracted devotion and prayer.
Then the clear light will gradually arise out of deep sleep.[182]

If you want to do the meditation of recognizing, changing, expanding, and purifying dreams,[183]

སྲིབ་འཐུག་འོད་གསལ་རིམ་བཞིན་འཆར་བར་འགྱུར། ༈ །རྨི་ལམ་འཛིན་བསྒྱུར་
སྤེལ་སྦྱོང་སྒོམ་འདོད་ན། །ཉིན་མོའི་སྣང་བ་ཐམས་ཅད་རྨི་ལམ་གྱི། །འདུན་པས་
ཟིན་ན་རྨི་ལམ་འབྱུང་བ་སླ། །ཉིན་སྣང་ཨ་འཐས་དབང་བཏང་མཚན་མོ་ལ། །རྨི་
ལམ་འཛིན་མོད་ལག་ཏུ་ལོན་པ་དཀའ། །དེ་ཡང་བར་དོ་ཆོད་པར་བྱེད་པ་ལ། །རྨི་
ལམ་ཆོད་དགོས་དེ་ལ་ཉིན་སྣང་ཀུན། །སྒྱུ་མ་རྨི་ལམ་ལྟ་བུར་མ་རྟོགས་ན། །
འཁྲུལ་པ་རྒྱ་འབྲུམས་གཅིག་གིས་གཅིག་ལ་སྒྲིབ་བསྒྲིབ། ༈ །སྤྱིར་ནི་འཆི་བ་མི་
རྟག་བྱམས་སྙིང་རྗེ། །མོས་གུས་བསྐྱེད་རིམ་རྨི་ལམ་སྒྱུ་ལུས་དང་། །བར་དོ་ལ་
སོགས་གོམས་འདྲིས་དགོས་ཚད་ཀུན། །སྤྱོད་ལམ་རྣམ་བཞིར་མི་བརྗེད་གསལ་
འདེབས་བྱ། །མྱུར་དུ་འབྱོར་ཞིང་རྒྱུད་ལ་སྐྱེ་བར་འགྱུར། །བདག་འདྲ་སྙིང་ནས་
ཆོས་སྒྲུབ་མ་དྲན་པས། །རང་རྒྱུད་ཆོས་དང་འདྲེ་བར་མི་འདུག་ཀྱང་། །སྔོན་
བསགས་རྣམ་དཀར་ལས་ཀྱི་འཕྲོ་བཟང་པོས། །སངས་རྒྱས་བསྟན་ལ་སྙིང་ནས་
དད་པའི་ཕྱིར། །འདི་ཙམ་གྱིས་ཀྱང་གཞན་ལ་ཕན་པའི་བློས། །རྒྱུར་བྱས་བཅས་
བསྒྲུབ་གསུམ་རྣམ་དག་དགེ་བའི་ཆཤེས། །ཤྲཱི་ཀླན་ཞེས་བྱས་གསུང་བསྐུལ་རྐྱེན་
བྱས་ཏེ། །རང་ལ་མེད་པར་ནེ་ཙོའི་ཆོས་སྐད་བཞིན། །བྲིས་པའི་དགེ་རྩས་དཔལ་
ལྡན་ཀརྨ་པ། །ཡབ་སྲས་བརྒྱུད་པར་བཅས་པའི་ཞབས་བརྟན་ཅིང་། །མཛད་ཕྲིན་
འཕེལ་དེས་མཁའ་ཁྱབ་སེམས་ཅན་རྣམས། །ཚེ་གཅིག་རྡོ་རྗེ་འཆང་དངོས་འགྲུབ་
གྱུར་ཅིག །

you must maintain an attitude during the day that all appearances are dreams,
and then it will be easy to deal with dreams.
If you tend to solidify appearances during the day,
then at night, even if you recognize dreams, the practice will be difficult.
Also, to cut through the intermediate existence[184]
you need to have cut through the dream experience.
If you don't realize that all waking appearances are like dreams or illusions,
then one vast mass of delusion will obscure another.

In general, impermanence, love and compassion,
devotion, creation stage, dream yoga, illusory body yoga,
intermediate existence yoga, and so on; all those practices that require habituation,
should be conscientiously applied during the four daily activities.[185]
Quickly assimilating them, they will become part of your being.
Someone like me who cannot remember to practice Dharma sincerely
has not mixed the Dharma with his being.
However, due to the good influence of previously accumulated virtuous karma,
I do have sincere faith in the teachings of the Buddha,
and with just this I have the intention to benefit others.
This is the primary cause [for this composition], and the secondary cause was the encouragement of the spiritual friend Shrimen, who perfectly possesses the three trainings.[186]
I wrote it not through my own gifts, but rather like a parrot mimicking Dharma talk.
May the roots of this virtue render service to the glorious Karmapa[187]
and the lineage of gurus and disciples.
May the expansion of their enlightened activities bring all beings throughout space
to the mastery of the state of Vajradhara in a single lifetime.

ཞེས་པའང་རྒྱལ་དབང་ཐམས་ཅད་མཁྱེན་པ་བཅུ་བཞི་པའི་ཞབས་གྲུས་ཀྱི་དགེ་བའི་བཤེས་གཉེན་ངེས་དོན་ལ་ཐུགས་ཤིན་ཏུ་གཞོལ་བ་ཀརྨ་དཔལ་ལྡན་ནས་གསུང་བསྐུལ་གནང་བ་ལྟར། ཤཱཀྱའི་དགེ་སློང་རྟགས་ཙམ་འཛིན་པ་ཀརྨ་ངག་དབང་ཡོན་ཏན་རྒྱ་མཚོ་ཞེས་པས་རང་ལོ་ཉེར་བདུན་པར་སྨྲས་རིམ་བཞིན་དུ་བསྐུལ་བ་པོ་ཉིད་ཀྱིས་བྲིས་པ་འདིས་ཀྱང་བསྟན་འགྲོ་ལ་སྨན་པའི་དཔལ་ཡོན་འབྱུང་བར་གྱུར་ཅིག །སརྦ་ཀཱ་ལ་དེ་ཀྲྀཥྞི་ཡཾ་སི་སྠི་ཏ་ཧྲ་བ་ཏུ།། བཀྲིས་དཔལ་འབར་འཛམ་གླིང་རྒྱན་དུ་ཤོག། །།དགེའོ།། །།དགེའོ།།

Colophon

At the request of the spiritual friend Karma Palden, an attendant of the fourteenth Omniscient Lord of the Victorious Ones (Karmapa), and whose mind is totally devoted to the definitive meaning, I, Karma Ngawang Yönten Gyamtso,[188] bearing merely the signs of a Buddhist monk, at the age of twenty-seven, gradually dictated this text, and he transcribed it. May it send forth glorious healing qualities for the doctrine and for beings. In all times and directions may glory prevail. May the glorious blaze of good fortune adorn the world. Virtue! Virtue!

Commentary by Khenchen Thrangu Rinpoche

Introduction

In this essay, I will discuss the creation (or generation) and completion stages according to the text *The Essence of Creation and Completion,* which was composed by Jamgön Kongtrul the Great. In particular, between the two topics, the creation stage and the completion stage, we will be concerned primarily with the creation stage. Although in a sense our main practice is the completion stage, the practice of the completion stage depends entirely upon the stability and blessing of the creation stage, just as for example the practice of *vipashyana,* or insight, depends upon the attainment of stable *shamata,* or concentration.

This is a very appropriate topic for study. It is easy to talk about *shamata* and *vipashyana* and to listen to explanations of mahamudra or explanations concerned only with the completion stage. However, it is important not to choose the topic that sounds good, but instead to choose the one that will be of the most practical benefit, that will actually enable students to progress in their practice of meditation. Therefore, it is appropriate to address subjects that are more difficult to understand, because it is these, especially, that need the most complete explanation.

When you examine your mind, some impurities you might discover in your motivation for study and practice are competitiveness, arrogance, and selfishness. In a sense, an impure motivation is not a serious problem, but at the same time, it is necessary to let go of it and replace it with a pure motivation. A pure motivation is the motivation of wishing to study and practice in order to be able to benefit both yourself and others. Given that normally we are mostly concerned with benefiting only ourselves, it is especially important to emphasize the wish to benefit others. Even when we wish to benefit others, we tend to restrict that wish to a few others, such as our family and friends. The wish to benefit a few others is not an impure motivation—it is pure—but among pure motivations it is a fairly minimal one. Here we are trying to develop the motivation of practicing and studying in order to benefit all beings who fill space, since all beings, without exception, equally wish to be happy and free from suffering, and yet lack the knowledge necessary to enable them to achieve these goals. So if you have the motivation for both study and practice in that you are doing it in order to establish all beings without exception in a state of happiness, this motivation is not only pure but also vast in scope.

Essential Points for Approaching the Path

Our text begins by explaining eight essential points for approaching the path: gaining certainty in the Dharma; renunciation; understanding what Dharma is (view, meditation, conduct, and fruition); defining creation and completion; faith and devotion; pure vision; the two truths; and understanding the qualities of the path.

Gaining Certainty

The first point is that, in order to practice Dharma, you need to be certain about its validity. Cultivating that certainty has to be done in three steps: cultivating the wisdom or knowledge of hearing, cultivating the wisdom of thinking about what has been heard, and then finally cultivating the wisdom that comes from meditation. It is pointed out that people of the highest faculties, which means extremely rare and highly gifted individuals, do not necessarily need to go through the preliminary stages of hearing and thinking about the Dharma. An example of this type of person is King Indrabhuti of Uddiyana, who received instruction from the Buddha and was liberated on the spot. Most of us, however, need first to hear instruction, then to think about it very carefully, and only thereafter to implement it in meditation practice.

Why do we have to begin by hearing the Dharma? Because Dharma practice is not primarily concerned with or limited to the experiences of this life. Therefore, it is sufficiently different from what we are used to that before we have heard it explained, we really have no idea what it is, let alone how to go about practicing it. We therefore require instruction. What do we take as the sources of our instruction? What Dharma do we try to hear? Generally speaking, there are two classes of scripture or texts used in Buddhadharma. One is called "the dictates of the Buddha," which means the teachings that the Buddha gave when he taught in India. The others are called the "commentaries," or *shastras*, which are commentaries on these teachings composed by the great masters of India and other countries.

The custom in the *Vajrayana* tradition is to emphasize the study of the commentaries rather than the study of the Buddha's original teachings. Casually considering this, you might expect that we would emphasize the Buddha's teachings themselves in our study because, after all, is not the Buddha the most important teacher in the Buddhist tradition? Historically some scholars also have objected, saying, "Why study the commentaries rather than the Buddha's original statements?" The reason is that the Buddha's original statements are vast in extent and number. Furthermore, they are not necessarily organized for easy study or reference; they are organized on the basis of the occasions on which they were delivered. In addition, because these teachings given by the Buddha were made at the request of and for the needs of specific individuals in specific contexts, they represent different styles of teaching.

The Buddha's teachings are principally classed as either provisional or definitive in meaning. Simply by studying these original texts themselves, it is impossible for a beginner to determine which statements are provisional and which are definitive. On the other hand, the commentaries distinguish clearly between provisional and definitive statements of the Buddha; for easy reference, they assemble similar teachings or those that need to be used together; they explain the hidden meanings or subtleties the Buddha's teachings; and they summarize especially long treatments of topics that can be understood with a briefer explanation. In short, it is really through the commentaries that we approach the Buddha's teachings themselves.

Within the commentaries on the Buddha's teachings there are two main types. Some are elaborate explanations employing a great deal of logical reasoning that are intended as guides for acquiring tremendous knowledge of the teachings. The other commentaries do not have elaborate presentations of logical reasoning but are fairly straightforward guides on how to practice the Buddha's teachings. These tend to include references to the Buddha's statements and also refer a great deal to the actual experiences discussed in those texts with practical instructions. It is principally these that we emphasize in our study.

Within the general class of texts that give practical instructions, again there are two varieties. Some of these texts are elaborate explanations of the methods of practice, and some are very brief, very pithy statements on the essence of practice. The latter tend to be in the form of songs and are referred to in Sanskrit as *doha.* They are the most important type of texts to emphasize in your study, because, given their form, they are easy to remember. Being easy to keep in mind, they are easy to use in actual practice. They combine the two virtues of profundity and brevity. Among the Indian dohas, we study those of the Indian *mahasiddhas* such as Tilopa and Naropa. Among the Tibetan songs, we study those of the masters of the Kagyu lineage, especially those of Jetsun Milarepa. Whether you read them or hear them, they are the most important basis for study.

Through hearing the Dharma, you come to a very basic idea or understanding of what it means. You come to think, "Things are like this, this is how things are." This understanding is the first level of *prajna,* or knowledge—knowledge that comes from hearing. But it is only the first level. In general there are two kinds of practitioners. One kind is called a "follower of faith," which means someone who basically believes what they are told simply because they have been told it. The other kind is a "follower of Dharma," or someone who does not take anything on authority, no matter who was supposed to have said it, but tries to discern why they said it, what it really means. Taking this second approach—looking for the real meaning of a statement—you go beyond the knowledge of hearing. Whether you study the Buddha's teachings or the commentaries upon them, the texts of instruction or the dohas, you are concerned with the question, "What does this really mean? What is this really trying to say to me? Why did the person who wrote or sang this express it in this way?" Through that type of analysis, you generate much greater certainty and understanding than you would by simply taking the statement at face value. This greater certainty is called the "knowledge (prajna) of thinking." If you meditate after having generated this knowledge of thinking, then your practice will go much better, because you will actually know how to meditate. You will also understand why you are meditating, why it is beneficial, and why it will work, which will give you much more confidence to go on with the practice. It is principally for this reason that the practice of meditation needs to be preceded by the practice of hearing and thinking.

Renunciation

The next topic our text deals with is the importance of renunciation. There are two vital things that you need at the very inception of your practice. One is trust in Dharma, in its validity. The other is renunciation—revulsion for samsara. In order to create these, in order to generate true certainty about Dharma and revulsion for samsara, it is necessary to begin by contemplating what are called "the four thoughts that turn the mind," or the *four reminders.* They are the difficulty of acquiring the freedom and resources of a precious human life; death and impermanence; the results of actions; and the defects of samsara. The generation of this type of renunciation and certainty in the Dharma is what is called "your mind going to the Dharma."

Understanding What Dharma Is

The next step in your practice is to come to an understanding of what Dharma is, an understanding of the topics of view, meditation, conduct, and fruition that make up Buddhadharma. The root of all of these, as the Buddha himself said, is taming the mind. The Buddha's 84,000 teachings are concerned with taming the 84,000 types of mental afflictions, or *kleshas.* Taming the mind means taming the kleshas, because your mind is sometimes very rough, very wild, full of selfishness, afflicted by all kinds of coarse and negative thoughts. Whether or not we succeed in taming our minds, this taming is the topic with which all Dharma is concerned.

Everything depends upon your mind. Any qualities that you attain through the path, you attain through your mind. Any defects that you remove through the path are removed from your mind. Therefore, what is called "the recognition or realization of the view" is taming your mind. What is called "the cultivation of meditative absorption" or "meditation" is taming your mind. You engage in certain modes of behavior of body and speech—conduct—in order to tame your mind. Taming is the fruition, or result, of your practice. If you understand this, then you understand that view, meditation, conduct, and fruition are all founded upon the mind.

According to Buddhadharma, a person consists of the three faculties of body, speech, and mind. How do we think about these? The body is composed of physical substances such as flesh and blood. What we regard as our body, from the top of the head to the tip of the toes, seems very powerful, very real. Speech seems much less substantial. Speech consists of all of the positive and negative things that we say. But the root of all of the deeds of body and speech is our mind. Now, if you were asked to say which of these three—body, speech, or mind—is primary, you might say the body because the body seems the strongest, the most active or effective. Then you might say that speech is second because speech, after all, can communicate. Nevertheless, it is not as strong or as stable as the body. And mind seems the weakest because it doesn't achieve anything except to think. However, in fact mind is in charge of body and speech. Body and speech don't do anything at all without mind telling them to do it. So mind is the root. It is therefore said by the siddhas of our tradition that your body and speech are like servants who perform the virtue and wrongdoing that the mind, like a boss, instigates. So, of these three, mind is in fact the most powerful. Therefore, it is of the greatest importance that we take hold of our mind, that we fix our mind. Hence all Buddhist practices, including view, meditation, and conduct, are concerned with fixing or taming the mind.

Taming or fixing the mind means abandoning the kleshas, the mental afflictions. Everyone's mind has two aspects, one pure and the other impure, and the impure aspect is called klesha. If you abandon kleshas, then all of your actions of body and speech will automatically become Dharmic or pure. As long as you have not abandoned them, then no matter how good your actions of body and speech may appear, you will still never be happy. Abandoning kleshas is the aim of Dharma, but for this to succeed, it is necessary that the remedy, the practice, actually encounter the kleshas. In order for this to occur, you need to take an honest look at your own mind. You need to see which klesha is your biggest problem. For some people, it is anger; for others it is jealousy, or attachment, or bewilderment, or pride. It can be any one of the five main kleshas, which are usually called the *five poisons.* (In fact, it is in order to tame these that wisdom deities manifest as the buddhas of the five families.)

When you have discovered which klesha is the strongest, you dedicate your practice to its amelioration. For example, if you are meditating on the four reminders, such as the difficulty of acquiring a precious human existence, you think, "I am doing the meditation in order to abandon such and such klesha." Or if you are practicing the uncommon preliminaries, such as the refuge and *bodhichitta* practice, the Vajrasattva practice, mandala practice, or guru yoga, then you think, "I am doing this in order to tame this klesha that afflicts my mind." This is especially effective in the Vajrasattva practice, wherein you can visualize the ambrosia coming from his heart and entering the top of your head to purify you and think: "Such and such klesha is being purified." Thus, by specifically directing the intention of your practice to your biggest problem, the Dharma becomes an effective remedy for your kleshas, and your kleshas will weaken over time.

Some people do not have any particularly dominant klesha and are not particularly involved with anything overtly unvirtuous. They are more afflicted by a basic fundamental fixation on their own existence. Or they might be afflicted by doubt and hesitation. They might always wonder whether "such and such is like this, or like that." Or they might be afflicted by meaningless regret, constantly questioning their own actions. Or they might be mostly afflicted by a state of neutral sleepiness, or simply by the presence of a great many thoughts that aren't particularly kleshas or negative in themselves. If any of these is your principal problem, then direct your practice to that. Dedicate all of your practice, whether it is the visualization of deities, the recitation of mantras, or the practice of meditation, to the eradication of that problem. Directing your practice in this focused way will weaken and eventually eradicate the problem.

Defining Creation and Completion

The next topic addressed in the text is a definition of the creation stage and the completion stage, which, in effect, distinguishes between them. The term "creation" or "creation stage" refers to the creation of something, the generation or origination of something. "Completion" refers in general to carrying that which has been generated to its completion, or to its perfection. In practice, creation stage refers to the visualization of the deities, including radiating and gathering light rays, the visualization and recitation of mantras, and so forth. Completion stage refers to the dissolution of such visualizations into emptiness.

However, in another sense, the meaning of the term creation is "something that is fabricated." In creation-stage practice you think that things are such and such, that "things are like this." The completion stage, by contrast, refers to something that is natural or unfabricated, because in the completion stage, rather than thinking that things are like such and such, you discover them as they are. However, the statement that the creation stage is the cultivation of some kind of fabrication, as true as it is, is really only true of the beginning of creation-stage practice. Nevertheless, as artificial as the creation stage may appear to a beginning practitioner, it is still necessary.

In practicing we are trying to ameliorate the traces of our previous wrongdoing, especially our obscurations, which consist of the *cognitive obscuration* and the *afflictive (or emotional) obscuration.* Because of the presence of these obscurations, we experience the world in an incorrect and deluded way; our experience of what we call samsara consists of deluded projections. What we are trying to do in our practice is to transcend these deluded projections and experience the pure reality, or pure appearances, that lie behind them. It is not sufficient simply to tell ourselves, "I know that what I am experiencing is adulterated by delusion," and then to stay with these deluded projections. As long as you continue to invest energy in them they will continue, even though you recognize them, at least theoretically, to be invalid. We have to reject, to cast aside, our involvement with delusion and actually consciously attend to and cultivate attention to pure appearance. By doing so you can gradually transcend and abandon delusion.

It is for this purpose that we make use of iconography, or, in other words, deities. In the Vajrayana the deity is something very different from what we normally mean by that term. Normally when we say "deity," we imagine some kind of external protector or higher power, something superior to us, outside of us, that can somehow lift us up out of where we are and bring us to where we want to be. Therefore, concurrent with our conventional idea of deity is the assumption of our own inferiority to deities. In comparison to the deity, we consider ourselves as an inferior, benighted being that has to be held up by something outside ourselves. But the Vajrayana notion of deity is not like that, for in the Vajrayana, practitioners visualize themselves as the deities with which they are working.

This body that you now consider to be so impure and afflicted is an extension of the nature of your mind. Therefore, in practice you consider this apparently impure body to be the body of your *yidam,* the deity upon whom you are meditating. Since buddha nature is the most fundamental essence of your mind, and since your body is the projection of that mind, your body is pure in nature. You acknowledge that fact in practice by imagining your body to be pure, not only in essence, but in appearance. Through cultivating this method, eventually the actual appearance or experience of your body comes to arise in purity. The creation stage is necessary in order to work with the deluded projections in this way.

Devotion and Pure Vision

In order to practice the creation and completion stages, it is essential to have devotion, to have faith, and to have pure vision or sacred outlook. Devotion has two aspects: one is enthusiasm, the other is respect. This means being interested in and enthusiastic about the Dharma, and having the respect that comes from understanding its validity and significance. One extends this same attitude toward one's root guru and the gurus of the lineage, being interested in them, and having respect.

Another important disposition is the attitude of pure or sacred vision. Pure vision is one of two ways that we can look at the world. You can look at anything in a way that sees what is good about it, that sees the purity of it; and you can look at anything in a way that sees what is wrong with it, that sees it as impure. Any action can be conducted either with an attitude of purity or of impurity.

For example, a simple act of generosity, giving something to someone, could be done mindlessly, simply to get rid of something you don't need, or done without checking to see whether it actually is appropriate for that person. That attitude is not one of pure vision but of carelessness—an impure outlook. Or you can give consciously. You can carefully evaluate the situation and determine that the gift you are giving is actually what the person needs. The same is true of any action or situation. For instance, you could be very patient with a situation simply through thinking, "This person who is abusing me is pathetic anyway, and I can't do much about it, so I might as well be patient." But this is not a pure vision. Instead you could have an attitude of courage, thinking, "Even if there were some way I could get back at this person, I would never do it." That would be a pure or sacred attitude. The point of a pure vision is to emphasize positive qualities rather than defects; especially, to be free from the type of projection that causes you to see others' qualities as defects. If you have this kind of pure vision, then through it and from it devotion will arise. If you possess devotion, then devotion itself will bring you the results of practice.

Devotion is necessary because fundamentally we need to practice Dharma, and if you have one-hundred-percent confidence in Dharma, then your practice will be one hundred percent. If you have less confidence, then your practice will be less intense. The less intense your practice, the less complete the result. Therefore, it is essential to have confidence in, and devotion for, Dharma itself. For that to occur there has to be trust in the individuals who teach you Dharma. There has to be trust in the guru. If you trust the guru, then you will trust the Dharma, and if you trust the Dharma, then you will practice it.

However, faith in one's guru does not mean blind faith. It does not mean believing "My guru is perfect," even though your guru is not perfect. It is not pretending that your guru's defects are qualities. It is not rationalizing every foible of the guru into a superhuman virtue. After all, most gurus will have defects. You need to recognize them for what they are. You don't have to pretend that your guru's defects are qualities, because the object of your devotion is not the foibles, quirks, or defects of your guru, but the Dharma that your guru teaches you. You are not practicing the guru's foibles. As long as the Dharma you receive is authentic and pure, then that guru is a fit object for your devotion. The result that you get, you get from the Dharma that you practice. You need to recognize the defects of your guru as defects—you don't need to pretend that they are otherwise. The guru's defects cannot hurt you, because it is not they that you create and cultivate. You follow the teaching of the guru, and "trust," meaning trust principally in the validity of the teachings themselves.

The Two Truths

The next topic the text addresses is that of the two truths: relative truth and absolute truth. Basically, understanding the two truths is seeing that, in their nature, all things are empty and like magical illusions. This should not be misunderstood to mean that therefore nothing has any moral value, that nothing has any meaning. Relative appearances, because of their consistencies within their own context, do have a moral value, but ultimately their nature is emptiness.

Understanding the Qualities of the Path

Finally, the last of the eight topics a beginner needs to know is understanding of the qualities of the gradual path itself. This means that you will know how to practice based upon an honest assessment of your own spiritual state. You may be a beginner, or you may be an advanced practitioner, someone who has grasped a very exalted view. If you look at yourself and you feel like a beginner, then you are a beginner. If you look at yourself and you discover that you have a very high view, then you have to accept that you should do the practices appropriate for someone with a very high view. To force yourself to do the practices appropriate for a beginner would be inappropriate.

This completes the eight topics one needs to know about in the beginning in order to approach this path.

Question: Regarding the last point, assessing one's own self in terms of one's development, what if you think you have a high view but you are actually very stupid and just arrogant? How can you determine this?

Rinpoche: It is possible to deceive yourself in that way, but if you look at your own situation completely, then you will be able to detect that self-deception. From among the types of pride, considering yourself to possess qualities that you lack is called "full-blown pride." Fully manifest, full-blown pride. Full-blown pride is not difficult to detect. If you look to see whether this pride is present in your way of thinking and in your motivation, then you can usually spot it very easily.

Question: What are some examples of beginning practices, middle practices, and advanced practices?

RINPOCHE: One begins with shamata practice, meditation on the four reminders, and cultivation of the preliminary practices in order to accumulate merit. Then one undertakes the meditation of the creation and completion stages. Finally, one engages in the conduct of a siddha in order to attain full awakening.

Essential Points for Traversing the Path

Now, following the text, we will look at what is necessary once one has entered onto the path.

First of all, all of the Buddha's teachings are included within two paths. They are the stable and gradual path of the *sutras* and the quick and especially effective path of the Vajrayana, or the *tantras.* Both of these take as their root the taming of the mind, or pacifying the thoughts and kleshas that afflict our minds. With respect to their aim, the paths of sutra and tantra are the same, but they differ in their methods. The methods for pacifying thoughts and kleshas can be divided into the techniques of abandonment, transformation, and recognition.

THREE TECHNIQUES FOR PACIFYING KLESHAS

The sutras in general teach the path of the rejection or *abandonment* of the kleshas, which is based on seeing the kleshas as a problem and therefore being motivated to let them go. Exactly how to let go of the kleshas is taught in the sutras. Now, there are many kleshas, but principal among them, and at the root of all the others, are what are called the three poisons of attachment, aversion, and bewilderment. If we use attachment as an example, in the path of abandoning the kleshas you determine that you must reject or relinquish attachments. Our attachments and cravings come from a mistaken assumption that the things to which we become attached will endure and that they will retain lasting characteristics. Therefore, in order to remove this attachment, you meditate on the impermanence of things, and come to recognize that they are constantly changing and are ultimately destructible and impermanent. You also meditate on the unpleasant nature of all the things that you assume are pleasant.

The third of the root kleshas is bewilderment, which essentially refers to ignorance itself. Ignorance occurs in two forms, mixed ignorance and unmixed ignorance. Mixed ignorance is the ignorance that always accompanies any klesha; it is called *mixed ignorance* because it is the arising of ignorance mixed with the arising of another klesha. No klesha can arise in the absence of ignorance; therefore, when attachment arises, for example, it is based upon some ignorance, some fundamental mistake about the characteristics of the object of attachment. When anger arises, it never arises alone, because anger by itself in the absence of ignorance would be powerless. The same is true of pride and jealousy. There is always some fundamental confusion that is the condition for the arising of that particular klesha. Unmixed ignorance is ignorance in itself, not knowing or not being aware of the nature of things. That unknowing is the most fundamental aspect of ignorance. The unknowing becomes a misconception or a mistaken understanding when, on the basis of unknowing, we cultivate a mistaken view through incorrect reasoning. Therefore, while bewilderment in itself is not as vivid or as immediately unpleasant as the other kleshas, it nevertheless is the root of all kleshas and of all suffering.

The reason that bewilderment feeds, nourishes, and reinforces the kleshas is because bewilderment fixates upon the perceived characteristics of objects as either pleasant or unpleasant. When you perceive an object upon which you fixate as pleasant, you generate attachment. When you perceive an object that you fixate upon as being unpleasant, you generate aversion. When you fixate upon something as being extremely unpleasant, you generate manifest suffering. In order to abandon fixation you meditate upon interdependence. Through the recognition that all things lack independent existence and are but interdependent arisings, your fixation on their perceived characteristics diminishes. Through diminishing that fixation your ignorance diminishes, and through that the kleshas are pacified. That is the path of abandonment of the kleshas. This type of abandonment meditation is used whenever kleshas arise and whenever there is a problem of mental misery or physical discomfort or pain.

The second approach, that of *transformation,* is characteristic of the path of secret mantra, or the Vajrayana. In this approach whenever a klesha arises, or any other kind of difficulty, pain, or problem, instead of attempting to abandon it, you visualize yourself as a deity manifesting it. It could be any deity, or it could be a deity particularly connected to the klesha or problem with which you are dealing. For example, it could be one of the five buddhas: Vairochana, Akshobhya, Ratnasambhava, Amitabha, or Amoghasiddhi. In dealing with desire, it could be a deity shown in sexual union. In dealing with anger, it could be a deity shown in a wrathful form. The idea is that you stop conceiving of yourself as yourself and you think of yourself as the deity. Through visualizing yourself as the deity, the emotional state ceases to be a klesha, because your attitude has been changed. The emotion itself is transformed into something pure.

The third approach to the kleshas is the path of *recognition,* which means recognition of the nature of whatever klesha arises. In this approach, when a klesha arises in your mind, it is recognized as merely a relative and dependent thing. We experience the arising of kleshas accompanied by all kinds of suffering, sadness, misery, and depression; but if you actually look at the nature of what is arising, you will see that what is occurring is not what you normally consider to be occurring. For example, when I become angry, I generate a thought of anger that has a particular object. I think, "This person is my enemy," and I am aware of this thought of being angry. When I don't look directly at the anger, the intensity of the anger and its attendant suffering seem intolerable. But if, while this thought of anger is arising and is present, you look straight at it, look to see how it arises, where it comes from, where it is while it is present, and exactly what it is in substance, you find that there is nothing you can point to. There is nothing in your mind anywhere that you can point to and say, "This is my anger." Anger in its nature is empty of any kind of true existence. When, in the midst of the emergence of the anger, you see and experience its emptiness directly, then it is naturally pacified. This works with any other kind of suffering or with any of the other kleshas as well. It is simply the recognition that there is really no thing there. This is the path of the recognition of the nature of kleshas.

According to the teachings given by the Buddha in the sutras, the beginning of the path of abandonment of the kleshas is a process called "distancing," which means to distance yourself from the kleshas. Normally when various thoughts and kleshas arise in our minds, we generate a further fixation on them. We become attached and addicted to them. The first step in letting go of the kleshas is therefore letting go of this fixation. The fixation is based upon thinking of them as something valuable, and identifying with them. Thus we have to recognize that kleshas are problems, that they are useless and harmful. Recognizing this is not simply being aware of it theoretically, but cultivating the habit of recognizing it all the time. Doing so will not immediately eradicate the kleshas. But gradually, by not identifying with them and not valuing them, you will become distant from them in the sense that you will have less fixation on them when they arise, and this will make them easier to abandon.

Having cultivated distancing, you can go on to employ the various methods of transcending the kleshas: abandonment, transformation, and recognition. According to the great teacher Gyalwang Yongdrupa, it is best to combine these three methods rather than to select one among the three. For example, he taught that when a klesha arises, first recognize it as a problem, recognize it as something you do not wish to cultivate. Then generate the aspiration, "May I never again generate this klesha from this moment until my attainment of buddhahood." As much as possible, generate this sense of commitment to never doing so. That is abandonment.

Then you go on to employ transformation. Whatever the klesha may be, you transform it into altruism by changing your attitude. You think, "May all of the kleshas that are present in the minds of all sentient beings, and especially this klesha, be absent from their minds and be added on to this klesha of mine. May whatever suffering that all beings, especially practitioners of Dharma, have through the affliction of this klesha be experienced only by me. May this klesha of mine substitute for all of their kleshas." In that way the presence of the klesha itself becomes an occasion for the generation of an especially good intention. Then, having generated that intention with the attitude that you are doing so in order to pacify or remove this particular klesha, you visualize yourself as a deity. Those two steps of accepting the kleshas of others and visualizing yourself as a deity comprise the process of transformation.

Next you practice the recognition of the klesha's nature. Continuing to visualize yourself as the deity you have chosen, you think that in the center of your body, at the level of your heart, resides your root guru, who is majestic and beautiful in appearance. Visualizing the root guru there as vividly as possible, you supplicate, asking that you be granted the blessing of the nature of the klesha to arise as wisdom—that you may actually see the nature of that klesha, which is wisdom. After having supplicated in that way, you look at the single nature of three aspects of the meditation: the deity you are visualizing as yourself, the guru visualized in your heart, and the klesha that has arisen and is the occasion for the meditation or practice. Through looking at the single or unified nature of these three things, you come to recognize the nature of the klesha, which causes it to be naturally pacified. That is the approach or path of recognition.

Outline of the Creation Stage

Having presented the instructions for the practices common to both sutra and tantra, the text now turns to the issues surrounding Vajrayana practice in particular. These include the practice of the creation and completion stages in general, and especially the practice of the tradition of uncommon or special instructions. The text goes first through the creation stage, then the completion stage, and lastly through the tradition of uncommon instruction.

Beginning with the creation stage, it is important to remember that while we practice what is called self-generation (visualization of oneself as the deity) and front generation (visualization of the deity in front of oneself), it is self-generation that is principally important. This involves visualizing yourself as the deity as vividly as possible, including the deity's color, costume, implements, and so forth. The details of each specific deity practice are explained in the liturgy and commentaries of that particular practice, so in this text no specific instruction is given. This text is concerned more broadly with the background and theory surrounding the practice of the creation stage; therefore this stage is presented in four topics: 1) the basis of purification, 2) that which is to be purified, 3) that which purifies it—the methods, and 4) the result of this purification process.

In order to understand the difference between the ground of purification and that which is to be purified or removed, you need to understand that there are in a sense two aspects to your mind. There is how your mind is, in its nature, and how it appears or manifests in your experience. From the point of view of how your mind appears, you could say that your mind is full of kleshas, of suffering; full of all kinds of confused or deluded projections. But from the point of view of how your mind really is, there is nothing in any of this confusion that cannot be abandoned, because this confusion is secondary or adventitious to the nature of mind itself.

Therefore, confusion can be purified and removed, and the innate wisdom of your mind can be revealed and expanded.

The nature of your mind, what your mind really is, even the nature of what appear as kleshas, is called *sugatagarbha* or *buddha nature,* the seed of all the qualities of buddhas, the seed of all wisdom. This is always present but is obscured by the presence of the kleshas and other obscurations. The process of the path consists of revealing just this. It does not need to be created but to be revealed. Therefore, the basis or ground of purification is buddha nature, which is the innate presence of the qualities and wisdoms of buddhas and therefore of yidams.

That which purifies the obscurations of innate buddha nature is the creation stage of the yidam. The confused projections that make up *samsara,* including the kleshas, can be abandoned because they are secondary to the fundamental nature of mind itself. But in order for you to abandon them, there has to be a shift in your attitude. As long as you invest energy in the impurity of the projections, and as long as you view these appearances and experiences as impure, you maintain them. If you change your attitude and view them as pure, actually meditate upon them as pure, then you no longer maintain them.

When you begin the practice of the creation stage as an ordinary individual, the approach to practice is called "taking aspiration as path," which means that preliminary to actually seeing things as pure, you aspire to see them as pure. Through this process of taking aspiration as path, eventually you will generate what is called the "clarity of appearance," or the vivid direct experience of the purity of phenomena. This activity will naturally purify the delusion. The technique consists essentially of visualizing yourself as the yidam and visualizing the place in which you find yourself as the *mandala* or abode of that yidam. When one begins this practice, the thought will arise, "I am pretending to be other than what I am." You may even know through your study of Dharma, your understanding of buddha nature, and your confidence in the theory of the practice, that this is not really true, that in fact you are not pretending to be other than you really are. However, because we have a strong habit of conceiving of ourselves and everything around us as impure, these thoughts may continue to arise. In order to counteract them, there are specific techniques built into the practices that serve as remedies. For example, in order to counteract the thought, "I'm visualizing myself as this deity, but I'm not really the deity; the deity is really something or somewhere else," you invite this real deity into yourself. There are other techniques as well, such as repeating a mantra, radiating and gathering light rays, and so on, all of which are aspects of the creation stage. As you practice the creation stage, over time you approach the result or fruition, which is the experience of the innate purity of both body and mind. That is essentially an outline of the practice of the creation stage.

Three Elements

The practice of the creation stage consists of the cultivation of three elements: clarity, purity, and stability. *Clarity* means the clarity of the visualized image, which is the technique of the creation stage. This element consists simply of visualizing the deity as clearly as you can. Some people, because of the constitution of their channels and so forth, find it easy to generate a very clear image. Other people do not. In any case the technique is the same. With a relaxed mind, you visualize the form of the deity. In doing so it is natural to develop hope that the form will be intensely vivid. In fact, you would like the image of the deity to be as vivid as what you see with your physical eyes.

In practicing visualization you are not using the eye consciousness but rather the mental consciousness, and the mental consciousness is conceptual. Unlike the eye consciousness, which experiences the individual characteristics of forms, the mental consciousness produces an abstraction or a generalization; therefore, the visualization will tend to remain something vague. However, if you continue the practice with a relaxed mind, then gradually the image will increase in stability and in clarity or vividness. To rest within this continued clear visualization of the deity (the deity's form, color, position, costume, ornaments, implements, and so forth) is the practice of the first element of the creation stage, the clarity of image, or clear visualization.

When you are cultivating clarity in the visualization, sometimes you will find that the visualization is less clear, vivid, or stable than usual. There are things you can do to correct this. For example, the text suggests that you concentrate for a while in your visualization on one specific detail, such as the *vajra* held in the hand, or a scepter, or the jewel on top of the deity's topknot. Depending upon the nature of what is preventing clear visualization, there are some choices to make in what you direct your attention to. In general, if many thoughts are running through your mind and preventing you from concentrating on the visualization, then it is recommended that you direct your attention to something toward the bottom of the visualization, such as the lotus seat on which the deity is seated or standing. If, on the other hand, a kind of torpor or depression prevents the emergence of clarity or vividness, then it is generally recommended that you direct your attention to something toward the top of the visualization, such as the top of the deity's head, the jewel, or the topknot.

The second element of creation-stage practice is *purity*, or the recollection of purity. This is often explained as the enumeration in your mind of the symbolic significance of each aspect of the deity's appearance, i.e., what each aspect of the appearance represents. But our text points out that if you do this, it may become too conceptual and can actually disturb your mind and harm the meditation. What is recommended, practically, to implement the recollection of purity is to keep in mind that this appearance of the deity is a vivid or clear appearance without any existence, that it is the unity of clarity and emptiness, like the appearance of a rainbow in its vividness and insubstantiality.

The third element in the practice of the creation stage is *stability*, which means the stable pride of being the deity. In this practice you identify with the deity, actually thinking, "I am this deity." This is very important, as it is the aspect of the creation stage that actually serves as a remedy for our ordinary fixation on a self. The practice or cultivation of stable pride consists of abandoning the sense of being different from or other than the deity that you are meditating on as yourself.

QUESTION: In the meditations in the book *Progressive Stages of Meditation on Emptiness*, you view emotional reactions as evidence of fixation on self. Specifically, in the case of grief, one can view grief as something like physical pain in the form of suffering, or on the other hand, view it as a klesha, such as anger, based on attachment, duality, and fixation on self. In examining my own grief, I've come to some understanding of the nature of interdependence and impermanence and how they are an antidote to the attachment and duality that lead to grief. But I find only a small level of understanding. The pain and the suffering are very clearly still there. I am wondering if this process is the same as that in which one examines something like anger. The anger dissipates; it goes away. In the context of something like extreme grief, what does it mean to abandon it? Does it mean that it goes away, or that it's still there as a matter of relative truth but understood to be empty?

RINPOCHE: Grief is not a klesha. It is not considered a cause of suffering but rather *is* suffering. One does not need to abandon it in the way that one abandons kleshas, which cause future suffering. One abandons grief in the sense of allowing it to be pacified, because maintaining it can cause suffering upon suffering. But whether or not grief can be transcended depends upon the power of your meditation. When you look directly at the nature of your grief, it will probably not disappear. However, through seeing its nature, while the grief will remain present, it will be less overwhelming. In a sense the heaviness of it will be somewhat pacified, so that although you will still grieve, your position with respect to your grief will be different from that of an untrained person. Theoretically, when you see the nature of grief, it can be totally abandoned, but practically speaking this doesn't happen. Because our minds are not habituated enough to seeing the nature of whatever arises, to abandon it, the grief and sadness will just be somewhat lessened in their heaviness, but will still be there.

QUESTION: With regard to abandoning the klesha of bewilderment, you have said that the remedy is meditation on interdependence. I want to see how that actually works. Say, for example, I perceive that I'm fixated on perceiving the sound of the birds and the rustling trees as being pleasant. If there were twenty motorcycles roaring around, I would perceive that as unpleasant, and yet the nature of the sound is just sound—movement and vibration. I understand that, but I still have the experience of one being pleasant and one being unpleasant. How, practically speaking, would one meditate on interdependence?

RINPOCHE: The perception of things as pleasant and unpleasant is itself not a problem. The problem only occurs when, for example, in thinking of something as unpleasant, we develop an aversion to it, which is the point at which we actively wish to get rid of it. Or, thinking of something as pleasant, we develop an attachment to it, which means we actively wish to acquire it or prolong it. It is those things that cause us suffering.

The reason why meditation on interdependence is beneficial in this instance is that interdependence is, at the same time, relativity. By recognizing the relative nature of these perceived or imputed characteristics, one becomes free from fixation upon them. For example, if you were to become actually tormented by the sound of twenty motorcycles, thinking how awful and disturbing that sound is, then in that context you would reflect upon worse sounds. And there are indeed worse sounds that you could be hearing. By thinking about worse sounds, such as screaming, you would no longer be fixating on the unpleasantness of the motorcycles. Or, if you were tormented by being attached to the pleasant sound of birds, then you could reflect upon the fact that there are far more pleasant sounds you could hear, and in that way let go of your fixation on hearing the birds.

QUESTION: What is meant on page 41 by the marks and signs of the body of reality?

RINPOCHE: First of all, the *dharmakaya* is what is referred to in this passage as the "body of reality." It does not in itself possess any physical characteristics, but the quality of the dharmakaya manifests as the *rupakaya,* or form bodies, and they do possess physical characteristics that are normally enumerated as thirty-two major and eighty minor marks of physical perfection. The thirty-two major marks of physical perfection are that the bodies of buddhas are always beautiful, have certain very specific types of features, and have certain extraordinary characteristics, such as that the clothing or robes worn by buddhas will never actually touch their body but will always be four finger widths away from it, the body of a buddha always has an extensive halo, and so on. The eighty minor marks of physical perfection are less pronounced, wonderful physical characteristics that are similar to the thirty-two major ones.

QUESTION: I have a friend who gets very angry, and his anger has value to him. If someone harms him, he feels he can avenge himself. He seems to find satisfaction in just being angry. It's not enough to say to him, "You're going to cause yourself more suffering." He thinks, "I want revenge." How can I talk with him?

RINPOCHE: A distinction can be made between anger itself and holding a grudge. Holding a grudge comes about from having invested in and cultivated anger. If you continually invest in anger, then anger will develop into this tendency to hold grudges, which is the next step or development of it. Holding a grudge basically consists of never letting go of anger. Whenever you get angry, it becomes somehow deeply entrenched, and you hold on to it because you are so used to being angry. The remedy for this is to cultivate the remedies for anger in general. That will prevent its becoming entrenched.

One thing you can say to your friend is that he is better off being patient than seeking revenge, because revenge becomes perpetual. It is self-maintaining, simply because the act of vengeance itself usually involves doing more back than what was done to you. This is an illustration of the fact that kleshas such as anger always include ignorance. In this case, the ignorance lies in part in that when you seek revenge, you don't stop to think that the person on whom you are exacting revenge will probably feel victimized by your exacting more than is fair, and will want to get revenge on you in return. If this goes on long enough, eventually both people will regret it, because they will have harmed each other without either really ever being satisfied by what they have done.

QUESTION: On page 49, the text reads, "Do not meditate on pride, cut through the root of ego-clinging." The following line says, "When ego-clinging is destroyed, wherever one's mind focuses, its essence arises vividly." Could you comment on the phrase "wherever one's mind focuses, its essence arises vividly."

RINPOCHE: It means that when fixation on a self has been eradicated, wherever the mind is directed, that selflessness, that absence of self that is the mind's nature arises vividly in your direct experience.

QUESTION: On page 45, in the section that begins, "In some of the highest yogatantras of secret mantra," what is meant by "the emanation from the organs in union"?

RINPOCHE: This is in a section of the text discussing the technical details of different types of deity practice. Here it describes a specific type of creation stage, a gradual development of the visualization of the deity in which, in some practices, the deity is actually generated twice. First, through whatever gradual process, you generate yourself as the deity. Then that deity dissolves and melts into a sphere of light, and from that sphere of light you re-emerge as the deity. These deities are called the "causal vajra holder" and the "resultant vajra holder." What is referred to as the vajra holder corresponds to the mind of luminosity or clear light that occurs at the death of the previous life and that subsequently emerges from the bardo into conception and birth in the next life. In a *sadhana* practice where the text says "from the secret space...," the deity who is generated in this dual way has a retinue before the causal vajra holder. In that case there will be a father and mother in union, and before they melt into light, from the secret space of the mother, the other members of the mandala will have merged and taken their places in the palace. Then the father and mother causal vajra holder, the central figures, will melt into light and then re-arise.

The basic idea here is that you are purifying the way you are conceived and come into the world. At the end of the previous life, you are alone and then you die. Before you are reborn, there are already the parents, and so on. The body that you have is a mixture of three things: the white constituent, which is the sperm from the father; the red constituent, which is the ovum from the mother; and the wind element, which is the mount for your consciousness as it actually enters the womb and combines with the other two. The function of these visualizations is to correspond to, and thereby purify, fixation on the mixing or combining of these three elements.

QUESTION: What does it mean that "the vital drops purify the white and red appearances"?

RINPOCHE: In this section [page 45] Jamgön Kongtrul is giving a list of different elements, not all of which are likely to be present in the same practice. For example, when he says that "through the gradual disappearance of the three syllables, appearance, increase, and attainment are purified," he's talking about something that occurs in some practices in which you visualize the three syllables and then they disappear, and the visualization proceeds from there. When he says, "through the drops, the appearances of white and red are purified," he is referring to the visualization of the sphere of light that occurs when the causal vajra holder has dissolved before the resultant vajra holder has arisen. What you are purifying is your attitude about the white and red constituents, the sperm and the ovum, which are the substantial, or physical, basis for the emergence of your own body.

QUESTION: Are the vital drops the same thing as the white and red appearances?
RINPOCHE: It is not so much that the drops are the same. It's that they correspond. The visualization of this white and red sphere intermingled, which then becomes the resultant vajra holder, is a way of representing, and therefore purifying, your fixation on the white and red drops that you received from your parents.

QUESTION: So the vital drops are the causal vajra holder?
RINPOCHE: No, when the causal vajra holder melts into light, he or they or she, depending upon what the deity is, become a sphere of light that is mixed white and red.

QUESTION: And those are the vital drops?
RINPOCHE: That's what is referred to here as the "drop." It represents the vital drops, but here the visualization is of a sphere or drop. The word *tig-le*, which the translator here translated as "vital drop," can also mean sphere.

Purification

The structure and format of creation-stage practice corresponds to the way we are born. Being born is the acquisition of a new body. A new body, of course, does not mean your first body, just your latest body, your most recently acquired body. There are four different ways that sentient beings can be born. The first is womb birth, as with humans and other mammals, where you are born from the womb of your mother. The second, which is very similar, is egg birth, where you are hatched from an egg that has issued forth from the womb, as is the case with birds and reptiles. Those two types of birth are fairly coarse in manner. The third one is a little more subtle, and although it is often presented as a separate type of birth, it can also be understood as a variation of either womb or egg generation—birth from heat and moisture.

These first three types of birth correspond to three types of creation-stage visualization that are principally designed to purify the habit of these types of birth. Womb birth is purified by the style of generation called *five enlightening factors,* egg birth by what is called the *four vajras,* and birth from heat and moisture by what is called the *three procedures* or *three rituals.*

The fourth type of birth is the way that beings in certain realms who have particularly subtle bodies appear. It is an instantaneous birth occurring in the absence of womb, egg, or even heat and moisture. This instantaneous birth is purified by what is called *instantaneous generation,* or "generation that is complete in an instant of recollection." In this case the meditation on the deity does not begin with the establishment of the mandala and the seat of the deity, then the placement of the seed syllable on the seat, its transformation into an implement, and of the implement into the deity, as is usual in other visualizations. Rather, in an instant of recollection, you simply visualize yourself as the deity. However, although these four types of visualization (five enlightening factors, four vajras, three rituals, and complete in an instant of recollection) do correspond individually to the four types of birth, practicing any one of these purifies all four.

Once you have generated the deity's form through any of these four procedures, then you visualize that deity with its particular position, color, costume, ornamentation, implements, with the father, the mother, the retinue, the mandala in which they abide, and so on. From that point onward the practice will vary. Depending upon the specific practice, there may be many other steps and stages. In all cases, the practice will conclude with what is called the "dissolution phase." *Dissolution* refers to the dissolution or withdrawal of the mandala into the clear light, or emptiness. The entire practice can either be very elaborate or very simple and concise. Either way, the entire practice, beginning with the generation of the deity and culminating with the dissolution of the deity and mandala into the clear light, corresponds to all the events of one life, from the time the consciousness enters the womb until the dissolution of death.

Nyingma and Sarma

There are many variations in the procedure, style, and content of these creation-stage practices, as I have mentioned. For example, in Tibet there were two periods in the introduction of Buddhism. The initial spread of the teachings in the eighth and ninth centuries led to what is called the old, or *Nyingma,* tradition. The subsequent renewal of the doctrine with the introduction of new translations from India in the eleventh century led to what is called the new, or *Sarma,* tradition. The procedures and style of the practices of the creation stage in the Nyingma and Sarma traditions vary somewhat, at least in appearance and in method, but there is no difference in their effectiveness in the actual purification of the kleshas. If, for example, one had an illness of the eyes, one might treat it with a surgical procedure or one might treat it with medication. In either case, one could remove whatever is obstructing or obscuring one's vision. In the same way, although the actual methods vary slightly, the focus of both the Sarma and the Nyingma creation-stage practices is identical.

Next the text gives a description of how a creation-stage practice works. The type of creation-stage practice that the text uses for an example is basically a Nyingma model, but it will give you an idea of a creation-stage procedure. The characteristic of a Nyingma approach to the creation stage is the cultivation of what are called the *three samadhis* or *three meditative absorptions.* These correspond to the *dharmakaya,* the *sambhogakaya,* and the *nirmanakaya.* The first samadhi, connected with the dharmakaya, is called the *samadhi of suchness,* and essentially consists of meditation on emptiness. It corresponds to and purifies one's death in the preceding life, up to the point at which the appearances of the preceding life have vanished and there is an experience of nothing whatsoever, which is like emptiness.

Following this meditation on emptiness, which is the samadhi of suchness and corresponds to the dharmakaya, is meditation on the compassion that has the characteristics of a magical illusion. This is called the *all-arising samadhi.* It corresponds to the sambhogakaya, and it purifies the subsequent experience of the *bardo* (one's experience after one's previous death and before one's conception in this life). The function of this second samadhi is to form a link between the dharmakaya and the coarse or full manifestation of the nirmanakaya. Therefore, it forms the basis or prelude to the generation of the mandala.

The third samadhi, which is connected to the nirmanakaya, is called the *samadhi of cause* and is the initial visualization of the seed-syllable of the deity. This corresponds to the emergence of your consciousness from the bardo and its actual entrance into the womb. Therefore, along with visualizing the seed-syllable, one visualizes the seat of the deity, which will consist of either a lotus with sun and moon disks or a lotus with either just a moon or just a sun. One begins by imagining this lotus, sun, and moon seat; this corresponds to and purifies the white and red elements, the sperm and ovum that come from the parents and are the physical or substantial basis for your physical body. Then you visualize, on top of this, the seed-syllable of the deity; this corresponds to and purifies the entrance of your consciousness from the bardo into the womb at the time of conception.

Next, visualize the seed-syllable changing into the deity's characteristic implement, which is marked at its center by the seed-syllable; this corresponds to the period of gestation in the womb. When the implement, together with the seed-syllable, is transformed into the complete body of the deity, this corresponds to and purifies the moment of birth. Having visualized yourself as the deity, you imagine the three syllables of OM, AH, HUNG in the three places of the deity's body; this purifies the habits from this life of body, speech, and mind. This procedure is characteristic of the Nyingma school, beginning with the three samadhis and culminating in the gradual generation of the deity from syllable, implement, and the entire body.

In the tantras of the Sarma school, one often finds the generation of the "causal vajra holder" and "resultant vajra holder," which is a different way of generating the deity. The more elaborate practices of the Sarma school tend to include two generations of the deity. First, through a gradual procedure, the deity is generated as the causal vajra holder. This first form of the deity is generated in order to purify the death process of one's previous life. The causal vajra holder form of the deity that has been generated will then melt into light, becoming a sphere of light. From that sphere the deity is generated a second time, and this deity is called the resultant vajra holder. This visualization corresponds to and purifies the arising of the mental body in the bardo, as well as the entrance of that consciousness arisen as a mental body into the womb—the process of gestation and birth.

The details of these practices can vary quite a bit. For example, in some practices with causal and resultant vajra holders, when the causal vajra holder emerges, the other deities of the mandala will emanate from the secret space of the consort of the principal deity. Then the causal vajra holder, father and mother, will melt into light and become a sphere of light. At that point the *dakinis* and other emanated deities of the retinue will request the central deity, now in the form of a sphere of light, to arise from emptiness for the benefit of beings, in response to which that sphere of light will turn into the resultant vajra holders. Furthermore, in some other practices, rather than using the causal and resultant vajra holder, the end of one's previous life is purified by visualizing the gradual dissolution of the three syllables OM, AH, HUNG. These correspond to the stages of death called *appearance, increase,* and *attainment.* Thus, there are many variations within the Sarma school creation-stage practices.

Whether the practice is of the Nyingma or Sarma style, once the deity has been generated completely, usually you will visualize that, from the heart of yourself as the deity, rays of light shoot out and invite the wisdom beings, or *jnanasattvas,* which are the actual deity. You imagine that these are invited and dissolve into you, at which point you rest in the confidence that the jnanasattvas have actually entered into your being. This corresponds to and purifies the learning process you go through after birth. Following that, usually you will again invite the five male and female buddhas, who will bestow empowerment upon you as the deity. This is done in order to purify your family inheritance, everything that you inherit from your parents. Then there will be homage, offerings, and praises to yourself as the deity. The function of these stages of the practice is to purify all of your interactions throughout this life with the various objects of experience, including your possessions, and so on. In short, every step of the creation-stage practice is designed to correspond to and purify something upon which we project impurity.

Mantra

Next comes the repetition of the mantra. The mantra repetition purifies all of your talk and conversation throughout your life, especially talk connected to attachment, aversion, and bewilderment. Following that comes the dissolution of the visualization into emptiness and finally the re-arising of yourself as the deity. These processes correspond to your death at the end of this life and to your re-arising in a mental body in the bardo. Hence the procedure of any one creation-stage practice completely corresponds to all of the events of one life cycle, starting with the bardo and the entrance of the bardo consciousness into the womb, going through your whole life and ending with your death, and again your entrance into the bardo.

Invariably such practices are preceded by going for refuge and generating bodhichitta, and are followed by the *dedication of merit* and the making of aspirations. These are essential for the practice to be a Mahayana practice. Going for refuge and generating bodhichitta establish your intention for the practice at the beginning, along with making aspirations for the benefit of beings and, at the end, dedicating the merit to all beings. These Mahayana practices are used to enhance the technique of the creation-stage practice and make it a proper Mahayana practice.

In many creation-stage practices there will be additional elements, such as the consecration of the offerings and sometimes a *feast offering*. The purpose of the consecration of offerings and the making of feast offerings is to gather the two accumulations, the accumulation of merit and the accumulation of wisdom. Although the text says "to gather the two accumulations," principally these lead to the accumulation of merit. In the general context of Mahayana, merit is accumulated by means of the first five *paramitas:* generosity, morality, patience, diligence, and meditation. In the specific context of Vajrayana, the methods by which merit is accumulated emphasize the practice of visualization. This means, a small thing can be magnified or multiplied in its power so that one accumulates vast amounts of merit without much difficulty. For example, in feast practice you use a very small offering as a basis for meditation, and in meditation you multiply it extensively. It therefore becomes a basis for an accumulation of merit that is far greater than the offering itself. The idea here is that through perfecting or completing the accumulation of merit, you also come to accumulate wisdom. But the most direct effect of these feast offerings and offering consecrations is principally the accumulation of merit.

The Nature of Deities

The fourth topic concerning the creation stage is the result of purification: Everything that obscures the pure ground is removed, and the sugatagarbha, or buddha nature, that is itself the ground of purification is fully revealed. The view of the creation stage is that this buddha nature itself contains all of the qualities of the deities. So when you visualize yourself as a deity, you are visualizing yourself as something that is a similitude of, that has the same characteristics as, your own buddha nature. By doing this you familiarize yourself with buddha nature and therefore allow buddha nature to reveal itself. It is not that through the creation stage you are creating a result. You are revealing the ground as a result. The result is that through this process of familiarization, taking the appearance of the ground as the path, you come to fully reveal that ground. When everything that obscures it has been removed, then that ground fully revealed is itself the fruition or result. In other words, the result does not come from outside; it is revealed from within.

The creation stage is the practice of a yidam, and you do that specific yidam practice exactly as it is prescribed in the liturgy for it. If the liturgy prescribes a long and elaborate series of steps to the visualization, that is what you visualize. If it is concise and prescribes that the deity be visualized complete in an instant of recollection, then that is what you visualize. In either case, in the principal or main practice of a yidam, you visualize yourself as that deity, as that yidam.

We also do other practices where the emphasis is not on visualizing yourself as a deity but on visualizing deities external to yourself. For example, when we visualize the sources of refuge as part of refuge or prostration practice, we visualize them in front of ourselves. When we visualize Vajrasattva in the Vajrasattva preliminary practice, we visualize Vajrasattva seated above our head. When we do the Chenrezig practice, we commence with the visualization of Chenrezig above our head. The reason that, in these three types of practices, the visualization is different from a conventional creation-stage practice of self-visualization is that they are designed for beginners. You cannot start by simply revealing your own inner wisdom, which is the principal reason for self-visualization. You have to begin by visualizing external deities and their qualities.

We should be clear about the nature of the deities in the Vajrayana, especially because it seems we almost externalize them in some practices. We should view them primarily as something internal, something that is within us. First of all, a distinction needs to be made between the use of a deity in a nontheistic tradition such as Buddhism and in a theistic tradition such as Hinduism. In Hindu practices that work with the iconography of deities, the deities are considered to be external and essentially to have the role of creators of the universe. It is believed that these deities have the power to make you happy and to make you suffer. These deities, if pleased, have the power to bring you to liberation, to grant you all kinds of attainments, supreme and common. Therefore, the practice in such a tradition consists of praying to deities with the greatest faith and devotion, making offerings to them with the understanding that if they are pleased, they will grant you attainments, and that if they are not pleased and become angry, they can actually cast you into the lower realms.

The Buddhist view of deities is entirely different. First of all, the Buddhist tradition holds that your happiness and suffering come about because of your own previous actions, and that no other being can actually cause you to experience what you have not caused yourself karmicly. What you experience comes about because of your own previous actions and habits of perception. Ultimately, from a Buddhist point of view, no deity can grant you siddhi, or attainment. You receive attainment through your removal of the obscurations of your innate wisdom. Therefore in the Buddhist tradition, we do not assert that attainment is actually given to you by the whim of an external being.

On the other hand, there also exist traditions that say that there is no help whatsoever from outside, that the path consists entirely of one's own internal work, and that any supplication of any awakened being is meaningless. But this is not exactly the Buddhist view either, because while it is true that no buddha can hand you the result of this path, they can help. For example, if you consider this life, up to a certain point you had no knowledge of Dharma whatsoever. Then, through some series of circumstances, you approached a guru and received instruction; this guru became your root guru and something changed, and that is called *the blessing of Dharma.* Before, you didn't know what Dharma was, and then you did. Before, you didn't know how to practice, and then you did. Many things changed as a result. Maybe you had no confidence in Dharma, and then came to have confidence. You had no devotion, and then you came to have devotion. You came to have more compassion than you did before. Your meditation improved. Now, none of these things were precisely given to you by your root guru, but nevertheless something happens surrounding your relationship with the root guru, and this is what we call the blessing of the guru.

This change is easy to understand because it is concerned with your relationship or interaction with someone you have met, someone who is another human being. But you also supplicate gurus of the past, gurus you have not met, gurus who are not visible to you at present. So when you supplicate them, even though, like your root guru, they cannot hand you attainment or fruition; yet, like your root guru, they can influence and help you. It is not particularly that by supplicating them they are pleased and therefore decide to share their spiritual wealth with you. It is rather that the devotion you generate in your supplication causes this blessing simply to occur. Therefore the guru can still grant blessing even when he or she is not physically present in your perception. That is the first of the *three roots,* or three sources, of Vajrayana practice, the guru, which is the root of blessing.

The second root is the yidam, the deity, which is the root of attainment. Essentially, yidams are the forms of the sambhogakaya that buddhas take in order to communicate with and train beings. It is not the case that literally speaking your yidam, any more than your guru, can bestow on you supreme attainment, but, like gurus, yidams can influence you. They grant you their blessing in the sense that through working with a yidam, a new clarity dawns in your meditative absorption, and you come to gradually realize something or attain something. To be precise, we would say that in calling yidams the root of siddhi, we do not mean that they grant it, but that they facilitate it.

The third root is the *dharmapalas,* or Dharma protectors, who are the root of activity. The function of dharmapalas is to help you free yourself from anything that impedes your practice and path. They help to encourage your exertion, encourage your devotion; they help you find ways to purify your obscurations and your wrongdoing. Dharmapalas are basically buddhas who take this type of role for the aid of practitioners. So while it is not the case that any external being can grant you supreme siddhi, still these three roots—the gurus, yidams, and dharmapalas—if you supplicate them, can bestow blessing and can help remove obstacles on your path.

For these reasons, as you will discover when you do the intensive practice of the creation stage in retreat, most creation-stage practice consists of visualizing yourself as the deity, because the most essential thing in our practice of the creation stage is to reveal and expand our own innate wisdom. While that is the principal practice, in the special circumstances of feast practice, particularly of self-empowerment, in which you give yourself the empowerment of that specific practice upon its completion, you not only do the visualization of yourself as the deity, but you also visualize the deity in front of you. You do so because making offerings to the deity visualized in front of you, as in the context of feast practice, is a powerful way to accumulate merit. By receiving a blessing or empowerment from the deity visualized in front of you, you will be especially confident that you have actually received it.

QUESTION: How important is it to visualize the deity exactly as the liturgy says? For example, if some of the icons of the culture I was raised in come into the visualization, is that something that I should make sure not to let happen?
TRANSLATOR: Could you give a specific example of what you mean?
QUESTION: An example is Saint Francis of Assisi as an image of compassion, as well as Avalokiteshvara. Would a visualization of Saint Francis of Assisi take away from the power of the visualization of Avalokiteshvara?
RINPOCHE: It is acceptable from time to time to remember Saint Francis of Assisi if it gives you a clearer idea of compassion, but at the same time, when you are doing a formal practice of visualization, everything in the visualization is there for a reason, and by working with the details exactly as they are set out, they will enhance the stability of your mind. In other words, the creation stage will become a practice of shamata and also of clarity, not only of the visualization but of the revelation of the mind's characteristic clarity itself. Ultimately there is more benefit in working with the practice exactly as it is set out.

We find a reference to this topic in the autobiography of Mipham Rinpoche in the nineteenth century. He says in his autobiography that he had some degree of recognition of this mind's nature, which is called the "clear appearance of the completion stage," since he was a small child. But he felt that in order to stabilize this and to expand its clarity, he would have to use the methods of the creation stage. He felt that the technique of the creation stage, with all of its otherwise troublesome details, was actually an ideal method leading to the clarification of whatever recognition of your own mind's nature you possess. In his autobiography Mipham Rinpoche said that he was unable to achieve enough of a practice of the creation stage to fulfill his wish. But he felt that the most important method for generating stable completion-stage realization was the intense practice of the clear visualization of the creation stage.

QUESTION: When it is said that the white and red elements in the form of the vital drops, in the head and the navel, meet at the heart and dissolve together when one dies, are these something other than egg and sperm?
RINPOCHE: Actually the original sperm and ovum have grown to form your whole body. The drops are not so much the original sperm and ovum as they are the essence or kernel of them, or you could say the kernel or essence of what has grown out of them. During your life, according to tantric physiology, the kernel of the white aspect, which you received from your father, is housed inside your head, close to the top. The kernel or essence of the red aspect, which you received from your mother, is seated below your navel, in the abdomen. In between these two is the basic *prana* that keeps you alive. These two actually keep the prana from escaping. When you die this prana collapses in on itself, into the heart. While these two keep the prana from escaping, the prana itself keeps the one up and the other down. When the prana withdraws into the heart, they then go in with it. The white drop comes down from the head, the red drop comes up from the abdomen, and they meet at the heart.
QUESTION: So the prana is going between the two?
TRANSLATOR: The specific prana—it is called the life wind.

QUESTION: Are there particular deities that one uses, for instance, to combat pride, or some of the other kleshas? Or can any one of them overcome all of the kleshas?
RINPOCHE: Both are true. There are specific deities that are connected with the wisdom that lies at the root of each klesha. For example, the text suggests that if afflicted by desire, visualize yourself as Amitabha. By extension we would say, if afflicted by bewilderment, Vairochana; by anger, Akshobhya; by pride, Ratnasambhava; by jealousy, Amoghasiddhi. The text mentions Chakrasamvara as an example, but that doesn't mean that you specifically need to use that deity. Still, visualizing yourself as Chakrasamvara with his consort will serve not only as a remedy for the affliction of desire but for any other affliction as well.

QUESTION: Since the yidam is initially visualized outside of yourself and only very late in the practice do you become the deity, does that mean that all the various purifications of womb birth and prior bardos and prior death occur at the time of the visualization of the external Chenrezig?
RINPOCHE: Through the power of your faith in the Chenrezig visualized above you, at a certain point in the practice, you and all beings take the form of Chenrezig. In that case, the visualization of yourself is the form of the deity complete in an instant of recollection. So there's no specific correlation here with at which point of the practice it purifies which event. However, you could say that when you become the deity, that is purifying this birth.

QUESTION: At what level does supplication work? When we talk about supplicating gurus of the lineage who have died and dharmapalas, how does that work?
RINPOCHE: Supplication produces blessing, and although the blessing is understood as something given to you, something that somehow engulfs you from outside, in fact blessing really isn't given to you at all. When you supplicate, you generate faith and devotion. That faith and devotion cause the appearance of what we call blessing.

QUESTION: Creation practice seems to be dealing with body, speech, and mind. I'm curious as to what part of creation-stage practice actually purifies relationships with our world and the inhabitants in it, family and friends and those around us?
RINPOCHE: Because your connections to others, whether positive or negative, are a part of your interaction with the world, in general your interactions are all purified by the homage, offering, and praise sections of the sadhana.

QUESTION: Could a person settle on one deity to complete this process? Or does one try to practice with as many deities as possible?
RINPOCHE: It doesn't matter. It is a question of individual taste and interest. Some people naturally find themselves utterly devoted to the practice of one deity. It is perfectly possible to pursue that one practice until you attain the final result. Other people find that they are naturally attracted to

combining the practices of different deities. They might practice two or three or even more. There is nothing wrong with that either. By combining the practice of these different deities, they will achieve the same result another person does with one.

QUESTION: Purifying relationships with others by paying homage and making offerings has to do with pure vision, the way one looks at other beings. It is hard to maintain a pure vision of others while witnessing the suffering that we inflict upon one another in this life. Is there a key to doing this?
RINPOCHE: Pure vision is something you cultivate in order to remove your own confusion. It is not really a method for helping others directly. Whatever arises in your own ordinary perception is as deluded as what arises in anyone else's. Also, negative situations are not more difficult to purify than what you experience normally. Whatever you experience is a deluded projection, and has to be acknowledged as such and transcended or transformed with the application of pure vision. This is no more or less true of any one type of deluded perception than any other.

QUESTION: You said that dharmapalas help us with our activities. This is intriguing. Could you say more?
RINPOCHE: Dharmapalas are what we would call great beings who sometimes manifest as humans and sometimes—especially when we refer to them as dharmapalas or Dharma protectors—manifest as nonhuman. In their nonhuman manifestation, which is a manifestation in external form of their wisdom, they are in a position to actively assist us. So if you ask for their assistance in removing impediments to your practice, they can actually provide some help. However, for this process to occur, there has to be some kind of a connection made between you and the dharmapalas. Principally this connection is made by your involvement with Dharma itself. Through practicing Dharma, you become in some sense their responsibility, and then they will be responsive to your requests for assistance.

QUESTION: Are they what we call devas?
RINPOCHE: First of all, the term "deva" is just the Sanskrit term for deity or god. It is used to refer to two types of beings. One type is a mundane

being called a deva. Devas can be gods of the desire realm, gods of the form realm, or gods of the formless realm. They are mundane, samsaric beings. The other type of being, referred to as *lha* or *deva* or *deity*, is supermundane, beyond the world. These are beings who have such wisdom, and especially such stable bodhichitta, such commitment to the welfare of others and to benefiting the teachings, that they are entirely unlike a mundane being. Dharmapalas can be thought of as beings who are completely and utterly committed to the welfare of others and therefore are very active in accomplishing their welfare.

You could say that dharmapalas are included within the class of things that we call "devas," just as some awakened people are included within the class of what we call "humans." But not all humans are awakened, and not all devas are dharmapalas. There are all different sorts of people. Some people are wonderful and some are horrific. It is the same way with devas. There are wonderful devas, horrific devas, and everything in between. Dharmapalas are a kind of wonderful deva.

QUESTION: Thinking about science and DNA and how we're altering beings, as with cloning, would a clone be the same being as its source, since the clone has the same DNA?
RINPOCHE: In the case of cloning, the clone would be a different sentient being. You don't have to go as far as cloning. It is really the same process as when someone is conceived as a human being. The substances come from the parents, but the child is a different being from the parents. Similarly, if you clone somebody, then the substance would come from a parent's body, but that doesn't mean that the cloned person is the same person as the parent.

QUESTION: When the Buddha is visualized and reappears from the drop, is the Buddha an adult, a child, or an infant?
RINPOCHE: In the creation stage, even though the rituals correspond to the different stages of life, you don't visualize the deity first as a little baby deity and then as a child deity, an adolescent deity, and a mature deity. You don't take it that far. You're trying to purify all of those appearances. In order to do that, there has to be some degree of correspondence, but not to that degree.

QUESTION: Now scientists are capable of fertilizing eggs and keeping them in a frozen state for a long time. What becomes of the mental consciousness in that state?
RINPOCHE: I don't know. You'd have to ask the scientists who are doing that.

The Emergence of Confusion

SHAMATA AND VIPSHYANA

Our most common practice is tranquility meditation, or shamata. As is well known, we need shamata practice because our mind is normally agitated by thoughts; we practice shamata in order to generate a state of mental stability. While the technique of shamata and the technique of the creation stage are distinct in that, in the one, your mind is resting on a very simple and neutral object, and in the other your mind is immersed in the elaborate visualization of the deity, the function of these two techniques is really the same.

In the practice of shamata, you cultivate a state of attention that transcends the two defects of excessive tension and excessive relaxation. You do the same thing in the practice of the creation stage. In the visualization of the form of the deity, or the visualization of the syllables of the mantra, if your mind is too tight, too tense, then the natural clarity of the visualization is diminished; and if your mind is too relaxed, you become distracted. So while the techniques are distinct, the function of shamata and the function of the creation stage are fundamentally the same.

However, the creation stage does have a feature that is not overtly present in shamata practice. Through the practice of the creation stage, you not only generate the ability to rest the mind at will, but you also bring out the mind's innate clarity or capacity for lucidity. This is brought out especially in the creation stage, not only by the technique of visualization, which obviously uses and augments the mind's clarity, but also by the variations in visualization. In creation-stage practice you move from one thing to another. For example, at one point you visualize the invitation of the jnanasattvas, and at another point you visualize the radiating and gathering of light rays. This change of focus in the visualization actually produces new meditative absorptions at each step. These enhance the development of mental clarity and the stability of samadhi in general. So the creation stage is a technique that not only can generate a state of shamata but also assists in the development of mental clarity. For that and other reasons, it is absolutely necessary to practice the creation stage. However, the creation stage is never practiced alone or in isolation. It always has to be combined with, and succeeded by, the practice of the completion stage.

The relationship between the creation and completion stages in the Vajrayana is very similar to the relationship between shamata and vipashyana in the Sutrayana. In fact, we would have to say that the completion stage in Vajrayana is in some respect identical to the vipashyana that is taught in the Sutrayana. "In some respect" means that although the techniques of the completion stage are not necessarily identical to the techniques of vipashyana, the function of the completion stage and the function of vipashyana are the same. Therefore, we can consider the completion stage to be a variety of vipashyana, or insight meditation. In that context what we mean by vipashyana and by the completion stage is in both cases meditation on the nature of one's mind. When we use the term vipashyana to refer to the completion stage, we are talking about that style of meditation that is characteristic of the tradition of uncommon instruction.

To make this clear, there are two types of vipashyana practice. One takes *inferential valid cognition* as the path, and the other takes *direct valid cognition* as the path. Generally speaking, the sutras advance the technique of inferential valid cognition. This technique consists of using logical reasoning to determine the emptiness of all things; starting with the fact that all relative truths are interdependent, one reasons the validity of emptiness. In that type of practice emptiness is not an object of direct experience. One examines phenomena and gradually comes to a conviction that everything is empty. One then cultivates and stabilizes that conviction until after a long time it becomes a clear and definite recognition of emptiness. Sometimes this practice of taking inferential valid cognition as the path is also called "analytic meditation." Analytic mediation is very stable and helpful, but it is not quick; it takes a long time. Therefore, in Vajrayana practice, one does not do analytic meditation. One emphasizes the practice of direct valid cognition.

If one takes direct valid cognition as the path, one does not emphasize thinking about the nature of external things. From the point of view of

Vajrayana meditation, we don't particularly worry about whether external things are empty or not, because the source of all of our experience, what we use in practice, what experiences pleasant and unpleasant things, is our mind. Therefore, in Vajrayana practice we are concerned principally with the mind itself. In fact, the mind is not only more important to ascertain the nature of, but is also easier to ascertain. The mind, just as it is, is an obvious embodiment or demonstration of *dharmata,* an obvious embodiment of emptiness. This means that whereas you cannot in the beginning directly see the emptiness of external things, you can from the beginning directly see the emptiness of your own mind. When you take the path of direct valid cognition as a practice, the view of the mind as empty is not determined through some kind of analysis or logical reasoning but by looking directly. This is the characteristic approach of all Vajrayana meditation. Therefore it is said that if you know the nature of your mind, this alone will accomplish your aim and practice. As long as you do not, no other practice and no other knowledge will be of any significant help. The many renowned traditions of this type of meditation—mahamudra, the great perfection, the great middle way—and terms such as "simplicity" and "freedom from elaboration" all refer to the practice of this meditation on the empty nature of mind. Meditating on the nature of mind is essential.

The Nature of the Mind

Up to this point the text makes no distinction between what we could call the pure and the impure aspects of mind. Now it points out that there are some individuals who, because of their intense devotion, have spontaneously recognized or realized the mind's nature. Such a person, having attained that recognition, has no need to learn the difference between the pure and impure aspects of mind, how they work, how they manifest; they already understand what learning those distinctions is intended to reveal. However, for most people, it is difficult to generate a realization spontaneously through devotion alone. Most practitioners need to learn at least a little bit about how mind works. Otherwise, there is a danger that your meditation will not be a recognition of the mind's nature but will be simply immersion in some kind of blank neutrality or abstraction. While that is not particularly harmful, it is also not particularly helpful; it is somewhat of a shame, a waste of time. Therefore, the text proceeds to explain how mind works.

What we could call the impure or deluded aspect of mind is referred to as "consciousness." Consciousness is enumerated as being of eight classes or groups. Before going into the details of consciousness, it is necessary to understand the basic view of cognition that is characteristic of Buddhadharma. The term cognition in Sanskrit is *jnana.* Jnana just means cognition, the capacity to cognize. Literally speaking, in Tibetan one would translate jnana as *shepa,* or "knowing." However, it is interesting to observe that when the teachings were translated into Tibetan, jnana was usually translated not as shepa, but as *yeshe. Ye* means primordial. The prefix "ye" was added by the Tibetan translators to point something out about cognition, which is that cognition, mere clarity, cognitive clarity in and of itself, has been there from the very beginning. Therefore they translated "cognition" as "primordial cognition." But the term "jnana" in itself does not include this word "primordial," so it refers simply to cognition.

The term for consciousness, which is a specific type of cognition, is *vijnana.* It is the term for cognition, jnana, with the prefix "vi," which means complete, or fully developed. This is a more specific term than cognition; and although "fully developed cognition" may sound positive, in this context it is actually somewhat pejorative, because it refers to cognition that has developed in the sense of becoming coarsened. This type of cognition, full cognition, is the consciousness that is divided into eight kinds. All of these consciousnesses are considered manifestations of the mind's impurity. They are eight conditions that arise when a mind does not recognize its own nature.

The basic idea of the development of consciousness is that when a mind does not recognize its own nature, its inherent lucidity, it runs wild, and running wild, it develops a coarse, deluded consciousness characteristic of samsara. Nevertheless, in the midst of all of this confusion, the nature of these consciousnesses, the nature of this deluded mind, remains unchanged. This unchanging nature of the mind is called the *pure all-basis,* as opposed to the *all-basis consciousness,* one of the eight consciousnesses. That pure all-basis is mere cognition, fundamental jnana itself. Therefore, when you wish to make a distinction in Tibetan between the mind in its impure manifestations and the pure nature of the mind itself, then impure mind will be called *sem*, and the mind itself, mere cognition, will be called *sem nyi*.

The Eight Consciousnesses

There are different ways that the eight consciousnesses can be explained. In this text the style of explanation follows that of the third Gyalwa Karmapa, Rangjung Dorje, especially his book *The Profound Inner Meaning,* which was written as an explanation of the theoretical underpinning of the Six Dharmas of Naropa, and as a clarification of certain points concerning the Six Dharmas called *Distinguishing Between Consciousness and Wisdom.*

According to these teachings, the first five of the eight consciousnesses are called the "consciousnesses of the five gates." The gates are the five senses. They are called "gates" because they are the means by which your mind encounters what is outside your body, the means by which your mind can project itself or expand itself beyond the body. The first of the five gates is the eyes. The eyes are the organic basis for the eye consciousness. They encounter as their object visible form—color and shape. When they encounter these, what is generated is called the "eye, or visual, consciousness."

Visual consciousness is the first of the eight consciousnesses. The other four are similar. The second consciousness is connected with the ears; when the ears encounter their object, which is a sound of any type, what is generated is called the "ear consciousness" or "auditory consciousness." The third is connected with the nose; when the nose encounters its object, which is a smell of any type, what is generated is called the "nose, or olfactory, consciousness." The fourth is the tongue; when the tongue encounters its object, a taste of any type (such as sweet, sour, or bitter), what is generated is called the "tongue, or taste, consciousness." The fifth one is the whole body as an organ of tactile sensation; when the whole body encounters its object, a tactile sensation, what is generated is called the "body, or tactile, consciousness." These five consciousnesses operating through the five senses, or five gates, experience their objects directly. The eye consciousness actually sees shapes and colors, the ear consciousness actually detects sounds, the olfactory consciousness actually smells, and so on. It is direct experience, therefore these consciousnesses are nonconceptual. "Nonconceptual" means that they don't have any thought about the characteristics of what they experience. They do not conceptually recognize the things that they perceive.

That which thinks about what is experienced by the five senses, which conceptually recognizes them as such and such, which conceives of them as good and bad, is the sixth consciousness, the mental consciousness. The mental consciousness does not work with, or appear on the basis of, a specific sense organ like the other five. It inhabits the body in a general way. It is normally enumerated as the sixth consciousness, after the other five. The fundamental distinction between it and the others is that the five sense consciousnesses, since they engage only in the direct experience of their objects, can only experience the present. For example, the eye consciousness only sees what is there now. It does not see what was there in the past. It does not see what will be there in the future. This is also true of the ear consciousness and so on. The five sense consciousnesses are not capable of thinking about their objects. Not only can they not think about the past or the future, they do not even conceptualize or think about the present.

The sixth consciousness on the other hand can and does think about things. It thinks of the past, both distant and recent. It thinks about the present and about the future, both proximate and distant. But while it is capable of thinking, it is not capable of directly experiencing things the way the sense consciousnesses do. It produces a generality, or abstraction, on the basis of the things that are experienced by the five sense consciousnesses. This means that when the five sense consciousnesses experience something, it becomes an object of thought for the sixth consciousness, not in the form of what is *actually* experienced but in the form of a concept created by the sixth consciousness as a replica of the sense experience. For example, when I look at the glass on the table in front of me, my eyes see it directly, but my mental consciousness does not. It produces a generality or abstraction, based upon what my eyes have seen, which it recognizes, conceives of as having such and such a shape, considers as good or bad, and so on.

These six consciousnesses are relatively easy to observe because they are vivid in their manifestation or function. The other two consciousnesses are less easy to observe. For one thing, the six consciousnesses start and stop in their operation. They are generated by certain conditions, and, when those conditions are no longer present, they temporarily stop functioning.

Therefore the six consciousnesses are called "inconstant" consciousnesses. They are created as they arise. The other two consciousnesses are called "constant" consciousnesses. Not only are they constant, or always operating, but they are also much less observable.

The seventh consciousness is called the "afflicted consciousness." This refers to the most basic level of mental affliction, or klesha. It refers not to coarse kleshas, but to the root of kleshas. Specifically, the afflicted consciousness is the most subtle level of fixation on a self. Again, this is not coarse fixation on a self. This is the subtle level of fixation on a self that is unfluctuatingly present even when one is asleep. When sometimes you have a sense of self, and you think "I," that is an operation not of the seventh consciousness but of the sixth. The seventh consciousness is omnipresent until you attain a higher level, such as with a first-level bodhisattva. Although it is not itself directly observable, the afflicted consciousness is the basis for all coarse fixation on a self and therefore for all coarse kleshas.

The eighth consciousness is called the *alaya vijnana* or *all-basis consciousness.* It is so called because it is the basis or ground for the arising of all other types of consciousness. It is that fundamental clarity of consciousness, or cognitive lucidity, that has been there from the beginning. As the capacity for conscious experience, it is the ground for the arising of eye consciousness, ear consciousness, etc. Like the seventh, it is constantly present, constantly operating, and it persists until the attainment of final awakening, or buddhahood.

Along with the eight consciousnesses, there is something else that is called the *instantaneous mind.* Many texts present this mind as that which is generated by the cessation of a previous instant of consciousness and which links one type of consciousness to another. In the particular presentation found in the *Profound Inner Meaning* by the third Gyalwa Karmapa, Rangjung Dorje, the instantaneous mind is presented as that which causes the lack of recognition of dharmata or of the nature of things, in which case it would be considered an aspect of the seventh consciousness. The seventh consciousness in that way has an inward-directed aspect, an aspect that causes the other consciousnesses to arise and function; that is the instantaneous mind. The instantaneous mind is thus not a separate consciousness, but an identifiable function of the impure mind; therefore it is not a ninth consciousness.

In certain sutras you will see, also, the use of the term *receptive consciousness.* Receptive consciousness refers to the capacity of the all-basis consciousness to receive and store impressions. Therefore, it is synonymous with the all-basis consciousness. In short, all of the functions or manifestations of the impure or deluded mind are included in the eight consciousnesses.

Consciousness and Meditation

Which consciousness performs meditation? Since the first five sense consciousnesses are nonconceptual, they neither require nor are capable of meditation. In the case of shamata practice, which is concerned with the pacification of thoughts, the sixth consciousness is that which meditates. In the case of vipashyana, however, meditation is performed by and involves the sixth, seventh, and eighth consciousnesses.

From the point of view of meditation, one would have to say that although one can distinguish the sixth, seventh, and eighth consciousnesses as distinct in their degrees of manifestation or obvious cognitive clarity, from their own point of view, they are internally basically the same. The practice of vipashyana consists of protecting the sixth, seventh, and eighth consciousnesses from delusion: rather than allowing them to run wild in delusion, one allows them instead to rest in their natural or basic state. Through doing this you come to experience or know the nature of all three, i.e., the mental consciousness, the afflicted consciousness, and the all-basis consciousness. In vipashyana practice the most important thing is to recognize the nature of these consciousnesses. Therefore, in vipashyana, they are the object of meditation.

The eight consciousnesses are impure in how they manifest, since they manifest as delusion based upon the mind's projection of objects. But in their nature, they are unchanging. The basic nature of the mind, of which they are the permutations, is pure. Therefore, we find the oft-repeated phrase "the all-basis is virtuous or good in its nature." This idea of the fundamental goodness of the all-basis refers not to the deluded all-basis consciousness but to the all-basis wisdom, which in the context of delusion is the pure aspect of the all-basis consciousness. This pure aspect has never been lost in delusion, meaning that the nature of the mind has been mistaken, but that nature itself has never been changed or corrupted by the mistake. While the manifestation of your mind as a plurality within cognitive clarity seems to be deluded, if you look for some actual substantial presence of this delusion, you won't find it anywhere. Yet you cannot say that your mind is a dead or static nothingness, because there is the experience and presence of cognitive clarity. This basic way the mind really is, the fact that it is a cognitive lucidity free of any kind of substantial existence, is what is called buddha nature, and that, of course, is pure. That is what we attempt to realize or fully experience through the practice of meditation.

Hence, because the eight consciousnesses are the deluded aspect of mind, yet their nature is buddha nature itself, in practice it is important not to follow confused or deluded projections but to look at the nature of the mind instead. If you attend to the delusion, then it will be reinforced, but if you look at the nature of the delusion, of that deluded mind, then you see through it. By means of this you gradually become free from delusion, leading both to attainment of extraordinary samadhi and eventually to buddhahood. In these states, because of the recognition of the mind's nature, the thoughts and kleshas that arise have no effect; they do not in any way obscure or prevent the recognition of that basic nature.

This does not mean that the lucidity that is manifested as delusion is going to cease, because it is not the case that by seeing the emptiness of mind, the manifestation of mind disappears or stops. It has always been empty; seeing this does not make it more empty. What is recognized is that while mind is empty of any substantial existence, it is a cognitive lucidity. While being lucid, it is empty; and while being empty, it is lucid. That is how it remains.

You might ask, "Since the mind's nature is always pure and unchanging, why does the confusion of the eight consciousnesses arise in the first place?" The confusion or delusion of the mind is like mistaking a mottled rope for a snake. From the point of view of confusion, we would say that at the moment at which you first mistake that rope for a snake, confusion starts; and at the moment at which you come to recognize that the mottled rope is merely a mottled rope and not a snake, you are liberated from confusion. From the point of view of your delusion or your confusion, there is a period of delusion, and there is the possibility of liberation. Nevertheless, as strongly as you might believe that that mottled rope is a snake, the mottled rope itself has never been turned into a snake by your delusion. It retains its own nature.

Similarly, one would say that although we mistake mind to be the eight consciousnesses, and thus generate the appearance or experience of these eight consciousnesses and their delusion, the mind has always been empty. Even though we do not experience that emptiness and instead experience the mind as the eight consciousnesses, in fact the mind has always been that emptiness, or buddha nature. Not experiencing the mind as it is, we look away from it, and looking away, we generate delusion. As to when this deluded activity began, it is beginningless. The delusion has always been there along with the fundamental nature of the mind.

To use another image, the mind in itself, as inherently nondeluded cognition, is like a mirror. The nature of the mirror is to reflect; it is not its nature to be obscured. Nevertheless, this mirror, from the very beginning, has been covered by some kind of rust or grime. The grime is like the all-basis consciousness. Because there is a little bit of tarnish, over time the tarnish increases, and it accrues the grime of further habits in the all-basis, generating the obscurations that are the mental afflictions. Nevertheless the nature, not only of the ground itself but also of the all-basis consciousness, has always been emptiness. What occurs in the absence of recognition, in the absence of awareness of the true nature of one's mind, is that the emptiness of mind, not being recognized as what it is, is mistaken to be a self. So the empty essence of mind is the basis for designation of the imputed self.

But, again, mind is not just empty. It is cognitive lucidity that is empty. The cognitive lucidity, in its intensity, is mistaken to be an object, is mistaken to be external to this imputed self. On the basis of the two main characteristics of mind, emptiness and lucidity, there is the designation of self and other, or subject and object.

The way in which we generate the presence or assume the existence of objects on the basis of the lucidity of mind is like what happens to us when we go to sleep. When you go to sleep there is a state that in English is called "hypnogogic." Before you start to dream, the images that will eventually arise as dream images are still thoughts. During the period when they are thoughts, they are simply things that are arising in your mind. But as you become more deeply asleep, you mistake these thoughts for actually occurring events. In other words, the thoughts themselves become images that are experienced as objects; this is how thoughts become dreams. The process is similar to the way in which, under the sway of ignorance, we mistake the lucidity of mind to be an object external to ourselves. On the basis of that dualism—that imputation of self and other—the six consciousnesses are activated through the function of the instantaneous mind.

When the six consciousnesses arise in this way, there occurs the appearance of the sense organs encountering their objects. As far as the way things appear to function, there is definitely the appearance in our experience of external objects that are encountered by the sense organs, producing consciousness or awareness of those objects. Actually, what we perceive as external objects and what we perceive as internal faculties are really aspects of the consciousnesses themselves.

For example, when your eyes see form, what we would normally say occurs is that there is an external object that your eyes are capable of encountering; through the encounter between the eye and the object, a visual consciousness is generated. From the point of view of the way things really are, what you perceive as external form is the objective or lucid aspect of the visual consciousness itself; i.e., eye consciousness appears as form. The empty aspect of the eye consciousness is what you experience as, or presume to be, the subject experiencing an object. The way a consciousness actually manifests as its apparent object is like, for example, when you dream of mountains and react to them with fear or happiness or joy or boredom. In our normal daytime experience, mountains do seem external to us. We really think and believe that this lucid aspect of the mind is out there, is an external form. We really believe and really experience it this way—that the empty aspect of mind is in here and is experiencing the object.

The interaction of all these factors—the emergence of the six consciousnesses and therefore the appearance of subjects and objects in those six consciousnesses—is all arranged or brought about by the instantaneous mind. Nevertheless, the experience of the five sense consciousnesses is direct and nonconceptual. As I explained earlier, it has no connection with past or future. On the basis of the experience, some sensation is generated. The sensation causes the emergence of the sixth consciousness, which then generates concepts about the experience. The sensation is labeled as pleasant, unpleasant, good, bad, and so on, and then there is a recognition of the characteristics of the object. That is how confusion happens.

QUESTION: On page 53 the text explains that "The instantaneous mind moves the six consciousness groups and causes the meeting of object and organ," and then further down it discusses mistaking the luminous aspect for form and the empty aspect for the organ. What is the meaning of "organ"?

RINPOCHE: It means the sense organs themselves. The projection of the existence of sense organs is based upon the mistaken apprehension of the empty aspect of consciousness as a subject and therefore as a sense organ. As far as how things appear, we do have sense organs. For example, the structure of the eye—the optic nerve, I believe—is said to be like a flax flower. The ears are said to be like a pattern in birch bark. There is an image for each one of the sense organs. That is how they appear. We have functioning senses. So the organs from that perspective are the organic basis for sense perception. But as far as how things are, the development and experience of sense organs, like the development and experience of sense objects, is a projection based upon the mistaken apprehension of the emptiness of consciousness as a self.

QUESTION: Could you explain the point about mistaking luminosity for an external object? Is this mistake thinking that phenomena are real? If so, would that be to deny that there is a tree outside when there really is a tree outside?

RINPOCHE: There appears to be a tree, but the reason there appears to be a tree is that we have a strong habit of conceiving the appearance of trees; therefore we experience their appearance. For example, in a dream there also appears to be a tree. The tree in a dream might be just as vivid as a tree we experience during a waking state, but we know that there is no tree in the dream. It is possible that the tree we experience in the waking state might be a projection also, because we experience what it is our habit to experience.

QUESTION: Is it true that the person who knows dream yoga can approach the real world in the same way as one would in a dream? For instance, could one make the tree disappear?

RINPOCHE: I have no experience of this, but they say so.

QUESTION: How is it that we all see the tree in the same place?
RINPOCHE: Common experience is the experience by different individuals of a similar object or event that they can agree upon as a shared perceptual experience. It is like having a vase in the middle of a table surrounded by one hundred mirrors. Each of those mirrors is reflecting the same vase, but the image contained in each mirror is particular to that mirror. In the same way, even though different people may see the same thing, what I experience in my mind is particular to my mind, as it is my experience, and what you experience in your mind is particular to your mind, as it is your experience.

QUESTION: What is the relationship of compassion to the eight consciousnesses? Can the function of instantaneous mind be used to liberate oneself?
RINPOCHE: Manifest compassion arises in the sixth consciousness. The habit of compassion resides in the eighth consciousness. In a sense, one could say that even the seventh consciousness presents some kind of compassion. The five sense consciousnesses are nonconceptual and have no particular connection to compassion. With regard to the role of the instantaneous mind in the path, it cannot be used for the accumulation of wisdom, because the accumulation of wisdom is accomplished through the meditative state, in which all of the processes of delusion are at least temporarily shut down, revealing one's innate wisdom. So the manner of accumulating wisdom, the manner of liberation itself, is the antithesis of the linking process that is the instantaneous mind.

On the other hand, the other aspect of the path, the accumulation of merit, does make use of the instantaneous mind. The instantaneous mind is used in the accumulation of positive karma when one makes offerings to buddhas and bodhisattvas, just as it is used in the accumulation of negative karma. The reason that the instantaneous mind has its place in the merit aspect of the path but not in the wisdom aspect is that the merit aspect is concerned with the appearances of relative truth, not with the realities of absolute truth. Since the instantaneous mind is part of the workings of relative truth, it can still be used in that context.

QUESTION: Is it possible to have direct experience through all five of the senses in the same instant?
RINPOCHE: The five sense consciousnesses, when they are functioning, all

function simultaneously. What is not functioning simultaneously is the apprehension of the experience of the sense consciousnesses by the sixth consciousness, which tends to apprehend them only one at a time.

QUESTION: Does the presence of the instantaneous mind cause the experience of the five sense consciousnesses? Is the instantaneous mind always present?

RINPOCHE: Yes, because in the case of sensory experience, the instantaneous mind produces the experiences, bringing them out of the all-basis like a messenger and then also returning to the all-basis the habit reinforced by that experience. It is like when you go to the bank. The teller who brings out or puts in your money for you is like the instantaneous mind.

QUESTION: On page 53, at the bottom, the claim, "when the afflictive mind functions with the instantaneous mind, directed inward, it leaves habitual patterns in the foundation," seems to contradict the earlier statement that just the arousal of anger doesn't create an imprint.

RINPOCHE: When you simply have a thought of a klesha, that doesn't place a habit in the all-basis. The instantaneous mind does grab it, as it were, and deposit it into the all-basis, but it is not yet a karmic habit. There are several types of habit. Karmic habit is the imprint of an action and manifests as external experience. From among the various results of an action, this manifestation is a result of complete maturation. Klesha habit itself becomes a kind of obscuration, but it doesn't manifest as karma.

QUESTION: Does that make it easier for anger to arise again?

RINPOCHE: When the thought of anger arises and is recognized, then the type of habit that it places is very subtle and doesn't even particularly promote further arising of thoughts of anger—certainly not the arising of spite, which unrecognized anger normally would produce. The term "the thought is liberated" means not that it doesn't place any habit whatsoever, but that that particular thought is not leading to further such thoughts.

QUESTION: Going back to the discussion about the tree, if we leave aside language and habit and look at things without our known concepts or our known way of looking at things, just seeing the object for what it is, it doesn't have to be a tree. Is that what happens? Or are you saying that all things are imagined?

RINPOCHE: There are two ways to understand this. It depends on whether you are emphasizing the way things are or the way things appear. According to the way things appear, we would say that the imputation of the tree is a projection of your mind and that the basis for the imputation is not your mind, it is "out there." But viewing it from the point of how things really are, we would say they are both your mind.

QUESTION: Of the eight different kinds of consciousness, are the seventh and the eighth those that move on into the bardo?

RINPOCHE: No, all of them do. In the bardo you have a mental body that has its own mental forms of the five sense consciousnesses as well as the sixth mental consciousness. In the bardo you still sometimes see things from your previous life, the places and people and so on.

To be more precise, there are several stages to the interval of the bardo. First, what happens as you die is that there is a dissolution process where the appearances of this life dissolve and then temporarily cease. Really there are two dissolutions: a physical dissolution and a mental dissolution. At the end of these—the coarse and subtle dissolutions immediately after death—dharmata appears, the direct experience of the nature of things. However, if the person has not cultivated a recognition of dharmata in the preceding life, then they will not recognize it in the bardo. Its mere appearance will not produce liberation. Nevertheless, in that phase of the bardo at which the dissolution process is complete and the appearance of the dharmata occurs, the six consciousnesses temporarily cease and only the seventh and the eighth are still functioning. However, after that, when they re-arise from that bardo of dharmata in a mental body, then all eight are back again.

Working with Confusion

Next the text instructs us in how to work with the emergence of confusion in our practice. Practitioners (people practicing shamata, vipashyana, the creation stage, and the completion stage), when the immediate mind first arises from the all-basis consciousness, attempt to rest in the practice, to rest in the samadhi that they have cultivated. If they do so, then the development of confusion or delusion that arises along with the instantaneous mind will not progress beyond the instantaneous mind's arising itself. Essentially what you attempt to do here is rest in an awareness of the buddha nature, in the recognition of the emptiness and manifest lucidity of your mind. In the beginning, this has to be mostly an aspiration. Then, as one gains experience, what are called the *example wisdom* and the *actual wisdom* will arise. The wisdom of example is not a full or direct recognition of the buddha nature; it is a recognition of something that is like buddha nature. When you rest in a basic recognition of the emptiness-lucidity of your mind, that's example wisdom. Through cultivating that, eventually you come to a decisive, direct insight into buddha nature; this is the actual wisdom. In any case, through resting in the meditative state, when the instantaneous mind arises from the all-basis consciousness, some liberation from the process of delusion becomes possible, simply because it will not continue and will not degenerate into coarse or fully manifest delusion.

For delusion to diminish, mindfulness and alertness have to be maintained. But at the same time, thoughts are the natural display of the mind, so this does not mean that thoughts of attachment, aversion, and bewilderment will not continue to arise. They will. But, if there is sufficient mindfulness and alertness, then upon their arising their nature will be recognized, and so will not be a cause for the accumulation of karma. The initial thought, being liberated through recognition, will not produce a second thought and a third thought. In other words, thoughts continue to arise as the mind's display, but they do not become the cause of the accumulation of further habits. The metaphor for this in the text is that of a vase with a hole in the bottom. Although you can still pour water into the vase, you will never be able to fill it. Everything that is poured in just flows right back out again. Similarly, when this kind of mindfulness and alertness are maintained, although thoughts come into the mind, they go right back out of it. If you can practice in this way, then gradually experience and realization will occur. The text treats this in some detail, but I have explained the essential point.

How To Practice

Next the text talks about how to actually practice. First of all, the essence of the completion-stage practice is to rest in that natural lucidity or awareness that characterizes the mind. If you rest in that without fabrication, even though external appearances will still appear to you, they will occur as appearances without any substance—as empty. This is the fundamental or essential practice of the completion stage according to the Vajrayana.

Within Vajrayana there are, broadly speaking, four classes of tantra. Within the highest there are three subdivisions, which are sometimes called the *father tantra of method*, the *mother tantra of knowledge*, and the *nondual tantra of the essential meaning*. The text says that from the father tantra and from the mahayoga on upward, i.e., for the three higher tantras (among the six tantras), there is a characteristic recognition that everything that appears, even samsaric appearances, is the natural display of the mind and therefore partakes of its essential purity. This view fundamentally distinguishes what are called the higher tantras from the lower.

How do you actually meditate in this way? I have explained how the eight consciousnesses function. The arising of thoughts within the mind is continuous and inexhaustible because of this functioning. Thoughts of past, present, and future continually arise in your mind, like waves on the surface of a body of water. While mind itself has no substance whatsoever, it manifests as an inexhaustible appearance, especially as the inexhaustible appearance or emergence of thoughts. The practice consists simply of not following thoughts but of resting your mind in shamata or vipashyana, in the creation-stage visualization, or in the completion stage itself—whatever your technique is. As for how you rest your mind, it needs to be in a way that is appropriate to your situation at that time, and this concerns the issue of effort, of the balance between effort and relaxation.

Sometimes you will find that you have a problem with fatigue in meditation. Typically, if fatigue is a problem, you will find that at the beginning of a meditation session the practice goes well, and by the end it becomes difficult. That indicates that your mind is too tight and you are becoming exhausted. The solution in that case is to relax. At other times you will find that the meditation session begins badly but goes well toward the end. In that case it indicates lack of effort. The solution is to try a little bit harder; to put more effort into it. At other times you'll find that the balance is fairly even throughout the session. In this case no adjustments should be made.

The key to being able to attend properly is the application of mindfulness, which keeps us from forgetting what we are doing. When you lack mindfulness, then you become distracted and forget the object of meditation. When you apply mindfulness, then this forgetfulness does not occur. Mindfulness in general is simply the faculty of memory, which is a normal mental arising. However, in this case, it is applied in a very specific and conscious way. By applying the faculty of memory as mindfulness, one's meditation remains free from error or deviation. The manner of application is to establish a gentle, watchful mindfulness. A mindfulness that is gentle and watchful means an alert mindfulness that is just enough. In other words, there is just enough intentional effort that you do not become distracted. If you maintain that, then over time the recognition of the lucid nature of mind will occur.

During this practice, however, a subtle problem can arise called "the dregs of mind" or the "dregs of awareness." This is the presence of subtle thoughts running through your mind even though your mind is basically at rest and there are no fully conscious thoughts present. These subtle thoughts are also called the "undercurrent," because they are an almost undetected current of thought that runs on a barely conscious level. The undercurrent is in fact a greater problem for meditation than either torpor or excitement and cannot be allowed to continue on its own. The solution to the problem of the undercurrent is to tighten up your mind a little bit; to bring out or enhance the lucidity of your mind, to strengthen or toughen the edge of your awareness. As important as being undistracted is, it is very difficult to develop a state of meditation for long periods of time in which you are never distracted. The reason this is difficult is lack of training. It is not particularly that we are doing it wrong, it is that we need to practice meditation a great deal in order to develop this level of freedom from distraction. So if you find that you still become distracted, don't be discouraged, just continue.

Typically your practice of meditation begins with shamata; this is true especially in the Kagyu tradition of mahamudra. We find in all texts of mahamudra instruction that one is to begin with establishing a stability or tranquility of mind as a basis for the emergence of the recognition of the mind's nature. However, in the uncommon branch of the tradition of dzogchen, there is a slightly different approach, wherein instead of taking mind as path, one takes awareness as the path. In taking awareness as path, if at the beginning one succeeds in correctly identifying or recognizing *rigpa* or awareness, then it is not, strictly speaking, necessary to begin with the practice of shamata, because the recognition of awareness has already been gained. One can simply rest in that and cultivate that. However, if there is no decisive and correct recognition of awareness, there is no way to go on with this path. Thus, for most practitioners it is essential to begin with shamata, as is done in the mahamudra tradition, so that there is a basis of tranquility in the mind that facilitates the emergence of that recognition.

The text advises at this point that when you are practicing in solitude, you should relax the mind and allow it to naturally come to rest in its own nature. When others are around and you might tend more to become distracted, you should exert more effort and strengthen the lucidity and alertness of your mindfulness. It is not really the case that mindfulness and alertness are actual things that are present within the mind; they are more accurately faculties or processes of mind. Nevertheless, although they are faculties or processes, they do affect very much the state of the mind in meditation.

QUESTION: Could you please say more about how to tighten up our minds and toughen the edge of our awareness?
RINPOCHE: Essentially the tough edge or sharp edge of awareness is what is meant by effort in meditation. Sometimes when we meditate, we practice it and experience it as conscious relaxation of the mind. At other times meditation involves a conscious and hard-headed refusal not to become distracted—the attitude, "I must not become distracted." At different times one should emphasize one or the other of these. When one slackens and needs to exert more effort, then one sharpens one's awareness through this hard-headed intention, which is the refusal to space out.

QUESTION: Is there any reason why one particular gate would provide the undercurrent, the dregs of mind? My undercurrent is music. There is always music going on in my mind. I will be meditating for several minutes and then discover I'm listening to *Ninety-Nine Bottles of Beer.*

RINPOCHE: It is probably happening either because of a strong, deeply-placed habit or because you like music a lot. The solution in either case is to generate the strong resolution, "I'm meditating now, not listening to music. I refuse to listen to this." If you resolve to cut your attachment to it, and if you *actually* do not want it to be there, then you can stop it.
QUESTION: It goes on before I'm aware of its going on. The only method I have found is to maintain a kind of steady sound in my mind as I'm meditating, to tie up that faculty so it doesn't produce music.
RINPOCHE: In that case it is because you are very attached to the experience of sound. Your mind is habituated to producing a replica of sound so that you can remember it, so that you can think about it. Therefore it does it even when you haven't particularly told it to.

QUESTION: The text on page 55 says that "it is impossible for thoughts of attachment and aversion not to arise. However, if you rely on mindful awareness, discursive thoughts cannot accumulate karma." Could you explain that?
RINPOCHE: The idea is that even as you maintain mindfulness and alertness, thoughts of attachment, aversion, and bewilderment will still arise because the habits that produce their arising have not yet been completely eradicated. Nevertheless, if you have some recognition of your mind's nature, then, when any one of those thoughts arises, you will experience the mind's true nature in that thought, because the mind's nature is also the nature of that thought. It is the display of that mind. Therefore, when you realize that, whatever the initial content of that thought may be, it is liberated. It will not produce a second thought that's connected with it. In that way the karmic chain of thoughts is broken.

The phrase, "although it is impossible for thoughts of attachment and aversion not to arise," refers to that point in one's training at which one has some recognition of the mind's nature but has not yet reached the ultimate state of liberation. When one reaches the ultimate state of liberation, the kleshas are exhausted and will not arise at all. For a beginner (someone who has some recognition of the mind's nature but is not yet fully liberated), these thoughts will still arise, but they need not be allowed to accumulate karma.

Question: If the thought is an angry thought, what happens?
Rinpoche: You don't accumulate karma just through one thought of anger. You accumulate karma when anger ripens and festers into spitefulness. For example, when you simply see someone who bothers you and you experience a thought of aversion, if you don't carry it any further, then you don't accumulate karma. You accumulate karma when that transient thought of aversion leads to the actual thought, "I would really like to beat up that person. I'd like to kill him." Then you accumulate karma.

Question: The normal or the conventional method of distinguishing sentient beings is by their physical basis, their bodies. If what we take as a physical object is merely lucidity and emptiness, what is it that distinguishes different sentient beings?
Rinpoche: Sentient beings are distinguished by their individual minds, which are not objects of your experience and therefore are not projections of your mind. The bodies of sentient beings are things you can see and are therefore projections of your mind.

Question: Is there a space that minds exist in?
Rinpoche: Basically what happens is that beings who have performed enough actions in common with other beings will come to experience the world in a way that is similar enough to all that it can be an agreed-upon reality. For example, you and I are likely to agree upon what we see in this room because we have gathered the types of karma that cause us to have similar types of physical perceptions.

Question: Sometimes when I'm meditating, I perceive a major denseness, a kind of fog. It doesn't feel like fatigue. I even feel it on the top of my head. I'll conk out and then I'll come back. Eventually by my just persisting, it leaves. What is that?
Rinpoche: That kind of a feeling of denseness, which is not uncommon, is one of a class of meditation experiences that come under the general category of torpor.

Question: If I don't have time during the day to meditate, and during the evening after I've helped my wife put the children to bed, I'm feeling a little tired, is it better to go ahead and rest or to try to work through that feeling of tiredness and practice at least for fifteen or twenty minutes?

RINPOCHE: It depends on exactly how tired you are. If you're just slightly exhausted then try to meditate, but if you're utterly exhausted then go to sleep.

QUESTION: I read that one should not exhaust oneself with things that are not going to be of benefit, but to me practice is of great benefit. That was the point of my question.

RINPOCHE: The most important thing to understand about exertion in practice is that the long term is more important than the short term. It is not as important to make a heroic effort on a given day to practice when you are exhausted as it is to practice steadily over a long time.

Cultivating Lucidity

So far, in discussing the completion stage, I have talked principally about one aspect of it. However, there are two aspects to the completion stage, two ends we are trying to accomplish. One is to discover or generate some tranquillity or stability in the mind. The second is to generate clarity or lucidity in the mind. The practice of generating stability is shamata meditation, and the practice of generating clarity or lucidity is vipashyana meditation. The significance of shamata is that, for as long as your mind is not at rest, there will be no clarity; there will be no lucidity. Therefore it seems necessary to practice shamata before one engages in the practice of vipashyana. As I have explained, however, in certain traditions, especially in certain aspects of dzogchen practice, there is the notion that because in that approach one takes awareness rather than mind as the path, it is not, strictly speaking, necessary to precede the practice of dzogchen with the practice of shamata. However, in that case, the practice depends entirely upon an authentic recognition of the mind's nature. Although the instructions for generating that recognition in the dzogchen tradition are especially profound, they will not necessarily work for someone who has not yet produced a stable state of shamata. Therefore, while it is theoretically unnecessary to precede the practice of dzogchen with the practice of shamata, practically speaking, for most people it is helpful to begin with shamata practice, which will enable one to generate a clear recognition.

Now I am going to talk about the vipashyana aspect of the completion stage, the cultivation of lucidity. In this text, the practice of cultivating lucidity is said to have two main aims: no meditation and no distraction. By "no meditation," we mean that there is no fabrication in the practice. One is not thinking, "I am meditating on this." One is not attempting to determine what one discovers in meditation. One does not tell oneself that the mind is empty and that therefore one will discover emptiness, or that the mind is lucid and that therefore one will discover lucidity. In this practice you simply see your mind as it is, and thus come to know it as it is. This lack of fabrication in the practice is what is meant by no meditation. On the other hand, it is possible to misunderstand this. When we say no meditation, you might understand this to mean allowing the state of ordinary distraction to continue. Therefore, along with no meditation one has to say no distraction. "No distraction" means that although there is no fabrication of some meditative state or realization, there is a maintenance of mindfulness and alertness. The function of mindfulness and alertness in this context is to protect one from being distracted from the recognition of the mind's nature. In that state one simply stays with the direct experience of whatever arises in the mind.

Different Approaches

There are two ways that this meditation can be presented to students. One way is through a sudden pointing out of the nature of the mind. This could occur, for example, in the context of pointing out the nature of thought. When this is done, then some students have a recognition of the mind's nature and some do not. But the recognition, as authentic as it is, is in some ways adulterated by conceptualization and therefore remains an experience rather than a realization. The problem with this is that, while the recognition is authentic as far as it goes, because it is incomplete and imperfect, it will at some point vanish. When it vanishes, the student does not know how to bring it back, because their initial recognition was experienced under the dramatic circumstances of receiving the pointing out from their guru. Therefore, in the Kagyu tradition, we take a slightly different approach. We use two situations of mind—abiding (the mind that rests) and moving (the presence of thought within the mind)—to enable students, through their own exploration, to come to a decisive recognition of the mind's nature. Students are taught first to look at the mind when it is still, and see how it is then, and next to look at the mind when thought occurs, and see how it is then. In that way they come to realize for themselves what the mind is like when it is at rest and what it is like when it is moving, or when there is thought. This leads to a more stable recognition of the mind's nature—a recognition that will not disappear, or even if it does, can easily be brought back by students because they gained it through their own exploration.

In the Kagyu tradition, this basic format of presentation of the mind's nature is called "abiding, moving, and awareness." With this approach, some students will recognize the mind's nature and some will not, but it is still the most stable and the best way to proceed. The basic idea is expressed in this text by the phrase, "To stay with whatever arises is the path of all siddhas," which means that, resting in an unfabricated way, you maintain an awareness of what arises in your mind. That is the path by means of which all have attained siddhi.

This practice of stabilizing the mind and attaining insight into what arises is the one root of all of the different approaches to meditation. Historically in Tibet the Vajrayana spread at different times. Therefore different lineages arose, each having their own specific emphasis and instruction. For example, there is the Middle Way school, which also teaches this approach to meditation. Then there is the school called *pacification,* which is the school of Padampa Sangye, who came to Tibet from India three times and each time taught something slightly different from before. So even within the school of pacification, three different approaches are taught. Then, connected with that, there is the approach called *severance,* which was taught by the great female disciple of Padampa Sangye, Machig Labdron, who was Tibetan. Based on the instructions she had received from him, and even more on her own spontaneous correct understanding of the *prajnaparamita* sutras, she started her own school, which has its distinct approach to meditation. There is also the mahamudra tradition, which was taught most typically by lords Marpa, Milarepa, and Gampopa. Then the dzogchen tradition, which was taught principally by Guru Rinpoche and by Vimalamitra. Within dzogchen there are two basic approaches: one called the common or ordinary dzogchen, which is very similar to mahamudra, and the other called uncommon or extraordinary dzogchen, which I discussed in part in the previous section.

The major distinction between all of these traditions lies between common and uncommon dzogchen. Dzogchen includes three classes of instruction. These are called the *mind*, *space*, and *instruction* classes. *Uncommon dzogchen* refers to the instruction class, which is considered by that tradition to be the highest level of instruction. Within that there is the essence of the instruction class, called the *heart-drop* or *nying tig* teachings. The distinction made in this text between the nying thig approach and that of these other meditative traditions is very subtle, and concerns what you do when a thought arises. In most traditions of meditation, as I have explained, when a thought arises, you look directly at that thought and thereby directly experience its empty nature. However, in the nying thig tradition, when a thought arises, rather than looking directly at the nature of the thought, you look directly at the nature of that which recognizes the thought's arising. This is obviously a very subtle distinction, but the idea is that by looking directly at the nature of that, or who, or what, recognizes the thought's arising, you directly encounter dharmata, the nature of all things. In the former instance, there is a slight sense of your awareness being directed outward at thought; and in the latter, there is a slight sense of its being directed inward back at itself. At this point you are relating to this distinction as theoretical understanding. It's not difficult to understand intellectually the difference between these two ways of looking, but the important thing, since this is meditation instruction, is to actually practice this. Whether you are looking at what arises or looking at that which recognizes what arises, in order to understand what the two approaches mean, you need to actually have attempted them. You need to attempt them again and again until you actually experience them, because the difference between them is profound.

Once you have gained some experience through actually practicing the instructions found in this text, then you can go back and study the text again and see how your experience compares with what you find in the text. Thus, by combining practical experience with the learning you have gained from studying this and similar texts, what you learn from this text will actually become useful to you as a practitioner. In this way the transmission of instructions has been kept as a lineage of practical experience rather than simply a lineage of transmitted information.

Evaluating Our Process

After further analysis of the three classes of instruction, the text discusses how to determine the degree of progress in meditation. It says that there is an external and an internal aspect to the samadhi that develops as you progress in practice. The external aspect, or the external sign of progress, is that you do not become distracted. The internal sign is that, not being in danger of distraction, you can relax. As a beginner, in order not to become distracted, you have to exert tremendous effort. As you go on it will take less and less effort, and this is the sign of progress. Therefore, what is called "no meditation," which is the final stage of meditation, is the exhaustion of the need for any effort. So the term "no meditation," in that context, means no need for intentional meditation. This is true because, in a sense, there is nothing to be meditated upon. However, there is something to be gotten used to. There being nothing to meditate upon means that meditation upon the nature of things is not the fabrication of any specific meditation experience. As we saw before, it is not pretending that what exists does not exist, or that what does not exist, exists. It is simply seeing things as they are. Meditation on the nature of things is simply seeing your mind as it is. However, there is a process of getting used to seeing it as it is, and therefore there is a process of cultivation or training. In order that this process continue, in order that there be progress in meditation, it is of the utmost importance that you not allow yourself to become distracted from the recognition of your mind's nature, not only during formal meditation sessions, but as much as possible in post-meditation as well. When you are eating, lying down, walking, sitting around, talking, whatever you are doing, you should try to maintain mindfulness of the fundamental nature of your activity.

Mind and Awareness

Next the text gives two sets of parallel instructions. The first comes from the dzogchen tradition, and the second comes from the Kagyu mahamudra tradition. The instruction from the dzogchen tradition reveals the essential point that makes this instruction section of the atiyoga or dzogchen teachings unique: distinguishing between mind and awareness. In the context of that tradition, the term *mind* is used to refer to what we would normally call thought or deluded mind. *Awareness* is used to refer to the innate nonconceptual cognitive lucidity of the mind. The point made in this tradition is that it is of great importance in meditation to properly distinguish between these two in your meditation experience. Since mindfulness, as a mental process, is a function of mind, intentional mindfulness itself cannot recognize the nature of mind. Mindfulness, as useful as it is, contains some conceptual dregs or impurities. The actual recognition of the nature of mind is distinct from mindfulness. It is a cognition without object, a cognition that is recognizing or experiencing itself.

To be more precise about this distinction between mind and awareness, mindfulness can be of two types. There is a kind of conceptual or intentional heavy-handed mindfulness that is a function of mind, and there is a kind of subtle mindfulness that is characteristic of awareness. The distinction is that the faculty of mindfulness that you use in your meditation is incapable of recognizing the mind's nature insofar as it tends to objectify what it experiences. When it seems to be experiencing something other than itself and therefore has that sediment of conceptualization, that is mind. When the faculty you are experiencing in meditation has no object other than itself, experiences its own nature as light, and has the characteristic of brilliant clarity, like a lamp flame, then that is awareness. The key point is that it has no object. Mind always has an object. Awareness does not have an object. The experience of awareness is like being frightened or terrified. It is that kind of intense nonconceptual experience. When you have recognized this, when awareness arises in your experience and you recognize awareness as awareness, then you will have certainty about what all of this means.

Such an experiential presentation of reality, as mentioned in the text, is very different from a theoretical presentation. The distinction between the two is the heart's blood of the lineage. It is the single key point and so is considered quite precious and rare. Therefore, the text admonishes one not to discuss the teachings with those who have broken *samaya* or who just talk about meditation. One may talk about these matters to people who actually practice meditation, but a distinction needs to be made between those who practice and those who just want to acquire jargon in order to impress others.

Mahamudra

Next Jamgön Lodrö Thaye presents meditation instructions from the mahamudra tradition, the Kagyu tradition. When in your practice you are attempting to have a continuous recognition of dharmata, of the nature of your mind, it is crucial that this be unfabricated. The mahamudra tradition counsels you not to try to force the recognition of it. If you do, you will have a momentary recognition of dharmata, and then you will try to adhere to it with force and vigor. That will not help. It is actually sufficient, according to the teachers of the Kagyu tradition, to have had that momentary glimpse of it. If you try to prolong it, you will only create a fabricated similitude of that experience. In any instant of actual meditation on the nature of mind, you are purifying the negative karma you have accumulated over innumerable eons. An instant of meditation on this nature causes all of your karmic winds to enter the central channel. In short, there is no limit to the benefit of this kind of recognition.

While you can't force it, nevertheless this kind of recognition of your own nature is the one thing that matters. In the Kagyu terminology, it is "the one thing, if known, that frees all." Another, related phrase is "knowing all, but missing out on the one." If you recognize your mind's nature, then that in itself is the recognition of the essence of everything else that is to be known. But if you don't recognize your mind's nature, no matter how much else you may know about Dharma, you are missing the point.

Next the text gives instructions for a method of enhancing one's meditation practice that is called "mixing of awareness and space." Essentially this consists of either looking into the midst of the sky or into the midst of a large body of water, such as an ocean, and mixing your awareness with where you are looking. By doing this mindfully, with some vigor to your mindfulness, you will have an experience of limitless awareness that is without substantiality; awareness without center or limit.

The Three States

Following that, the text addresses the question of how to determine what is happening in your meditation. Specifically, one might mistake any of the three meditation states for one another, because superficially they may resemble one another. These three states are the recognition or experience of emptiness, i.e., the states of vipashyana, shamata, and blank neutrality.

The experience of emptiness is occurring when there is a direct experience of or by your awareness that you cannot conceptualize. You cannot actually say it is one thing or another. You can't describe it to yourself; it is inexpressible. The experience of shamata, in contrast, is a state in which all of the agitation of thought is completely pacified, and there is a limitless experience of peace, stillness, and tranquillity. It is like a body of water without waves.

The experience of neutrality is different from these two in that your faculties of mindfulness, alertness, and awareness are weak. There is a feeling of obscurity. Neutrality differs from the experience of emptiness in the lack of recognition or direct experience. It differs from shamata in that there is some undercurrent of thought that is very subtle, that distracts you, that you only recognize after you have become distracted. So if there's a feeling of basic stillness but you are still being distracted by some undercurrent, that is neither emptiness nor shamata, but neutrality.

Of these three states, the realization of emptiness is what we are attempting to achieve, but shamata is also acceptable, especially if that is what you are trying to cultivate. If you are trying to practice shamata, then a state of shamata itself is not regarded as a defect, although a distinction needs to be made between a state of shamata and a state of realization. However, the third of these states, the blank neutrality in which the undercurrent is functioning, needs to be rectified. The way to rectify that is to recognize it and to strengthen or tighten up your awareness, to put more effort into mindfulness and into alertness and awareness. There is a particular variety of neutrality in which you have a feeling of dense obscurity or thickness to your mind, like being in a fog. That can be dispelled by vigorously breathing out all the stale air in your body and then breathing in. Other techniques such as the verbal repetition of mantras—the actual use of speech—and sometimes physical movement, can also dispel it.

Having recognized the presence of neutrality in your meditation, it needs to be overcome. There are steps for accomplishing this. The first is learning to distinguish neutrality—especially from shamata, but also from insight. The second is learning to recognize neutrality when it is occurring. The third is learning methods to get rid of it. Sometimes the state of neutrality afflicts our meditation, but at other times our meditation is impeded not by neutrality but by the presence of actual kleshas. So next the text explains how to deal with the kleshas that arise in meditation.

The klesha that is used as an example is anger. The reason that anger is used is because it is the easiest klesha to recognize, because it is the most vivid. When a thought of anger vividly arises in your mind, which through its intensity is easy to apprehend, look at it directly. Looking at it directly does not mean distancing yourself from it and looking at it theoretically or conceptually. When you conceptually examine kleshas from a distance, you are considering the characteristics and contents of the thought, creating the semblance of something there. You have an idea of who you are angry at, how you feel about them, and so on. That is not looking at anger directly. If you look at it nakedly or directly with nothing in between that which is looking and that which is looked at, then you will see the nature of it rather than the mere appearance of something there. When you look directly and rest within that looking without fabrication, without attempting to tell yourself anything about the anger, then the heavy-handed quality of the anger dissolves on the spot, and the thought is seen to have no benefit or harm. It no longer has any kind of negative energy.

QUESTION: What is the distinction between the teachings received by Machig Labdron and her own direct experience?
RINPOCHE: The difference between Machig's teachings and the teachings that she received from India is that the teachings that came from India take the approach of pacifying thought and delusion and letting it settle down, whereas Machig's approach, called *severance*, is very aggressive. Not aggressive in a negative way, but aggressive in the sense of "aggressively treating an illness." It is just slicing through thoughts—not waiting for them to settle down, but slicing through them or destroying them. The words "pacification" and "severance" themselves describe the difference. Rather than pacifying thoughts, you actually provoke the most difficult ones. In severance practice, you work especially with fear. You go to places where you feel unsafe, typically to charnel grounds. You trigger intense fear, and you cut through it.

QUESTION: My question concerns the arising of thoughts and directly experiencing them. When anger comes up for me, the next feeling or thought that comes up is guilt. Do I just keep on looking at these as they arise?
RINPOCHE: It doesn't matter what the thought is. While the thought of

anger is present, you can look directly at the thought of anger; if it is succeeded by a thought of guilt, you can look at the thought of guilt. In either case, what you discover when you look directly at a thought is that although there is something you can experience that you can call a thought—a feeling of anger—when you look at it directly, there is nothing there. Hence this is called the unity of clarity and emptiness. Clarity is the fact that there is an appearance or experience but it has no substantial existence. Thoughts are all the same. They are just like water bubbles. You see them, but then there is nothing there.

QUESTION: In the sutra tradition of the middle way, are there analytical meditations that specifically reveal the luminous nature of mind?
RINPOCHE: Not directly, because in analytical meditation you are always concerned with the maintenance and cultivation of some kind of conviction. Therefore it is very indirect. It takes a long time. If you persisted long enough with the maintenance and refinement of your conviction about the nature of mind, eventually there could be a discovery of the mind's innate lucidity, but it is not directly discussed in the sutra system.

QUESTION: Why are yidam practices done by accomplished realized beings? And why are empowerments given, such as the Kalachakra, that are so extensive and detailed that it would be very hard for me or other people like me to actually do?
TRANSLATOR: Those are two very different questions: Why people who have already attained enlightenment continue to do yidam practice, and why empowerments for yidam practice are given to people who are unlikely ever to do that yidam practice.
RINPOCHE: In answer to the first question, there are many different types of teachers, and they are not all necessarily at the same level, so it would be difficult to give a single answer for why they all would continue to do these practices. In the case of some of them, they do so because they still have some distance to go on the path; they do so for their own benefit, to expand their experience and realization. In the case of others who have already attained supreme siddhi, who in fact may be fully awakened buddhas, they continue to do formal practice as an example to others, to show the importance of formal practice.

In answer to the second question, giving empowerments has two aspects. One is called "actual" or "ultimate" empowerment, and the other is called "external" or "symbolic" empowerment. In the case of actual empowerment—what nowadays we would call an "extraordinary" empowerment—what happens is that the student actually recognizes on the spot the wisdom that that empowerment is designed to communicate. That is the fullest or most extraordinary instance of empowerment. It is not a particularly different type or ceremony of empowerment; it is a specific experience of empowerment.

Normally when an empowerment is given, the function is not only to empower people to do specific practices but to transmit the blessing of Dharma through the vehicle of that specific ceremony. In that spirit you might take the empowerment of Kalachakra or of Chakrasamvara or of Hevajra, or any other major or minor empowerment. The basic process of these is essentially the same: Some kind of blessing of Dharma is actually entering into you. To say that the blessing of Dharma enters into you does not mean that through receiving an empowerment you can immediately fly in the sky, or that you become intoxicated with some kind of mysterious spiritual drunkenness. It means simply that having received the empowerment, something changes. There will be at least a little increase in your faith and devotion, at least a little increase in your diligence. These changes in you are the principal blessing or benefit of the empowerment process. For example, many people have told me that they were previously unable to understand or settle on the validity of Buddhism, but then, for one reason or another, they received the Kalachakra empowerment from His Holiness the Dalai Lama and thereafter have been intensely involved in practice. That is an instance of the blessing of empowerment. It is not necessarily that they are practicing Kalachakra, but that, because of that empowerment, they are practicing Dharma.

QUESTION: In the sudden pointing out of the nature of mind versus abiding, moving, and awareness, you refer to the second technique as being specifically the Kagyu approach. Is there some flexibility in terms of how specific teachers deal with specific students?

RINPOCHE: Sure. There are different texts composed by different teachers, and present-day teachers following these different texts therefore guide their students slightly differently.

Question: On page 69 the phrase appears, "three things are said to pose the danger of misunderstanding." What does "danger" refer to?
Translator: The Tibetan says, "there is the possibility of mistaking one of these for another." The word that is translated as "danger" here, *nor dogs*, means something that possibly might happen.

Question: What are the ten winds?
Rinpoche: These are the five main and five minor energies or winds of the body. The five major winds govern the principal physical processes. They are called the *digestive wind;* the *eliminating wind,* which is connected with going to the bathroom; the *upward moving wind;* the *pervasive wind,* which enables you to move your limbs; and the *life wind* or *prana wind,* which keeps you alive, keeps you in your body.

Question: When the winds enter the central channel, is it one or all of them that enter?
Rinpoche: There are two mentions of this in our text. When it says "the ten winds become workable," it means that, as a sign of practice, they start to function in an ideal way. Generally speaking, the karmic energy or wind flows through the two side channels, the ones on the right and left of the central channel. The winds or energies that flow in the central channel are wisdom winds, not karmic winds. Through the cessation of the flowing of winds through the right and left channels, which brings the winds into the central channel, there is a transformation of karmic wind into wisdom wind. This is what the text refers to when it talks about the karmic wind being brought into the central channel. It occurs as a natural result of meditation, and there are specific methods to achieve it.

Question: How do the karmic winds that become wisdom winds relate to the five major winds that you named before?
Rinpoche: The ten winds are the energies of your physical body that enable it to do all the things it does. The karmic wind is actually what you breathe in and out. The point is that the karmic wind that you breathe in

and out has a little bit of wisdom wind mixed with it all the time. Therefore, especially at certain times, there is a presence of wisdom wind in your breathing. Through the practice of meditation in general and through certain specific processes or techniques, you can cause the karmic wind to be transformed into wisdom wind.

QUESTION: As the breath comes in or...?

RINPOCHE: Normally, as the breath is held, which is why there is the practice of holding the breath. The text talks about this also occurring as a natural result of meditative realization. Some people, if they develop an extraordinary state of shamata, have the experience of not having to breathe for a while.

QUESTION: On page 77 the text discusses breathing HUNG AH OM. Which is recited on the out, the pause, and the in-breath?

RINPOCHE: In this text, when you breath out, it is HUNG. Between breathing out and the next breathing in, it is AH. So the breath is actually held out rather than held in. Then, when you breathe in again, it is OM. In other teachings, the sequence sometimes varies.

Notes

1. *rdzogs:* I have used "completion" rather than "perfection" since it seems to imply a sense of wholeness and inclusion, whereas perfection might connote a thing perfected due to the elimination of its imperfect parts. In the case of dzogchen (see note 54) however, I have used "great perfection," which is in common usage by now, even though "great completion" might have been better. The reader should understand that the term in Tibetan is the same in both cases.
2. *Śākyamuni* means "the sage of the Shakya clan," and is the name usually used when distinguishing the historical Buddha from other buddhas. His personal name was Gautama or Siddhārtha. The dates of his life are generally given as 563 to 483 B.C.E., although various traditions offer a number of different datings. There are also many different perspectives on his life, the so-called historical version being only one possible interpretation.
3. *byang chub*, Skt. *bodhi:* the Tibetan term means purification *(byang)* of all obscurations, and realization *(chub)* of all qualities.
4. *thabs mkhas pa*, Skt. *upāya.*
5. *chos 'khor rim pa gsum*, Skt. *triparivartadharmacakrapravartana:* the early, the middle, and the last *(snga bar phyi gsum)* "turnings of the wheel of Dharma" are called, respectively, the Dharma turning of the four truths *(bden pa bzhi'i chos 'khor);* of absence of defining characteristics *(mtshan nyid med pa'i chos 'khor);* and of thorough distinction *(legs par rnam par phye ba'i chos 'khor).* The wheel is a metaphoric reference to the legendary universal king whose instrument of sovereignty is a wheel that subdues any territory without violence.
6. *'phags pa'i bden pa bzhi*, Skt. *catvāryasatya:* first recorded in the first sermon of the Buddha, *Dharmacakrapravartana Sūtra*, "Setting in Motion the Wheel of Dharma."
7. *rten cing 'brel bar 'byung ba*, Skt. *pratītyasamutpāda:* the interdependent relationship, or "dependent origination," that is the nature of all phenomena. This idea is at the core of all Buddhist philosophy.

8. *nyon mongs pa*, Skt. *kleśa*: the definition in the *Great Tibetan Dictionary (bod kyi tshig mdzod chen mo)* is: "mental events that incite one to unvirtuous actions and cause one's being to be very disturbed," *(mi dge ba'i las bskul bas rang rgyud rab tu ma zhi bar byed pa'i sems byung)*, vol. 2, p. 970. The three main afflictive emotions, or "poisons," are desire, hatred, and stupidity.
9. *bdag med*, Skt. *anātman.*
10. *dgra bcom pa:* one who has conquered *(bcom)* the enemy *(dgra)* of afflictive emotion.
11. *shes rab kyi pha rol tu phyin pa'i mdo sde*, Skt. *prajñāpāramitāsūtra:* the teachings on the perfection of transcendent intelligence first appeared in India beginning around 100 B.C.E., according to Edward Conze. There are about forty texts, varying in size from 100,000 verses to a single letter: A. They represent the evolution of the emphasis on emptiness and compassion.
12. *stong pa nyid*, Skt. *śūnyatā* and *snying rje*, Skt. *karuṇā.*
13. *don dam bden pa*, Skt. *paramārthasatya.*
14. *kun rdzob bden pa*, Skt. *saṃvṛtisatya*: these two truths *(bden pa gnyis*, Skt. *satyadvaya)*, the absolute and the relative, are to be understood as inseparable.
15. *byang chub sems dpa'*, Skt. *bodhisattva*: "hero of awakening," the ideal Mahāyāna paradigm, who is completely devoted to the awakening of all sentient beings.
16. *de bzhin gshegs pa'i snying po*, Skt. *tathāgatagarbha;* or *bde bar gshegs pa'i snying po*, Skt. *sugatagarbha:* literally, "the essence or womb of the one gone to suchness (or bliss)," in other words, a buddha.
17. Sūtras *(mdo)* are the discourses attributed to the Buddha Śākyamuni. They include the early teachings spoken directly by the Buddha, collected and preserved in the Pali canon during the early Buddhist councils, and texts that appeared much later, usually in Sanskrit, Prakrit, or Buddhist-hybrid Sanskrit, that are attributed to the influence of the Buddha and included in the Mahāyāna canon.
18. *rgyud*, "continuity": refers both to the class of literature, both Hindu and Buddhist, and the teachings contained in that literature.
19. *rdo rje theg pa*, Skt. *vajrayāna.*
20. *gsang sngags*, Skt. *guhyamantra.*
21. *dag snang:* the vision or outlook that recognizes the innate perfection or purity of all phenomena. In tantra, this means specifically regarding all beings as deities, the surroundings as the pure lands of the

buddhas, all sound as mantra, and all thoughts as intrinsic awareness. Also to always see one's spiritual teacher as a buddha.

22. *dkyil 'khor*, Skt. *maṇḍala:* literally, center and circumference. A stylized configuration of peaceful or wrathful deities, or enlightened attributes, usually formed by a circle with a four-doored square within, representing the pure abode of the deities; may also represent the universe, psychic energy centers, and other correspondences.
23. King Trisong Detsen *(khri srong lde btsan)* lived from approximately 730 to 798 C.E., although dates vary a great deal according to different sources and ways of calculating.
24. Śāntarakṣita *(zhi ba 'tsho)*, also called Abbot Bodhisattva *(mkhan po bo dhi sa tva)* by Tibetans.
25. *pad ma 'byung gnas,* Skt. *padmākara:* "Lotus Born," known more commonly in Tibet as Guru Rinpoche, Precious Guru, and many other names. He was an Indian tantric master considered to be the "second Buddha" and is credited with establishing Buddhism in Tibet and founding the Ancient *(rnying ma)* lineage.
26. *bstan pa snga dar:* "the early spreading" is also referred to as the *snga bsgyur rnying ma,* "the early translation [period of the] Ancient [School]."
27. *glang dar ma*, who ruled from approximately 841 to 846 C.E.
28. *bstan pa phyi dar:* also referred to as the *phyi bsgyur gsar ma,* "the later translation [period of the] New [School]." Since the Kagyu, Sakya, and Gelug traditions originated during this period, they are called collectively the "New (Sarma) School."
29. *sgrub brgyud shing rta chen po brgyad:* "the eight great chariots of practice lineages," they are the Nyingma *(rnying ma)*, Kadam *(bka' gdams)*, Kagyu *(bka' brgyud)*, Lamdre *(lam 'bras,* path and fruition, i.e., *sa skya)*, Shangpa *(shangs pa)*, Shije and Chöd *(zhi byed* and *gcod;* "pacification and severance"), Kālachakra *(dus 'khor;* also called *sbyor drug)*, and Orgyen Nyengyu *(o rgyan bsnyen brgyud)*.
30. *mdo lam sngags lam*, Skt. *sūtramārga* and *mantramārga:* "mantra" being short for the Secret Mantra Vehicle.
31. *sdig pa ci yang mi bya zhing /*
dge ba phun sum tshogs par spyad /
rang gi sems ni yongs su 'dul /
'di ni sangs rgyas bstan pa yin /
32. *'bras bu'i theg pa*, Skt. *phalayāna:* which makes the result the path, as opposed to the Causal Vehicle *(rgyu'i theg pa)*, which makes the cause the path—a method ascribed to the "lower" approaches.

33. *sbyang gzhi chos dbyings rtag brtan 'dus ma byas/*
bde gshegs snying pos 'gro kun yongs la khyab/
In Sanskrit, "realm of reality" is *dharmadhatu,* and "buddha nature" is *sugatagarbha.* See page 41.

34. *stong pa la bdag dang gsal ba la gzhan:* "on emptiness 'self' and on radiance 'other' [is imputed]," from "Kalu Rinpoche's Comments on Foundation Consciousness, etc." *(ka lu rin po che'i kun gzhi sogs khrid)* as well as innumerable oral teachings. The late Kalu Rinpoche was a supreme meditation master in the Kagyu tradition and lineage holder of the Shangpa tradition of Tibetan Buddhism. He was said to be a manifestation of Jamgön Kongtrul.

35. *mtshan nyid sdug bsngal du shar ba yin:* from *dam chos yid bzhin nor bu thar pa rin po che'i rgyan (Jewel Ornament of Liberation)* by Gampopa, f. 2.

36. Korlo Demchog *('khor lo bde mchog,* Skt. *cakrasaṃvara),* "Wheel of Sublime Bliss," a name for one of the tantric deities.

37. *de yang sbyang gzhi bde gshegs snying po nyid /*
rdo rje mtshan dpe gsal rdzogs skur bzhugs pas /
de dang 'dra ba'i rnam pa lam byed kyis /
sbyangs 'bras gzhi la yod pa'i lha sku nyid /
See page 47.

38. The *Ratnagotravibhāga,* more popularly known to Tibetans as the *Uttaratantra (rgyud bla ma),* a commentary on the ideas of buddha nature said to be written down by the great third-century Indian Acarya Asaṅga *(thogs med)* through the inspiration of the bodhisattva and future buddha Maitreya *(byams pa).*

39. *de dag yon tan gsum bcu ni /*
gnyis 'di chos skus rab phye ste /
nor bu rin chen 'od mdog dang /
dbyibs bzhin dbye ba med phyir ro /
Uttaratantra, f. 28 b.

40. The three bodies *(sku gsum,* Skt. *trikāya)* of a buddha: body of reality *(chos sku;* Skt. *dharmakāya),* body of perfect rapture *(longs spyod rdzogs pa'i sku,* Skt. *sambhogakāya),* and emanation body *(sprul pa'i sku,* Skt. *nirmāṇakāya).* There are a number of others as well, with similar or overlapping meanings, but this three-part classification seems to be the most common.

41. *phyag rgya chen po la rgyu med de /*
dad pa dang mos gus phyag rgya chen po'i rgyu yin /

phyag rgya chen po la rkyen med de /
bla ma dam pa phyag rgya chen po'i rkyen yin /
from *mnyam med rje btsun sgam po pa'i phyag rgya chen po lam gcig chod, (The Single Decisive Path, the Mahāmudrā of the Unequalled and Revered Gampopa)* ff. 1b–2. Gampopa was a master in the two lineages of Tibetan Buddhism, the Kadam and the Kagyu, and is seen as the founder of the established order of the Kagyu, being the first monk. Mahāmudrā (*phyag rgya chen po*, "the great seal") is the culminating formless practice in the Kagyu system and is also synonymous with its fruition—recognition of ultimate reality.

42. *dbang bskur*, Skt. *abhiṣeka:* the Tibetan term means to transfer power, especially in the sense of authority to do the practice concerned with the particular empowerment ceremony. The Sanskrit term means anointing or consecration. Most deity practices require that the practitioner first receive a ceremonial empowerment from a qualified master.
43. There are two classifications of the tantric literature in Tibet, either according to the Old Translation School *(Nyingma)*, in which case there are six classes, or the New Translation School *(Sarma)* (see note 28) with four classes. A thorough discussion in English can be found in Dudjom Rinpoche's *The Nyingma School of Tibetan Buddhism.*
44. Tulku Thondup Rinpoche, *Buddha Mind: An Anthology of Longchen Rabjam's Writings on Dzogpa Chenpo*, pp. 15–46.
45. These are called the *five actual enlightening factors (mngon byang lnga), four vajras (rdo rje bzhi)*, three rituals *(cho ga gsum)*, and instantaneously complete *(skad cig dran rdzogs)*. Each sequence covers the visualization process in greater or fewer stages, from the initial emptiness up to the full form of the deity.
46. These five are listed somewhat differently in different places, as Kongtrul himself notes. For instance, I have found differing lists in *zab mo nang don* [f. 41]; *bde mchog lha lnga rnam bshad; nor bu 'od zer* [f. 40]; and Dilgo Khyentse Rinpoche's *Pure Appearance,* pp. 18–30. Also see note 108.
47. In Khyentse's *Pure Appearance*, p. 24, the absorption of the cause includes the visualization of the seed syllable, or consciousness aspect, whereas here that visualization seems to come after the absorptions.
48. As all mental activity can be recognized as the pure radiance of awareness, the five basic emotions—ignorance, desire, anger, pride, and jealousy—are described as being essentially five aspects of pristine wisdom *(ye shes)*. They are the wisdoms of the realm of reality *(chos dbyings)*, of

discrimination *(so sor rtog pa)*, mirror-like *(me long lta bu)*, of sameness *(mnyam nyid)*, and of accomplishment *(bya ba grub pa)*. These are also discussed in terms of five families *(rigs nga)*, which are buddha, lotus, vajra, jewel, and action. Tantric deities are usually manifestations of one of these energies and are said to belong to that family.

49. *blo 'das brjod bral ba;* see page 51.
50. *mos gus stobs kyis nang nas shar ba la;* see page 51.
51. The eight aggregates of consciousness *(rnam shes tshogs brgyad)* are the five associated with the five senses *(dbang po lnga)*, plus the mental consciousness *(sems kyi rnam shes)*, the afflictive mind *(nyon yid)*, and the "foundation-of-all" consciousness *(kun gzhi rnam shes*, Skt. *ālaya-vijñāna)*. Kongtrul's explanation in this text is succinct but sufficient.
52. *dran pa*, (Skt. *smṛti*) or *dran shes*, "mindful awareness."
53. *mthar thug don la dran pa nyid kyang med*; see page 71.
54. Dzogchen *(rdzogs pa chen po*, Skt. *mahāsandhi):* "the great perfection" is the highest nonconceptual practice in the Nyingma School of Tibetan Buddhism and claims itself to be the culmination of all approaches. It is also called atiyoga, the highest of the six-part Nyingma division of tantra.

    Exceptional esoteric instructions *(man ngag sde)* are the third and highest of the divisions of the teachings of dzogchen. The other two are the mind class *(sems sde)* and the space class *(klong sde)*. See Dudjom Rinpoche, *The Nyingma School of Tibetan Buddhism*, pp. 319–45, and Tulku Thondup Rinpoche, *Buddha Mind*, pp. 47–81.
55. *de 'dras rim bgrod lam la 'bad na legs*, see page 63, *'grod* in the woodblock should read *bgrod*.
56. Channels *(rtsa*, Skt. *nāḍī)* through which the vital winds *(rlung*, Skt. *prāṇa)* and seminal drops *(thig le*, Skt. *bindu)* move. Chakras *(rtsa 'khor)* or "channel wheels" are areas where many channels join together.
57. Milarepa *(mi la ras pa)* (1040–1123) was a great yogi and poet in the Kagyu lineage whose trials and travails on the spiritual path and eloquent songs of realization make his life story perhaps the most popular of all stories of Tibetan saints.
58. Quoted in Thondup, *Buddha Mind*, pp. 113–14, translation by Tulku Thondup.
59. *des na lta ba nam mkha' bas kyang mtho /*
    las rgyu 'bras bag phye bas kyang zhib /
    attributed to Padmasambhava, quoted in *rdzogs pa chen po klong chen snying thig gi sngon 'gro'i khrid yig kun bzang bla ma'i zhal lung*, by

Patrul Rinpoche, f. 112. (Translated as *Kün-zang La-may Zhal-lung* and as *Words of My Perfect Teacher.*)

60. Information on Kongtrul's life has been taken from three sources: his autobiography, *phyogs med ris med kyi btsan pa la 'dun shing dge sbyong gi gzugs brnyan 'chang ba blo gros mtha' yas kyi sde'i byung ba brjod pa nor bu sna tshogs mdog can,* (*Jewels of Various Colors*, currently under translation by Richard Barron) in vol. 62 of *The Treasury of Precious Treasure (rin chen gter mdzod)*; E. Gene Smith's "'Jam mgon Kong sprul and the Nonsectarian Movement" in *Among Tibetan Texts*; and Dudjom Rinpoche's *The Nyingma School of Tibetan Buddhism*, vol. I, pp. 859–68.
61. Kongtrul had many different names given to him at different occasions. His first ordination name was Karma Ngawang Yönten Gyamtso Trinle Kunkhyab Palzangpo, his bodhisattva ordination name was Gyalsay Lodrö Thaye, his initiatory name was Padma Gargyi Wangchuk Trinlay Drodultsal, and his name as a tertön was Chime Tsenyi Yungdrung Lingpa. Any of these might be used to sign his compositions. He never signed Kongtrul, an abbreviation of his incarnation name, but occasionally "Jamgön Lama." Jamgön indicates the bodhisattva of transcendent intelligence, Manjuśrī, of whom Kongtrul was said to be an emanation. E. Gene Smith's "'Jam mgon Kong sprul and the Nonsectarian Movement" in *Among Tibetan Texts*, pp. 258–62.
62. *Jewels of Various Colors*, ff. 9 and 12b.
63. *Jewels of Various Colors*, ff. 17–18.
64. The late Dezhung Rinpoche, a great Sakya lama and proponent of nonsectarianism, said, "It was common in Tibet for the least spiritually developed adherents of each of the four great orders to nurture this spirit of sectarianism. Often monks and lay disciples of one order would refuse to attend the services of other orders. Monks would refuse to study or read the literature of others simply because they were writings of masters who belonged to another lineage—no matter how good the literature might be." From "Buddhism Without Sectarianism," translated by Jared Rhoton, p. 6.
65. The custom of recognizing the new incarnations of past great masters is widespread in Tibet. They are called *tulku*, (*nirmāṇakāya*, emanation body), referring to bodhisattvas who willingly come back in order to continue their work for sentient beings. It was a wonderful system to ensure the continuation of the lineages and education of its leaders. It was also vulnerable to abuse.

66. *Jewels of Various Colors*, f. 19.
67. Situ's name is invoked in the first line of the text translated here. Kongtrul lists a total of sixty teachers in one supplication prayer: ecumenical but loyal.
68. Hidden treasures (terma, *gter ma*) are teachings by the Indian tantric master Padmasambhava, who successfully introduced Buddhism in Tibet in the ninth century. Certain teachings were "hidden" for future generations in times when they would be appropriate. Then they are rediscovered by gifted individuals or emanations of Padmasambhava himself. All of the revealers (tertön, *gter ston*) were predicted by name in previous treasures.
69. Dudjom Rinpoche (Jigdral Yeshe Dorje, 1904–87), *The Nyingma School of Tibetan Buddhism*, volume I, p. 862.
70. Currently under translation by the Sonada Translation Committee established by Kalu Rinpoche. Parts of it have been published by Snow Lion Publications as *Myriad Worlds* and *Buddhist Ethics.*
71. "He only seems to want to bring some order into the chaos of this 'rediscovered' literature, to establish some criteria of authenticity for this genre that had often been reviled and rejected by Tibetan scholars of a more purist bent." E. Gene Smith, "'Jam mgon Kong sprul and the Nonsectarian Movement" in *Among Tibetan Texts,* p. 263.
72. *padma nyin byed dbang po:* the twelfth Tai Situpa (1774–1853), Kongtrul's principal teacher and head lama of Palpung Monastery, an important Kagyu center.
73. *mtsho skyes rdo rje:* Lake-born Vajra, a name for Padmasambhava; see note 25.
74. Vajra friends *(rdo rje mched po* or *mched grogs),* sometimes vajra brothers and sisters, refers to fellow practitioners of Vajrayāna, or tantric, Buddhism. It is an important relationship sanctified by the Vajrayāna commitment to honor one another. Various degrees of relationship are recognized, from students of the same guru who are initiated together up to the connection between all practitioners. It is significant that the author sites his vajra friend(s), whom he basically cannot refuse, as a pretext for the composition of the text. It would be considered presumptuous to decide on one's own to compose, and most Tibetan commentaries explain their inception in this way.
75. We do not have the personal good fortune to meet the Buddha, but we can actually encounter the teacher or guru, and so he or she is considered even more important than the Buddha for us personally, and not

essentially different. We call that buddha who we meet, the guru. It is also said, "before the guru, even the word 'buddha' did not exist."

76. *'khor lo bsgyur ba:* literally, "wheel monarch," ruler over a world system during the time when human life spans are exceedingly long. He gains his absolute power through the possession of a wheel that subdues beings without violence, and also has the marks of wheels on the soles of his feet, as do buddhas.
77. *dkon mchog gsum,* Skt. *triratna:* the Three Jewels, the Three Precious Jewels, or the Three Rare and Sublime Ones are the Buddha *(sangs rgyas),* or teacher; the Dharma *(chos),* or the teachings; and the Sangha *(dge 'dun),* or the community of practitioners. These are the three traditional sources of refuge and objects of faith of all Buddhists.
78. *rtsa ba gsum,* Skt. *trimūla:* the Three Roots are the guru *(bla ma),* root of blessings; the meditational deity *(yi dam,* Skt. *devatā),* root of accomplishment; and ḍākas, ḍākinīs *(mkha' 'gro),* and Dharma protectors *(chos skyong,* Skt. *dharmapāla),* root of enlightened activity. These are the second three sources of refuge (along with the Three Jewels), and are particular to the Vajrayāna Buddhism of Tibet.
79. *dkyil 'khor,* Skt. *maṇḍala:* see note 22.
80. *chos nyid,* Skt. *dharmatā:* reality, the essential true nature of all phenomena, which is emptiness.
81. Nāgārjuna *(klu sgrub),* a great master and scholar from southern India who lived approximately four hundred years after the Buddha's death. He is best known for his interpretation of the concept of emptiness, which led to the formation of the Madhyamaka school of philosophy.
82. *shes rab,* Skt. *prajñā:* this word carries the full range of connotations of perceptive and apprehensive abilities, from direct understanding or mastery of a single subject, to full realization of the ultimate nature of reality. The choice of "intelligence," or "transcendent intelligence," rather than the usual "wisdom" or "knowledge," reflects the active mode of that which apprehends, rather than that which is apprehended. Here the discussion is of the three kinds of intelligence that arise from listening, contemplating, and meditating.
83. Cyclic existence *('khor ba,* Skt. *saṃsāra)* and transcendence of its suffering *(mya ngan las 'das pa,* Skt. *nirvāṇa).*
84. *gnas lugs:* literally, the way of abiding. The true nature or natural condition of all phenomena.
85. Imaginary nature *(kun brtags,* Skt. *parikalpita)* and perfectly existent nature *(yongs grub,* Skt. *pariniśpanna)* are technical terms used in the

Cittamātra school of philosophy for the idea of the three natures *(rang bzhin gsum,* Skt. *trisvabhāva),* the third being the dependent nature *(gzhan-dbang,* Skt. *paratantra).* The two mentioned here seem to correspond to the relative truth *(kun rdzob bden pa)* and the absolute truth *(don dam bden pa,* see "second turning" section of the introduction). Here they are in relation to the contrivance *(bcos ma)* of the creation stage and the genuine condition *(rnal ma),* or true nature, in the completion stage, respectively. In other words, the creation stage deals with the vast array of phenomena on the relative level, and the completion stage deals with the essential nature of phenomena on the absolute level. For a practical discussion of the three natures and the two truths, see Khenpo Tsultrim Gyamtso's *Progressive Stages of Meditation on Emptiness.*

86. *sngags lam,* Skt. *mantramārga:* the approach or path of the Secret Mantra Vehicle is synonymous with Vajrayāna or tantra. (See the "tantra" section of the introduction.) It is also known as the *path of method (thabs,* Skt. *upāya),* for its many skillful techniques.

87. *drang nges lam:* usually, the conventional or provisional meaning *(drang don,* Skt. *neyārtha),* which is taught in order to guide common people in the right direction *(gdul bya thun mong ba rnams kha dran ba'i phyir du),* but which needs to be interpreted on a deeper level to understand the truth; and the definitive or certain meaning *(nges don,* Skt. *nīthārta),* which clearly states the absolute truth and needs no further qualifications. There has been much discussion and disagreement among Tibetans on which doctrines are which, but all agree that both are still valid. Here these two are applied to practice *(lam)* rather than doctrine.

88. *'dul* is translated in this section as "control," an unpopular word, but it seems close to the meaning. Other words might be "subdue," "master," or "conquer."

89. *nyon mongs pa,* Skt. *kleśa:* see note 8.

90. *rten 'brel,* short for *rten cing 'brel bar 'byung ba,* Skt. *pratītyasamutpāda:* see the "first turning" section of the introduction. Because of its profound and complex nature, contemplation on the subject of interdependent relationship is used as a remedy for stupidity.

91. *'od dpag med,* Skt. *amitābha:* Boundless Light, the name of a buddha—the head of the lotus family—that is associated with the transformation of desire into the pristine wisdom of discernment (*so sor rtog pa'i ye shes,* see note 48).

92. *khrag 'thung*, Skt. *heruka:* a general name for wrathful meditational deities, and also a name for Cakrasaṃvara *('khor lo bde mchog)* or "Wheel of Sublime Bliss," one of the tantric deities particularly associated with desire, as the name implies.
93. *phyag rgya chen po*, Skt. *mahāmudrā:* "the Great Seal," the culminating formless practice in the Kagyu tradition. The term is also synonymous with its fruition: recognition of ultimate reality.
94. *so sor rtogs pa'i ye shes:* see note 91 and note 48.
95. Gyalwa Yangön (*rgyal ba yang dgon pa rgyal mtshan dpal*; alias *lha gdon pa*, 1213–58), a distinguished disciple of the founder of the Upper Drukpa Kagyu tradition *(stod 'brug pa dkar brgyud pa)*, was born in the Dingri area of western Tibet. Three volumes of his collected writings *(gsung 'bum)* are published by Tango Monastic Community, Tango, Thimpu, Bhutan.
96. *rdo rje 'chang:* "Holder of the Vajra," the embodiment of the buddhas of the five families, and especially in the Kagyu tradition, the symbolic representation of the body of reality *(chos sku*, Skt. *dharmakāya)*, the ultimate state of enlightenment.
97. *'khor lo bde mchog:* see note 92.
98. *thig le 'chor ba:* loss of seminal drops. The word *thig le* (Skt. *bindu*) has a wide range of meanings, such as a tiny point of energy, the vital energy as embodied in the seminal fluids (as is the case here), meditational visions of spheres, and the totality of being. The general connotations are of vital energy and of an indivisible totality, being the seed or nucleus of enlightened mind.
99. *zung 'jug*, Skt. *yuganaddha:* "two into [one]." Here it is the two stages of creation and completion that must ultimately be integrated, just as form and emptiness, or relative and absolute, must be realized as essentially the same. Thus *zung 'jug* can also refer to the ultimate realization, or state of enlightenment.
100. *chos kyi dbyings*, Skt. *dharmadhātu:* realm of reality or absolute expanse-emptiness.
101. *bde bar gshegs pa'i snying po*, Skt. *sugatagarbha:* see the "third turning" section of the introduction.
102. *chos kyi sku*, Skt. *dharmakāya:* the ultimate and formless dimension of buddha. See the "deity practice" section of the introduction and note 40.
103. *dbyibs kyi rnal 'byor:* refers to the creation-stage practices of visualization.
104. *mngon byang lnga, rdo rje bzhi cho ga gsum:* names for sequences

covering the visualization process in greater or fewer stages from the initial emptiness up to the full form of the deity. See the "creation stage" section of the introduction.

105. *mngon rtogs:* literally means "actual realization," but here refers to the section in the liturgy of a deity visualization where the various attributes of the deity are described.

106. *bar do:* the time and state of being from death until the next rebirth.

107. *rnying ma* and *gsar ma:* see notes 26 and 28.

108. The three meditative absorptions or *samādhis* are *de bzhin nyid kyi ting nge 'dzin, kun nas snang ba'i ting nge 'dzin,* and *rgyu ba'i ting nge 'dzin.* See the "creation stage" section of the introduction. Kongtrul lists these three absorptions and then four additional stages of visualization, making the "five enlightening factors" somewhat difficult to count. One standard list of the five is enlightenment from the visualization 1) of emptiness, 2) of the moon (or sun, etc.) seat, 3) of the seed syllable or letter, 4) of the hand implements, and 5) of the fully complete form of the deity. This correlates with Kongtrul's list as follows: the first two absorptions represent the first enlightening factor; the third absorption is the second factor; the next two stages line up with the next two factors; and the final two stages combine as the final, full visualization. This scheme is according to Khenpo Tsultrim Gyamtso Rinpoche.

109. *bla med rgyud sde,* Skt. *anuttarayogatantra:* according to the New *(gsar ma)* Schools (see note 28), there is a fourfold classification of the tantras: *kriyāyoga, caryāyoga, yogatantra,* and *anuttarayogatantra*—the highest. This next sequence of five visualizations from highest yogatantra are a different style of creating the visualization but purifying the same life and death experiences as the first set of five enlightening factors.

110. *'od gsal,* Skt. *ābhāsvara:* not an actual light, it is the inner radiance or luminosity of mind itself. It is a way of describing the direct experience of mind's true nature. It also occurs during the death process, when it provides a good opportunity for enlightenment if it can be recognized.

111. *rgyu yi rdo rje 'dzin pa* and *bras bu'i rdo rje 'dzin pa:* according to my sources, usually the "cause vajra holder" is made up of the letters or vibrations that are visualized inside the celestial palace that will transform into the deity, and the "result vajra holder" is that fully formed deity.

112. *rlung,* Skt. *prāṇa* or *vāyu:* the vital energy or motility that moves through the body and mind on the subtle level.

113. *snang mched thob gsum:* three stages of experience pertaining to the

process of dissolution of the consciousness into emptiness that happens with every thought, with sleep, with death, and intentionally with advanced stages of realization. At death it leads to unconsciousness in an ordinary person, or, for a trained practitioner, to the state of clear light *('od gsal)*. The three stages can also describe the opposite process of consciousness emerging from unconsciousness.

114. *snang ba dkar dmar:* during the death process and the three stages of experience mentioned above, the white and red elements in the form of vital seminal drops (that a living being has received from the parents, and which together, with consciousness, constitute the basis of life) descend and ascend from their places in the head and navel and dissolve together. For the dying person, this is experienced as a vision of white and then of red.
115. *ye shes sems dpa',* Skt. *jñānasattva:* the actual presence of the deity that is invoked and enters the visualized form of the deity, the commitment being *(dam tshig sems dpa',* Skt. *samayasattva).*
116. Khenpo Tsultrim Gyamtso Rinpoche favors the spelling *'phrul spyod* over *'khrul spyod* in the woodblock text. This refers to the various sports, crafts, and stunts that a youth would need to master at this stage of life.
117. *dbang bskur,* Skt. *abhiṣeka:* this refers to the section in many deity practices for conferring the four empowerments on oneself as the deity. They are the same empowerments that one receives from the guru prior to beginning deity practice. See the "guru" section of the introduction and note 42.
118. *byang chub sems bskyed,* Skt. *bodhicitta.*
119. *theg pa chen po,* Skt. *mahāyāna.*
120. *tshogs gnyis:* the accumulation of merit *(bsod nams)* and wisdom *(ye shes).*
121. *rnam dag dran pa:* recollecting the purity refers to the various pure characteristics of the deity being manifestations of pure qualities; for example, the two crossed arms of Vajradhara manifest the inseparability of means and wisdom. See the "creation stage" section of the introduction.
122. *gsal snang:* luminous appearance. The text should read *gsal snang chung ngu yin* rather than the woodblock's *gsal snang chung ngu yis,* according to Khenpo Tsultrim Gyamtso Rinpoche.
123. *rnam par smin pa'i rig 'dzin:* "awareness" or "knowledge holders" *(rig 'dzin,* Skt. *vidyādhara)* are those who attain realization through the Secret Mantra Vehicle. They are often elevated to the status of the deities. The maturation knowledge-holder is the first of a classification

of four in the mahāyoga teachings of the Ancient tradition. See Dudjom, *The Nyingma School of Tibetan Buddhism*, vol. I, p. 260.

124. *rdzogs pa chen po*, Skt. *mahāsandhi* or *atiyoga:* see note 54.

125. *dbu ma*, Skt. *madhyamaka:* philosophy and practice of the Middle Way, beyond extremes of existence or non-existence. It is the term used to describe the highest teachings and meditational realization in the Gelug tradition.

126. *rnam shes tshogs brgyad*, Skt. *astavijñānakāya:* see note 51.

127. *kun gzhi*, Skt. *ālaya:* the pure, underlying basis of everything. This is not the same as the term "foundation consciousness" *(kun gzhi rnam shes*, Skt. *ālayavijñāna),* which has the sense of a straying from or overlaying of this fundamentally pure basis.

128. *sems nyid*, Skt. *cittatva:* "mind itself" or "mind-as-such," the essential nature of mind, not different from enlightened mind.

129. Rangjung Dorje (*rang byung rdo rje*, 1284–1334), the third in the Karmapa line of emanations who headed the Karma Kagyu subsect of the Kagyu lineage. Rangjung Dorje was a great yogi and scholar, a holder of the Kagyu and Nyingma lineages, and notable for his synthesis of the yogic meditation tradition of those lineages with the philosophical tradition of the Yogācāra school. A discussion of the eight consciousness groups may be found in his *The Treatise that Differentiates Consciousness and Wisdom (rnam shes ye shes ' byed pa'i bstan bcos).*

130. *de ma thag yid:* "instantaneous mind" refers to the function usually associated with afflicted mind that causes one mind moment to arise immediately after another, and provides mental continuity. Sometimes, it is counted separately from afflicted mind, making a total of nine collections of consciousness. Also see note 51.

131. The text reads *'du shes* (discrimination), a misprint for *'du 'byed* (formation) according to Venerable Bokar Tulku Rinpoche. This makes much more sense, as "discrimination" was just mentioned two lines above, and follows this discussion of what is basically the five aggregates *(phung po lnga*, Skt. *pañcaskandha),* that is: form *(gzugs*, Skt. *rūpa),* feeling *(tshor ba*, Skt. *vedanā),* discrimination *('du shes*, Skt. *saṃjñā),* formation *('du byed*, Skt. *saṃskāra),* and consciousness *(rnam shes*, Skt. *vijñāna).* Khenpo Tsultrim Gyamtso Rinpoche concurs with this interpretation.

132. *bral ba'i rkyen dang rnam smin rgyur:* the condition for fruition of freedom and the cause of the fruition of perfect maturity. These two

fruitions are discussed at length in the *Uttaratantra* in the sixth vajra point on qualities. The condition of freedom (from obscurations) is the accumulation of wisdom, and the result is the dharmakāya, which benefits oneself. The cause of perfect maturity is the accumulation of merit, and the result is the rūpakāya, which benefits others. The discussion in the text seems to be about perfect virtue *(zag med dge ba)* that cannot be imprinted on the foundation consciousness, so this is the interpretation offered by Khenpo Tsultrim Gyamtso Rinpoche. However, there is another interpretation based on imperfect virtue *(zag bcas dge ba)* offered by Bokar Rinpoche: that the virtuous imprint remains as potential "unless separated by conditions" *(bral ba'i rkyen),* such as anger or regret for those actions, or "used up through fruition" *(rnam smin rgyur),* that is, by enjoying the karmic result of those virtuous actions.

133. *'bur 'joms mgo thug:* literally "to flatten the swelling [and] meet the head." In other words, "to strike at first appearance."

134. For the twelve links, Tibetan just uses *rten 'brel bcu gnyis,* basically the same word as in interdependent relationship *(rten cing 'brel bar 'byung ba,* Skt. *pratītyasamutpāda),* whereas Sanskrit uses the separate term *nidāna* (link) for the twelve. They are: ignorance, karmic formation, consciousness, name and form, six faculties, contact, feeling, craving, grasping, existence, birth, and aging and death. In Tibetan iconography and for pedagogical purposes, these are portrayed as the wheel of life.

135. *rlung bcu,* Skt. *daśavāyu:* the five basic vital winds of breath, excretion/reproduction, speech, digestion, and metabolism/circulation/muscular movement. The five ancillary vital winds are those connecting with the eyes, the heart, the nose, the tongue, and the whole body. Here the winds maturing means that they have at least begun to enter the central channel.

136. *drod,* Skt. *ūṣman:* technically, one of the four signs of accomplishment of the path of application *(sbyor lam,* Skt. *prayogamārga),* where special insight into the four noble truths results in the meditative absorption of realization of absence of external reality. The "warmth" is likened to the heating up of a flint just before bursting into flame. It may also be used as a general term for a high level of realization, and does not imply actual heat.

137. *bde gsal mi rtog nyams:* the three meditative experiences arising from the practice of calm abiding *(zhi gnas,* Skt. *śamatha).*

138. *grub brnyes,* the same as *grub thob,* Skt. *siddha:* yogis with a high degree of accomplishment in meditation.

139. *rnal 'byor chen po*, Skt. *mahāyoga:* in the system of classification of the Ancient tradition *(rnying ma)*, there are six tantric vehicles: *kriyātantra, caryātantra, yogatantra, mahāyoga, anuyoga,* and *atiyoga*, each one "higher" than the last, culminating in atiyoga, or dzogchen.
140. This refers to the idea of the inseparability of the two truths, the relative and the absolute.
141. *rtse gcig:* one-pointedness is the first of the four realization stages or yogas of mahāmudrā *(phyag chen rnal 'byor bzhi)*; the others are: free of elaboration *(spros bral)*, single flavor *(ro gcig)*, and no meditation *(sgom med)*.
142. *bying rgod:* sinking and scattering are the two most obvious difficulties to overcome in calm abiding meditation *(zhi gnas*, Skt. *śamatha)*.
143. *sku gsum*, Skt. *trikāya:* the three bodies or dimensions of Buddha (see the "third turning" section and note 40). Here they are being introduced as the actual true nature of mind, corresponding with its three aspects of emptiness, clarity, and compassion (or unimpededness), respectively.
144. *khams gsum*, Skt. *tridhātu:* a threefold division of cyclic existence: the desire realm *('dod khams*, Skt. *kāmadhātu)*, form realm *(gzugs khams*, Skt. *rūpadhātu)*, and formless realm *(gzugs med khams*, Skt. *ārūpadhātu)*. The first includes our world of experience; the other two are god realms which are the result of various meditative trances.
145. *lhag mthong*, Skt. *vipaśyanā:* insight is the practice of looking at the nature of the mind once it has been pacified in the practice of calm abiding *(zhi gnas*, Skt. *śamatha)*. The two practices are the recommended preliminary to the practice of mahāmudrā in the "normal" Kagyu approach.
146. *man ngag sde:* see note 54.
147. *rig pa'i lam:* "Rigpa" is an important term in the dzogchen teachings, referring to the intrinsic, primordially pure awareness, completely beyond and before the functions of mind. Its recognition involves a different approach.
148. *sgro skur*, short for *sgro 'dogs* (exaggeration or projection) and *skur 'debs* (denial, underestimation, denigration): traditionally defined as projecting existence on what does not exist *(med pa la yod pa)* and denying the existence of what does exist *(yod pa la med pa)*.
149. *Pacification (zhi byed)* [of suffering] is a practice tradition founded in the twelfth century by Padampa Sangye *(pha dam pa sangs rgyas)*, and *severance (gcod)* is a practice of cutting through attachments initiated

in Tibet by his student Machik Lapdrön *(ma gcig lab sgron)*. Together pacification and severance form one of the eight main practice traditions (*shing rta brgad*, see note 29) of Tibetan Buddhism.

150. *snying thig:* a cycle of teachings in the class of esoteric instructions *(man ngag sde)* of dzogchen.
151. According to Khenpo Tsultrim, this refers to the three examples by Vimalamitra that follow.
152. A great Indian master who, along with Padmasambhava and Vairocana, brought dzogchen teachings to Tibet.
153. This is a play with the term "gom" *(bsgom)*, meditation, and the word from which it derives, "gom" *(goms)*, becoming habituated or getting used to something.
154. Atiyoga, the highest vehicle in the Ancient tradition, equivalent to dzogchen. See note 139.
155. *(chos skyong) srung ma*, Skt. *dharmapāla:* a class of wrathful deities that are oath-bound to protect the doctrine, particularly the secret mantra, or Vajrayāna, from external and internal dangers and corruptions, assuring its integrity.
156. *bka' brgyud:* "oral instruction lineage," one of the four main schools of Tibetan Buddhism that established a large monastic network. See the "Buddhism in Tibet" section of the introduction.
157. *rtsa dbu ma*, Skt. *avadhūti:* the main channel or energy pathway *(rtsa*, Skt. *nāḍī)* of the psychophysical body through which the vital winds *(rlung*, Skt. *prāṇa)* and seminal drops *(thig le*, Skt. *bindu)* move. It is visualized as being approximately along the inner side of the backbone. It is a goal of yogic practice to bring the vital winds into the central channel, causing the realization of true nature. Conversely, by recognizing the intrinsic nature of mind, the vital winds will enter spontaneously into the central channel.
158. *rlung ro bsal:* a practice of clearing out the "dregs" of the old vital wind by a specific yogic breathing exercise.
159. *rdo rje sems dpa'*, Skt. *vajrasattva:* "Indestructible Being," a sambhogakāya buddha, the lord of all the deity maṇḍalas, particularly associated with purity. Here the reference is to any deity, appearing and yet empty.
160. *dam tshig*, Skt. *samaya:* the "sacred word" or covenant in Vajrayāna between the disciple and the guru, and also the commitment to the practices received from the guru. There are different sets of specific commitments from different tantras. These are the "four great special commitments" *(khyad par chen po'i dam tshig bzhi)* associated with

atiyoga: non-existence *(med pa)*, evenness *(phyal ba)*, singularity *(gcig pu)*, and spontaneous presence *(lhun grub)*, although here it is *lhun rdzogs)*. Kongtrul addresses them further in his *Treasury of Knowledge (shes bya mdzod)*, vol. II, p. 194.

161. *lam khyer:* literally, carrying (the practice) on the path or as the path.

162. Here and elsewhere, the Sanskrit syllables or "letters" refer to the visualization of the letters themselves and sometimes also the utterance of their sound while visualizing some action or effect that is taking place due to their inherent powers. The mantra OM AH HUNG specifically embodies the power of enlightened body, speech, and mind, respectively.

163. *dkon mchog rjes dran pa'i mdo.* For *sūtra,* see note 17.

164. *rigs brgya'i lha:* according to *zab chos zhi khro dgongs pa rang grol las chos spyod bag chags rang grol,* a treasure text discovered by Karma Lingpa, there are 42 peaceful deities in the heart, 10 knowledge-holders (*rig 'dzin,* Skt. *vidyādhara,* note 123) at the throat, and 60 (or 58) wrathful deities in the brain. Generally, the 42 peaceful and 58 wrathful deities are known as the Hundred Deities of the Holy Family. (I am indebted to Tulku Thondup Rinpoche for this note.)

165. *mkha' 'gro ma,* Skt. *ḍākinīs:* female "sky-goers" who embody the feminine principles of emptiness and wisdom.

166. *tshogs kyi 'khor lo,* Skt. *gaṇacakra:* the tantric practice of a sacred feast where the special consecrated substances are enjoyed without attachment. Participants maintain the knowledge that the place, the food, and they themselves are all divine and perfectly pure.

167. *bla ma'i rnal byor,* Skt. *guru yoga:* an essential devotional tantric practice in which the guru is perceived as the essence of the buddhas, as the meditational deity, and as the nature of one's own mind.

168. *byang chub sems dpa':* "hero of awakening," bodhisattva activities fall under the classifications of the six perfections *(pha rol tu phyin pa,* Skt. *pāramitā):* generosity, moral discipline, patience, perseverance, meditation, and transcendent intelligence.

169. *bka' rtags kyi phyag rgya bzhi:* the four seals that indicate the Buddha's teaching are more usually stated as: all that is composite is impermanent, all that is corrupt is suffering, all phenomena are without self, and transcendence (nirvāṇa) is peace. Here, emptiness (replacing nonself) and peace are put together as qualities of nirvāṇa.

170. Torma *(gtor ma,* Skt. *bali)* are sculptures with specific shapes and colors made from flour and decorated with butter that are made for offerings during ceremonies or for representing the deities.

171. *dzam bha la*, Skt. *jambhala:* a wealth deity, who may also be propitiated in various manifestations for healing.

172. Trokma *('phrog ma)*, the plunderer, was a female spirit of the "harmdoer" class *(gnod sbyin*, Skt. *yakśa)*. According to legend, she had 500 hungry children to whom she had to feed 1500 beings every day. One day the Buddha Śākyamuni hid one of her children and struck a bargain for its return: if she would promise never to kill again, his followers would offer her (and her type) a specially consecrated bit of food from their meals every day from then on. To this day, monks and nuns and lay practitioners take a bit of food *(chang bu)* from their meal and pinch it in their hand, forming a shape with five ridges, representing Trokma's five hundred children.

173. Jurgek *('jur gegs)* and Kabarma *(kha 'bar ma)* are names for certain types of hungry spirits *(yi dvags*, Skt. *preta)*, a class of beings who are continually beset by sufferings of extreme hunger and thirst, the karmic fruition of former greed. The custom of offering them specially consecrated water also began with stories from the time of Buddha Śākyamuni. Disciples of the Buddha doing their begging rounds saw the hideous form of Constricted Throat *('jur gegs)*, a spirit unable to pass anything through its tiny throat. The Buddha explained that it had been a stingy (constricted) person in the past life, giving only water to others. Now it could only partake of absolutely pure water, so disciples of the Buddha are instructed to scrub their hands thoroughly and offer pure water by means of special mantras, which is the only way the suffering of these spirits can be somewhat relieved. The Buddha's nephew Ānandā encountered Blazing Mouth *(kha 'bar ma)*, a female hungry spirit with fire blazing out of her mouth, who told him that he would die in seven days and be born as a hungry spirit himself. The Buddha then consoled Ānandā with the prescription to redeem this karma through offering pure consecrated water to the hungry spirits using special mantras. (These stories have been taken from *gtor ma'i de nyid bdud rtsi'i dga' ston* [*A Festival of the Ambrosial Essence of Torma*] by the Fifth Shamarpa, Könchok Yenlak, 1525–83.)

174. *khams:* the territory of eastern Tibet. Generally, the native people called the east "Kham" and the west and central parts "Bö" *(bod)*, reflecting the ancient cultural differences. The term Bö has been translated as "Tibet," a foreign term, and come to denote both areas, which were seen as a national unit from the time of the Fifth Dalai Lama (1617–82) until the Chinese invasion of 1959.

175. *o rgyan,* Skt. *oḍḍiyāna:* a place in the western part of ancient India (perhaps present-day Pakistan) where Padmasambhava manifested in a lotus. Here, it is used as a name for Padmasambhava himself.
176. *thugs rje chen po,* Skt. *kāruṇika:* also called "Chenrezig" *(spyan ras gzigs,* Skt. *avalokiteśvara),* a deified bodhisattva, the very embodiment of awakened compassion, who is held dearly by the Tibetan people as the special protector and patron of Tibet.
177. OM MA NI PAD ME HUNG: the mantra of Chenrezig, the Great Compassionate One.
178. *bar gyi rlung:* there are many forms of breathing exercises involved in completion-stage yogas; holding the intermediate vital wind involves "joining" the lower and upper winds in the middle.
179. *ka ti:* a channel going from the heart to the eyes. These "three essential instructions" are mentioned basically in passing, and refer the practitioner to a whole set of detailed esoteric instructions that would be out of place here.
180. *dka' ba med par,* incorrectly spelled as *bka' ba med par.*
181. *mnyam med dvags po,* or *dvags po lha rje:* "the physician of Dagpo," a name for Gampopa (*sgam po pa,* 1079–1153, see note 41). The advice from Gampopa that is cited here seems to be a supercondensed method for doing these practices during daily activities: completion stage (holding a few gentle breaths), creation stage (mental or silent recitation), and their inseparability in the blending of one's mind with the guru's enlightened mind.
182. This refers to the yoga of clear light *('od gsal rnal 'byor),* in which one attempts to recognize the nature of the clear light during deep sleep.
183. Stages in the practice of dream yoga *(rmi lam rnal 'byor),* to recognize and gain control of dreams in order to apply that ability to phenomenal existence.
184. A reference to the yoga of the intermediate stage *(bar do rnal 'byor),* where one prepares for the recognition of the clear light during the intermediate experience of death. These yogas are all completion-stage practices, as found, for instance, in the six yogas of Naropa *(na ro chos drug),* first presented in English in W. Y. Evans-Wentz's *Tibetan Yoga and Secret Doctrines.*
185. *spyod lam rnam bzhi:* standing, walking, sitting, and lying down.
186. *bslab pa gsum,* Skt. *triśikṣā:* ethical discipline *(tshul khrims,* Skt. *śīla),* meditative absorption *(ting nge 'dzin,* Skt. *samādhi),* and transcendent intelligence *(shes rab,* Skt. *prajñā).*

187. The first Karmapa, Dusum Khyenpa (*dus gsum mkhyen pa*, 1110–93), was a disciple of Gampopa (note 41), and founded the subsect of the Kagyu school called Karma Kagyu. The second Karmapa, Karma Pakshi (*karma pak shi*, 1204–83), was the first recognized incarnate lama or "tulku" *(sprul sku)*, a tradition that rapidly flourished in Tibet. The Karmapas have continued to appear until the present time, which is the time of the seventeenth. Although Kongtrul is of course praying for the benefit of the entire lineage here, the specific Karmapa whom he may be addressing at this time (1840) would be the fourteenth, Thekchok Dorje (*theg mchog rdo rje*, 1797–1867).

188. *karma ngag dbang yon tan rgya mtsho:* one of the many names of Jamgön Kongtrul (see note 61). The style of this colophon and conclusion of the text, where the author states his inspiration and his own lack of worth, is quite traditional and stylized, and not particularly to be believed, although there is no reason to think that Jamgön Kongtrul was not truly humble.

Bibliography

Works in English

Ancient Tibet. Emeryville CA: Dharma Publications, 1986.

Conze, Edward. *Buddhist Thought in India.* Ann Arbor: The University of Michigan Press, 1967.

Conze, Edward. *The Perfection of Wisdom in Eight Thousand Lines and Its Verse Summary.* San Francisco: Four Seasons Foundation, 1973.

The Dalai Lama XIV, Tenzin Gyatso. *Dzogchen: The Heart Essence of the Great Perfection,* Translated by Geshe Thupten Jinpa and Richard Barron, edited by Patrick Gafney. Ithaca NY: Snow Lion Publications, 2000.

The Dalai Lama XIV, Tenzin Gyatso. *The World of Tibetan Buddhism.* Translated and edited by Geshe Thupten Jinpa. Boston: Wisdom Publications, 1995.

Dezhung Rinpoche. "Buddhism Without Sectarianism." Translated by Jared Rhoton. 1983, unpublished.

Gyaltrul Rinpoche. *Generating the Deity.* Translated by Sangye Khandro. Ithaca NY: Snow Lion Publications, 1996.

Dilgo Khyentse Rinpoche. *Pure Appearance: Development and Completion Stages in Vajrayana Practice.* Translated by Ani Jinba Palmo. Halifax, Nova Scotia: Vajravairochana Translation Committee, 1992.

Dudjom Rinpoche, Jikdrel Yeshe Dorje. *The Nyingma School of Tibetan Buddhism.* Translated by Gyurme Dorje and Matthew Kapstein. Boston: Wisdom Publications, 1991.

Evans-Wentz, W. Y. *Tibetan Yoga and Secret Doctrines.* London: Oxford University Press, 1958.

Gampopa. *The Jewel Ornament of Liberation.* Translated by Herbert V. Guenther. Boston and London: Shambhala, 1971.

Hookham, S. K. *The Buddha Within.* Albany NY: The State University of New York Press, 1991.

Jamgön Kongtrul. *The Great Path of Awakening: A Commentary on the Mahayana Teaching of the Seven Points of Mind Training.* Translated by Ken McLeod. Boston and London: Shambhala, 1987.

Jamgön Kongtrul. *The Torch of Certainty.* Translated by Judith Hanson. Boston and London: Shambhala, 1986.

Khenpo Tsultrim Gyamtso. *Creation and Completion.* Translated by Sarah Harding. Halifax: Vajravairochana Translation Committee, 1998.

Khenpo Tsultrim Gyamtso. *Progressive Stages of Meditation on Emptiness.* Translated by Shenpen Hookham. Oxford, England: Longchen Foundation, 1986.

Maitreya/Asanga. *The Changeless Nature.* Translated by Ken and Katia Holms. Scotland: Karma Drubgyud Darjay Ling, 1985.

Padmasambhava. *Natural Liberation: Padmasambhava's Teachings on the Six Bardos.* Commentary by Gyatrul Rinpoche, Translated by B. Alan Wallace. Boston: Wisdom Publications, 1998.

Patrul Rinpoche. *Kün-zang La-may Zhal-lung: The Oral Instruction of Künzag La-ma on the Preliminary Practices of Dzog-chen Long-ch'en Nying-tig.* Translated by Sonam T. Kazi. Upper Montclair NJ: Diamond-Lotus Publishing, 1989.

Patrul Rinpoche. *The Words of My Perfect Teacher.* Padmakara Translation Group. San Francisco: Harper Collins, 1994.

Pettit, John Whitney. *Mipham's Beacon of Certainty, Illuminating the View of Dzogchen, the Great Perfection.* Boston: Wisdom Publications, 1999.

Shabkar Tsogdruk Rangdrol. *The Life of Shabkar.* Translated by Matthieu Ricard. Ithaca, New York: Snow Lion Publications, 2001.

Smith, E. Gene. *Among Tibetan Texts: History and Literature of the Himalayan Plateau.* Boston: Wisdom Publications, 2001.

Stein, R. A. *Tibetan Civilization.* Stanford: Stanford University Press, 1972.

Thrangu Rinpoche. *Transcending Ego: Differentiating Consciousness from Wisdom: A Treatise of the Third Karmapa.* Translated by Peter Roberts. Boulder CO: Namo Buddha Publications, 2001.

Thrangu Rinpoche. *Everyday Consciousness and Buddha Awakening.* Translated and edited by Susanne Schefczyk. Ithaca: Snow Lion, 2002.

Tai Situ Rinpoche. *The Third Karmapa's Mahamudra Prayer.* Translated and edited by Rosemarie Fuchs. Ithaca NY: Snow Lion Publications, 2002.

Tulku Thondup Rinpoche. *Buddha Mind: An Anthology of Longchen Rabjam's Writings on Dzogpa Chenpo.* Ithaca NY: Snow Lion Publications, 1989.

Tulku Thondup Rinpoche. *Hidden Teachings of Tibet: An Explanation of the Terma Tradition of the Nyingma School of Buddhism.* Boston: Wisdom Publications, 1986, 1997.

Tulku Urgyen Rinpoche. *As It Is, Vol. I and II.* Kathmandu: Rangjung Yeshe Publications, 1999.

Zangpo, Ngawang, *Sacred Ground: Jamgon Kongtrul on "Pilgrimage and Sacred Geography"* Ithaca NY: Snow Lion Publications, 2001.

Works in Tibetan

bod kyi tshig mdzod chen mo. (The Great Tibetan Dictionary.) 3 vols. Beijing: mi rigs dpe skrun khang (Minorities Press), 1982.

Gampopa. *rje sgam po pa'i zhal gdams/ lam mchog rin po che'i phreng ba. (Precious Garland of the Sublime Path.)* Rumtek, Sikkim: Karmapa'i chos sgar, n.d.

Gampopa. *mnyam med rje btsun sgam po pa'i phyag rgya chen po lam gcig chod. (The Single Decisive Path, the Mahāmudrā of the Unequalled and Revered Gampopa.)*

Gampopa. *dam chos yid bzhin nor bu thar pa rin po che'i rgyan.* (See above, *The Jewel Ornament of Liberation.* Also *Gems of Dharma, Jewels of Freedom.* Translated by Ken and Katia Holms, forthcoming from Snow Lion Publications.) Rumtek, Sikkim: Karmapa'i chos sgar, n.d.

Gampopa, Mamgala. *gsang sngags rdo rje theg pa'i spyi don mdor bsdus pa legs bshad nor bu'i od zer. (Jewel Radiance.)* Delhi: Delhi Karmapa Chodhey Gyalwa Sungrab Partun Khang, n.d.

Jamgön Kongtrul. *phyogs med ris med kyi bstan pa la 'dun shing dge sbyong gi gzugs brnyan 'chang ba blo gros mtha' yas kyi sde'i byung ba brjod pa nor bu sna tshogs mdog can.* In volume 62 of *The Treasury of Precious Treasure (rin chen gter mdzod).* Autobiography of Jamgön Kongtrul *(Jewel of Various Colors).*

Jamgön Kongtrul (compiled by). *shangs lugs bde mchog lha lnga'i sgrub thabs kyi rnam par bshad pa zab don gsal byed.* Taranatha, from *gdams ngag mdzod shangs chos (The Shangpa Teachings in the Treasury of Instructions).*

Jamgön Kongtrul. *shes bya kun khyab mdzod. (theg pa'i sgo kun las btus pa gsung rab rin po che'i mdzod bslab pa gsum legs par ston pa'i bstan bcos shes bya kun khyab.) (Treasury of Knowledge.)* 3 vols. Beijing: Mi rigs dpe skrun khang (Minorities Press), 1982.

Kalu Rinpoche. *ka lu rin po che'i kun gzhi sogs khrid. (Kalu Rinpoche's Comments on Foundation Consciousness, etc.)* Unpublished.

Karmapa III, Rangjung Dorje. *rnam shes ye shes 'byed pa'i bstan bcos* and *rnam par shes pa dang ye shes 'byed pa'i bstan bcos kyi tshig don go gsal du 'grel pa rang byung dgongs pa'i rgyan.* (See above, *The Treatise on Differentiating Consciousness from Wisdom.)* Rumtek Sikkim: Dharma Chakra Centre, n.d.

Karmapa III, Rangjung Dorje. *zab mo nang gi don zhes bya ba'i gzhung* and *rnal 'byor bla med pa'i rgyud sde rgya mtsho'i snying po bsdus pa zab mo nang gi don nyung ngu'i tshig gis rnam par 'grol ba zab don snang byed. (The Profound Inner Meaning.)* Rumtek, Sikkim: Karmapa'i chos sgar, n.d.

Maitreya/Asanga. *theg pa chen po rgyud bla ma'i bstan bcos.* (See above, *The Changeless Nature.*) (Skt. *mahāyānottaratantrasāstra*). Rumtek, Sikkim: Karmapa'i chos sgar, n.d.

Patrul Rinpoche. *kun bzang bla ma'i zhal lung.* (See above, *The Words of My Perfect Teacher.*) Rumtek, Sikkim, c. 1968.

Shamarpa V, Könchok Yenlak. *gtor ma'i de nyid bdud rtsi'i dga' ston. (A Festival of the Ambrosial Essence of Torma.)*

Index

About the Translator

Sarah Harding was born in Malibu in 1951 and educated in Los Angeles, California. She studied English literature and anthropology at Prescott College in Arizona, and earned a degree in religious studies from Naropa University in Boulder, Colorado. Sarah spent three years traveling through Europe, Africa, and Asia, and while abroad, she studied Tibetan language and culture for two years in Darjeeling, India, and in Kathmandu, Nepal. In 1974, Sarah returned to the United States to continue her studies in Tibetan culture and language. Her interests in Tibetan and Buddhist studies culminated in her participation in the first traditional three-year meditation and study retreat for Westerners, which was conducted entirely in Tibetan, under the guidance of Venerable Kalu Rinpoche near Dijon, France.

Between 1980 and 1992, Sarah served as the resident Dharma teacher and translator in Los Angeles and later in Santa Fe, New Mexico. She has done extensive oral translation internationally for such renowned teachers as Kalu Rinpoche, Chagdud Tulku, Tenga Rinpoche, Khenpo Tsultrim Gyamtso, Khenchen Thrangu Rinpoche, and Gangteng Rinpoche. Sarah is a founding member of the International Buddhist Translation Committee and a member of the Nalanda Translation Committee. Her prolific career as a translator includes more than thirty-five translations of traditional Buddhist texts as well as the Tibetan Language Correspondence Course, co-authored with Jeremy Morrelli. From 1992 until the present, she has been a faculty member in Buddhist Studies at Naropa University. Sarah continues to make her home in Boulder, where she is currently working on her next book.

Also from Wisdom Publications

MIPHAM'S BEACON OF CERTAINTY
Illuminating the View of Dzogchen, the Great Perfection
Studies in Indian and Tibetan Buddhism Series
John W. Pettit
576 pp., 0-86171-157-2, $28.95

"Lama Mipham was one of the most extraordinary thinkers and meditators of the Tibetan Buddhist tradition. In his *Beacon of Certainty* he illuminates some essential points of Madhyamika philosophy according to the view of the Great Perfection (Dzogchen). John Pettit's translation and in-depth presentation is a major contribution to the field of combining Madhyamika and Dzogchen studies, that remains largely unexplored."—Matthieu Ricard, co-author of *The Monk and the Philosopher*

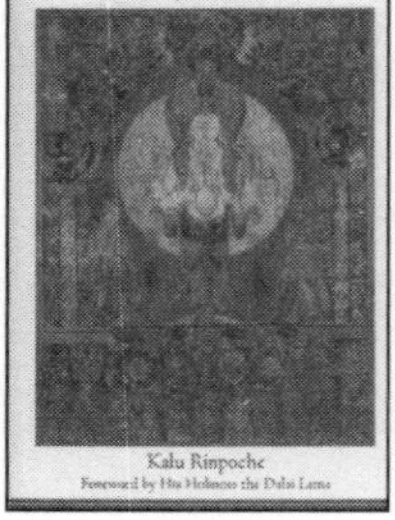

LUMINOUS MIND
The Way of the Buddha
Kalu Rinpoche
Foreword by the Dalai Lama
352 pp., 0-86171-118-1, $19.95

Drawn from the lucid writings and oral presentations of Kalu Rinpoche, who has been extolled as a "beacon of inspiration" and compared by the Dalai Lama to the great Tibetan saint Milarepa, this remarkable book presents the full range of Buddhist practice, from the basic analysis of the nature of the mind to its ultimate refinement in the teachings of the Mahamudra.

ORDINARY WISDOM

Sakya Pandita's Treasury of Good Advice

Translated by John Davenport

384 pp., 0-86171-161-0, $21.95

"The English translation of Sakya Pandita's *The Treasury of Good Advice (Sakya Legshe)* is indeed welcome as it presents the ancient wisdom in ordinary life. It became one of the most popular classics throughout Tibet and its cultural sphere. In my childhood, I memorized its verses, and they brought me solace during difficult times."—L.P. Lhalungpa, translator of *The Life of Milarepa*

PERFECT CONDUCT

Ascertaining the Three Vows

Ngari Panchen and Dudjom Rinpoche

192 pp., 0-86171-083-5, $18.00

"This timely book fulfills a crucial need for serious students of Buddhism.... At last we have a handbook in English that explains the full code of discipline [pratimoksa, bodhisattva, and tantric vows] along with an elucidation of philosophical principles and historical background."—from the preface by Tulku Thondup

THE FULFILLMENT OF ALL HOPES

Guru Devotion in Tibetan Buddhism

Je Tsongkhapa. Translated by Gareth Sparham

160 pp., 0-86171-153-X, $15.95

Tsongkhapa—one of Tibet's most revered scholar-practitioners—explains the core practice of devoting oneself to a spiritual teacher. Included is a complete translation of Tsongkhapa's commentary on the well-known *Fifty Stanzas on the Guru,* accompanied by the original Tibetan text.

Wisdom Publications

Wisdom Publications, a not-for-profit publisher, is dedicated to making available authentic Buddhist works for the benefit of all. We publish translations of the sutras and tantras, commentaries and teachings of past and contemporary Buddhist masters, and original works by the world's leading Buddhist scholars. We publish our titles with an appreciation of Buddhism as a living philosophy and with a special commitment to preserve and transmit important works from all the major Buddhist traditions.

To learn more about Wisdom, or to browse books online, visit our website at wisdompubs.org. You may request a copy of our mail-order catalog online or by writing to:

Wisdom Publications
199 Elm Street
Somerville, Massachusetts 02144 USA
Telephone: (617) 776-7416
Fax: (617) 776-7841
Email: info@wisdompubs.org
www.wisdompubs.org

The Wisdom Trust

As a not-for-profit publisher, Wisdom is dedicated to the publication of fine Dharma books for the benefit of all sentient beings and dependent upon the kindness and generosity of sponsors in order to do so. If you would like to make a donation to Wisdom, please do so through our Somerville office. If you would like to sponsor the publication of a book, please write or email us at the address above.

Thank you.

Wisdom is a nonprofit, charitable 501(c)(3) organization affiliated with the Foundation for the Preservation of the Mahayana Tradition (FPMT).